ONLINE COMMUNITIES HANDBOOK
BUILDING YOUR BUSINESS AND BRAND ON THE WEB

by Anna Buss
and Nancy Strauss

THE ONLINE COMMUNITIES HANDBOOK:
BUILDING YOUR BUSINESS AND BRAND ON THE WEB
ANNA BUSS AND NANCY STRAUSS

New Riders
1249 Eighth Street
Berkeley, CA 94710
510/524-2178
510/524-2221 (fax)

Find us on the Web at: www.newriders.com
To report errors, please send a note to errata@peachpit.com

New Riders is an imprint of Peachpit, a division of Pearson Education.

Copyright © 2009 by Anna Buss and Nancy Strauss

PROJECT EDITOR: Michael J. Nolan
DEVELOPMENT EDITOR: Margaret S. Anderson/Stellarvisions
PRODUCTION EDITOR: Becky Winter
COPY EDITOR: Gretchen Dykstra
PROOFREADER: Darren Meiss
INDEXER: Karin Arrigoni
COMPOSITOR: Danielle Foster
COVER DESIGN: Teri Bogaards
INTERIOR DESIGN: Maureen Forys

NOTICE OF RIGHTS
All rights reserved. No part of this book may be reproduced or transmitted in any form by any means, electronic, mechanical, photocopying, recording, or otherwise, without the prior written permission of the publisher. For information on getting permission for reprints and excerpts, contact permissions@peachpit.com.

NOTICE OF LIABILITY
The information in this book is distributed on an "As Is" basis without warranty. While every precaution has been taken in the preparation of the book, neither the authors nor Peachpit shall have any liability to any person or entity with respect to any loss or damage caused or alleged to be caused directly or indirectly by the instructions contained in this book or by the computer software and hardware products described in it.

TRADEMARKS
Many of the designations used by manufacturers and sellers to distinguish their products are claimed as trademarks. Where those designations appear in this book, and Peachpit was aware of a trademark claim, the designations appear as requested by the owner of the trademark. All other product names and services identified throughout this book are used in editorial fashion only and for the benefit of such companies with no intention of infringement of the trademark. No such use, or the use of any trade name, is intended to convey endorsement or other affiliation with this book.

ISBN 13: 978-0-321-60588-7
ISBN 10:   0-321-60588-8

9 8 7 6 5 4 3 2 1

Printed and bound in the United States of America

To Iñigo Izaguirre Ozámiz
—N.S.

To my grandma Minna who afforded a wonderful childhood to me.
—A.B.

Foreword

Online communities are playing an increasingly important role in marketing and brand management. In 2009, the online landscape is dramatically different from what it was ten years ago. No longer just for young people and techies, the Internet is being used by an ever larger portion of the population. Today's Internet users are no longer satisfied with merely reading content. Instead, people go online to communicate with others, meet friends on social networks, discuss brand experiences, and publish content of their own. The relationship between brands and consumers is undergoing a parallel evolution—more and more, consumers expect the chance to interact with brands. Rather than passively receiving brand messages, they want to be participants, and what used to be a monologue is turning into a conversation.

What does all of this mean for your brand? Should you immediately post a brand profile on Facebook? Or does it make sense to build an online community of your own? If you decide to build a community, what will be involved, and what can you expect to get back? How can you ensure that the project's a success?

All of these questions will be answered in this book, which we wrote as a practical guide for today's businessperson. Avoiding theoretical and technical discussion, we have focused instead on offering practical advice and tested techniques based on our own experience in the field and the experience of the experts who contributed to this book, including specialists in marketing and community building, and the founders, CEOs and managers of leading online communities.

We would like to take this opportunity to express our profound gratitude to all of the people who have contributed their time and valuable knowledge to this project. In particular, our thanks to Sabrina Bohnacker, whose bachelor thesis provided many important insights and ideas on the subject of social networks.

Many thanks also to (in alphabetical order): Leesa Barnes (Marketingfit.com), Helmut Bruendl (BMW), François Derbaix (Toprural.com), Klaus Eck (Imagecapital), Mark Gibson (BNI), Iñigo Izaguirre Ozámiz, Pedro Jareño (Minube.com), Tanja Kindler (Unilever), Debi Kleiman (Communispace), Wilhelm Lappe (Wlappe.com), Félix López Capel (Xing), María Marín Gregorio (Xing), Stephan Musikant (Ciao.com), Ulrike Piesch (Ciao.com), Penny Power (Ecademy.com), Nacho Puell (11870.com), Angela Rittig (Xing), Vihan Sharma (Ciao Surveys), Fernando Ujaldón (11870.com), Thomas Weber (Ciao.com), Wendy Weiss (Weiss Communications).

Finally, our very special thanks to Margaret Anderson, Michael Nolan, and everyone at Peachpit Press who turned our manuscript into this book. It has truly been a great pleasure working with you.

Nancy Strauss and Anna Buss

About the Authors

Nancy Strauss is a freelance consultant specializing in website communities, online communication, and globalization. She is also owner of William Victor (www.williamvictor.net), a global content and translation service with native writers and translators working in major world languages. Nancy's previous experience includes managing online community and panel communication for Ciao.com and Greenfield Online. A Cincinnati native, Nancy received an M.F.A. in Creative Writing from the University of Michigan, where she subsequently taught English composition. She resided briefly in the Czech Republic and for the last ten years has lived in Spain.

Anna Buss is a senior information architect and teaches online journalism at the University of Mainz. She started in 1996 as an intern and now has over ten years of experience with user-centered design, concept development, consultancy, brand strategy, CRM, and usability. Her clients come mainly from the automotive, financial services, and telecommunications industries. Nancy and Anna met at Ciao, where Anna worked as a user experience manager. Born in Berlin, Anna received her diploma in molecular biology from the University of Konstanz in 1995.

More information, online community tips, and useful downloads can be found at www.onlinecommunitieshandbook.com.

Contents

Introduction xi

Part One: **Online Communities**   1

ONE: What's An Online Community?   3

    What's An Online Community? 4

    Features Of An Online Community 9

    Types Of Online Communities 12

    The Power Of Online Communities 17

    The Chapter In A Nutshell 17

TWO: What Can An Online Community Do For Your Company?   19

    Business Benefits Of An Online Community 20

    What's The Downside? 31

    Preparing For Success 37

    The Chapter In A Nutshell 37

THREE: How To Set Up Your Community   39

    Define Your Community Strategy 40

    Get Started 42

    Analyze Your Competition 44

    Define The Role Of Your Brand 44

    Plan Your Website 48

    Plan Your Infrastructure 56

CONTENTS

A User-Centered Approach................................ 58
The Chapter In A Nutshell 59

FOUR: Member Recruitment **61**

Recruitment Strategies 62
Registration 71
Launch Strategy 75
The Chapter In A Nutshell 77

FIVE: Motivating Your Members **79**

Get The Most Out Of Your Members........................ 80
Managing the Membership Lifecycle....................... 92
The Chapter In A Nutshell 97

SIX: Care And Feeding Of Your members **99**

Community Management 100
Who Can Be A Community Manager......................... 100
What A Community Manager Does.......................... 101
What A Community Manager Needs......................... 105
Efficient Community Management 111
Peer Management 113
A Well-Managed Community............................... 114
The Chapter In A Nutshell 115

SEVEN: Monetizing Your Community **117**

Profiting From Your Community 118
Saving Money With Your Community....................... 119
Earning Money With Paid Subscriptions 120
Earning Money With E-Commerce 122
Earning Money With Advertising 123
A Project That Pays For Itself 127
The Chapter In A Nutshell 127

EIGHT:	**Growing Your Online Community**	**129**
	Measuring Success	130
	Keeping Your Website Fresh	131
	Keeping Community Management Fresh.	132
	Adapting Your Infrastructure	133
	Recruiting More Members	134
	Internationalizing	134
	An Asset For Your Company	140
	The Chapter In A Nutshell	140
NINE:	**Social Networks As A Platform For Your Brand**	**143**
	What's A Social Network?	144
	Why Market On Social Networks?	145
	What Can Your Brand Do On A Social Network?	149
	Are Social Networks Right For Your Brand?	153
	Chapter In A Nutshell	155
Part Two:	**Real World Lessons**	**157**
TEN:	**Ciao.com**	**159**
	Interview	163
	Lessons Learned	166
ELEVEN:	**11870.com**	**169**
	Interview	173
	Lessons Learned	177
TWELVE:	**M Power World**	**179**
	Interview	183
	Lessons Learned	185
THIRTEEN:	**Pro-Age Netzwerk**	**187**
	Interview	191
	Lessons Learned	192

FOURTEEN:	Xing	195
	Interview	199
	Lessons Learned	205
FIFTEEN:	Ecademy	207
	Interview	211
	Lessons Learned	216
SIXTEEN:	Minube.com	219
	Interview	223
	Lessons Learned	227
SEVENTEEN:	Toprural.com	229
	Interview	233
	Lessons Learned	236
EIGHTEEN:	Interview With Leesa Barnes	237
	Interview	239
	Lessons Learned	248
	Web 2.0 Glossary	251
	Index	259

INTRODUCTION

IS THIS BOOK FOR YOU?
Are you:

* Curious about the online communities trend and what it's all about?
* Interested in developing an online community for your brand?
* Looking for ways to promote your product on the Web?
* Hoping to take your online community to the next level of success?

If you answered "yes" to any of these questions, then the *Online Communities Handbook* is for you.

On the other hand, if you're a Web developer looking to deepen your technical skills, or a sociologist looking for a theoretical discussion of social dynamics on the Web, this book is probably *not* for you. There are many theoretical and technical books on online communities available; however, we aim to fill an important gap with a practical handbook written specifically for the business reader.

What you get

Even if you are not knowledgeable about the Internet—yet—this book will provide you with the essential tools to understand online communities and harness their power to grow your business.

We know that most of our readers are busy people, so we've structured this book to save you time with lists, dos and don'ts, and convenient chapter-end summaries. Our companion website contains ready-made PowerPoint slides to help you discuss online communities within your organization.

You'll learn what online communities are and how they work, and discover seventeen important business benefits that a community can bring to a brand. You'll find out how an online community can create brand loyalty, bring in new business, and offer a value to customers that your competitors cannot imitate. You'll discover how an online community can be an opportunity for free advertising and a way to get your message out into the world, as well as an invaluable source of market insights, giving you a direct line to your customer base.

But what about the price? We'll lay out the risks and costs that you must consider before embarking on an online community project, and show you how an online community can end up saving your company money and even become an important new revenue source of its own.

How to start? We'll take you step by step through the process of developing a community strategy for your brand and bringing it to life—from identifying your objectives, brainstorming about concepts, and planning the website and the infrastructure, to recruiting website visitors and turning them into loyal community members and customers. You'll find out the secrets of creating loyalty among your members, and techniques for cultivating word-of-mouth customer referrals. Learning from real-life examples of other website communities, you'll see how to avoid potential pitfalls and solve typical problems as they arise. And you'll benefit from insider tricks-of-the-trade, such as strategies for putting the community members to work for you.

Once you have a buzzing, lively, successful community promoting your brand, we'll show you how to keep it fresh and make it grow, opening up new markets for your company. You'll get tips on managing the membership life cycle and reenergizing members when they become less active. You'll learn how to convert your community into cash, different ways to monetize an online community, and essential dos and don'ts of website advertising and direct email marketing.

Throughout the first part of the book you will see terms in bold; these are included in our Web 2.0 Glossary at the end of the book.

Finally, you'll be inspired by exclusive interviews, where the management of thriving online communities share the lessons they've learned and the secrets of their success.

CHAPTER GUIDE
Part One: Online Communities

One: What's an Online Community?

Here we define Web 2.0 and online communities, explain how online communities are different from wikis, blogs, and message boards, and give an overview of the many types of online communities that can be found on the Internet.

Two: What Can an Online Community Do for Your Company?

This chapter presents seventeen business benefits of online communities, as well as eight business risks and how to avoid them. This is all essential information for anyone who is developing a community strategy or who wants to get the most out of an online community.

Three: How to Set Up Your Community

We walk you through the process of choosing the most strategic themes and activities for your community, analyzing your online competition, and planning your community website and infrastructure.

Four: Member Recruitment

This chapter presents different ways to bring members to your community. You'll learn how to use search engines for recruitment, strategies to make your website viral, ways to optimize registration forms, and tips for a low-risk website launch.

Five: Motivating Your Members

In this chapter, you'll learn how to get the most out of your members. We show you how to keep them on your website once you get them there, and how to motivate them to participate so that your community thrives. This chapter includes valuable tips on how to create a member loyalty program without spending money.

Six: Care and Feeding of Your Members

Effective community management is fundamental to the success of an online community. This chapter shows you how to set up an effective community management infrastructure, and ways to save money and resources by helping the community to manage itself.

Seven: Monetizing Your Community

This chapter covers different ways that you can turn community into a money machine, and explains how to do so without losing the goodwill of your members or customers.

Eight: Growing Your Online Community

In this chapter, we cover key metrics for measuring your community's success, and strategies to keep the community successful and growing over time. We describe the red flag signs that say you've outgrown your infrastructure. And we offer an internationalization checklist to help you promote your brand globally.

Nine: Social Networks as a Platform for Your Brand

Online social networks such as Facebook and Twitter are transforming the face of marketing. In this chapter, we explain the unique opportunities offered by these networks, and show how your company can use them in addition to a proprietary brand community or as a low-cost, low-risk alternative.

Part Two: Real World Lessons

Ten: Ciao.com

Ciao is Europe's leading shopping and price-comparison portal. Ciao Managing Director Stephan Musikant explains how a focus on quality and long-term thinking have contributed to Ciao's success. He also offers important strategic advice for anyone starting a new community.

Eleven: 11870.com

During its first week after launch, the European community 11870.com knocked Britney Spears out of the number one position on Technorati. The management of 11870.com explain their community strategy, which centers on effective Web design and personal communication with members.

Twelve: M Power World

Our interview with the manager of BMW's exclusive community for M model owners reveals the strategy behind this product-focused community, including the importance of offering community members product information that can't be found elsewhere on the Web.

Thirteen: Pro-Age Netzwerk

The German community Pro-Age Netzwerk is proof that the Internet isn't just for young people anymore. After making waves with their Pro-Age advertising campaign, Unilever's Dove brand have continued their emotional marketing strategy with an online community for women aged 45 and older. We spoke with Tanja Kindler, Senior Brand Manager at Dove.

Fourteen: Xing

With over 6.5 million members, Xing is one of the largest online networks of any kind. It has a highly effective business model, with three simultaneous revenue streams. Our interview with Xing highlights some of the reasons for their success. Félix López Capel of Xing also explains how companies such as IBM are using Xing's platform as a low-cost, low-risk alternative to building proprietary brand communities.

Fifteen: Ecademy

Founded in 1998, Ecademy was a pioneer in the world of online networking. In our interview, Ecademy's Founder and CEO explains the importance of starting with a clear idea of your target user and designing a community to meet that person's needs.

Sixteen: Minube.com

Our interview with this European travel community will show you ways to make your community more useful and, at the same time, more viral. Pedro Jareño of Minube also describes how a trip around the world was converted into a wildly successful viral marketing campaign.

Seventeen: Toprural.com

One out of every two Spaniards who researches rural accommodation online uses Toprural.com. From our interview, you'll learn how this rural tourism website focused on a narrow vertical market and came to dominate the niche.

Eighteen: Interview with Leesa Barnes

In our interview, social media marketing guru Leesa Barnes explains the keys to effective marketing on social networks and ways to avoid the kind of public relations mistakes made by brands such as Motrin and Starbucks.

PART ONE
ONLINE COMMUNITIES

ONE
WHAT'S AN ONLINE COMMUNITY?

QUESTIONS ANSWERED IN THIS CHAPTER

* What are online communities and community websites?
* What's Web 2.0, and how are online communities a part of it?
* What are wikis, blogs, and message boards, and how are they different from online communities?
* What types of online communities are out there?

WHAT'S AN ONLINE COMMUNITY?

An **online community** is a group of people who regularly interact with each other on a website. As in other kinds of communities, online community members are united by a common activity or interest; they can get to know who the other members are, relationships form, and a sense of connectedness develops.

FIGURE 1.1 Ourbania: This network for architects and real estate professionals shows typical elements of a community website.

The most basic characteristic of an online community is its focus on member-to-member interaction. Think of how a person not seriously interested in catching trout might go on fishing trips for the social aspect; similarly, people join an online community to meet others, and the specific activities they engage in are often secondary. This is an important point because it helps to distinguish real online communities from other types of websites that only look like communities.

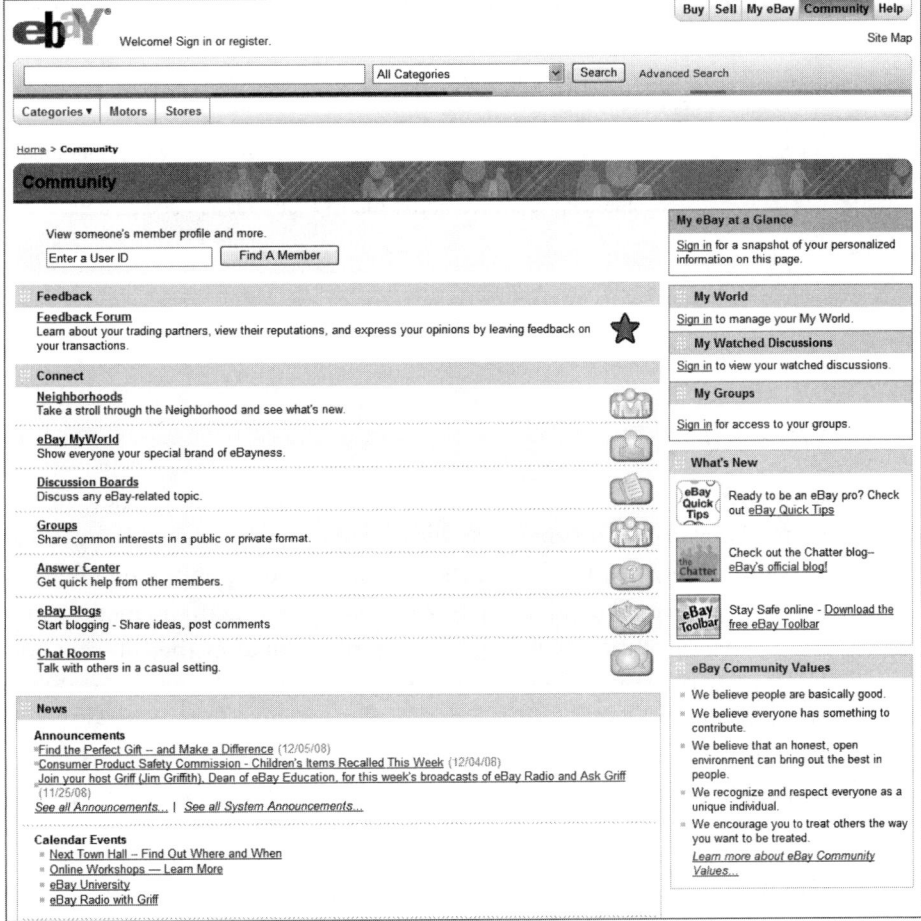

FIGURE 1.2 eBay: Although this section of eBay is called Community, it isn't one because people go to eBay to buy and sell, not to meet others.

> **"WHAT DOES AN ONLINE COMMUNITY MEAN TO YOU?"**
> **COMMUNITY MEMBERS RESPOND**
>
> * "On ParentsPlace, I met a lot of other new moms, and they've really given me a lot of support during Duncan's first year."
>   —Margaret, 26, ParentsPlace member
>
> * "By day, I'm a marketing manager, but I've always written poetry, and Gather lets me share this side of myself with other writers. Some of the friendships I've made there are more meaningful than my so-called real-life friendships."
>   —J.L., 48, Gather member
>
> * "It's something to do. It's better than TV, but not as good as a girlfriend."
>   —Jamie, 17, SecondLife member

Web 2.0

Community websites provide a context and tools for members to form relationships. They use technology that allows members to act visibly on the website; for example, by posting messages, voting in a poll, publishing photos, or reviewing a film. The idea of letting website users actually modify a website has been a revolution that began to take off right after the Internet bubble burst in 2001. Media consultant Tim O'Reilly coined a name for this new interactive use of the Internet: **Web 2.0**. Before Web 2.0, there was **Web 1.0**, where websites were typically collections of pages on which the owner published content and advertising—the communication was one-sided. Web 2.0 turns the Internet into a true dialogue.

Online communities are just one part of Web 2.0, or the Internet-as-dialogue. For a clearer understanding of what an online community is, it is worth distinguishing it from some other interactive uses of the Internet such as wikis, blogs, and message boards. Let's take a moment to review what each of these buzzwords really means and how it differs from the concept of an online community.

Online communities versus wikis

A **wiki** is a website that allows visitors to add, edit, and update content. Wikis offer a powerful tool for collaborating remotely on a document or developing an organized, expandable repository of information. A well-known example of a wiki is Wikipedia, an online encyclopedia to which anyone can contribute. Although wikis are interactive websites, they are not necessarily community websites. The term wiki is generally applied to websites that focus on the content, not on the authors. The identity of wiki authors often remains anonymous, and there is no direct interaction among them to permit relationships to form.

FIGURE 1.3 Wikipedia: This online encyclopedia is made up of user-generated content but is not a community.

Online communities versus blogs

The term **blog**, short for weblog, refers to a website where an author publishes content in a journal format: every time the author publishes a new entry, it appears with a date and time stamp on top of the previous entry, in a vertical list. Unlike wikis, only one or a small number of authors are creating the content, and the tone is often quite personal. Blogs are written in first person with short, informal entries, and the effect is that of a diary or a series of open letters. In general, visitors can comment on the entries. Sometimes the comments are published online; at other times they are seen only by the blog's owner.

> ### EXAMPLES OF FAMOUS BLOGS
>
> * Wonkette.com: Ana Marie Cox, a Washington, D.C. insider, publishes political gossip on this blog. She has also published a novel about (what else?) a Washington, D.C. insider with a political gossip blog.
> * ChocolateandZucchini.com: This blog by food writer Clotilde Dusoulier attracts millions of visits each month.

The intention of a blog is different from that of an online community. Like a journal, a blog is really about what the author has to say. Visitors may respond directly to the author, but a blog is not designed for direct interaction among the visitors or for the formation of relationships among them—even though connections do sometimes develop. The pattern of communication is much more hierarchical than that of an online community: it is closer to a monologue than an open conversation.

Although blogs are set up to be monologues, by including links to other blogs, they create the effect of a conversation among bloggers. The resulting network, composed of all interlinked blogs, is commonly described as the **blogosphere**. This is often called a community, but in a larger sense, in the same way we use the term "the business community" to refer to business people everywhere. Also, when we use the term online community or community website, we are referring to a community that exists on a single website, while the blogosphere involves relationships among sites.

Online communities versus message boards or bulletin boards

Many communities include what are known as **message boards** or bulletin boards—but a message board alone does not equal a community. A message board is a site that allows members or even the general public to publish their comments on specific topics or questions. As with blogs, the comments are normally displayed in reverse chronological order, in a vertical string with time stamps showing when each one was posted. Each topic, with its string of comments, is known as a **thread**. Message boards are normally supervised by a moderator who makes sure the comments stay on topic and that the conversation doesn't become abusive. Yes, a message board, unlike a blog, is a conversation. But it is not yet a community. The focus is on the thread's topic, not on facilitating relationships among the conversation's participants.

In the offline world, if you talk enough with someone about common themes of interest, a relationship may form naturally and organically, but on a simple message board this is not as easy. Users have little identity except as a nickname and sometimes an image or icon, and there is no way for them to have one-to-one conversations or discuss anything except the subject at hand. But if you give them the means to share more about themselves, to have personal homepages on your website, to have private chats or mailboxes where they can interact one-on-one, you're on your way to an online community!

FEATURES OF AN ONLINE COMMUNITY

Online communities are about human interaction and relationships. Most community websites share certain features that make it easy and satisfying for people to meet and communicate with each other on the Internet.

Community websites offer a common activity

Members of a community website need something to do there, whether it be discussing a specific topic such as travel or pets, publishing recipes, or playing an online game with other users. Otherwise, they have no reason to spend time on the website. In addition, their participation in the activity has to be visible to other members of the site, so that the members have a way to get to know each other.

Community websites offer online identities for their members

Frequently, members of an online community have an alias or nickname that they use (also known as a **user name**, **login name**, or **nick**), because most people don't want to publish their real name and email address on the Internet. The member's nickname is shown on a community website next to actions performed by that member; for example, if a member publishes a comment on an article, the comment appears with its author's nickname. The nickname therefore becomes an online identity for the member. The use of nicknames offers a kind of anonymity that many people find liberating and is a special attraction of Internet culture, even while it opens up the risk of abuse.

SOME OF OUR FAVORITE USER NAMES FROM COMMUNITY WEBSITES

* Shy riceball
* Eatpizza304
* Napoleonjunior

TRUE STORY
A member called RedHead1978 wrote to the community management of a popular website requesting an urgent user name change because she had just dyed her hair.

In addition to user names, community members are often identified with images, either real photographs of themselves that they submit, or pictures of other things. Some community websites provide a menu of cartoon figures, and members can select and even customize a figure that will stand in for him or her as an online face and body. These cartoons are called **avatars**. Habbo, Yahoo Answers, and SecondLife are some examples of communities that offer avatars to members.

> **SOME CURIOUS AVATAR STATISTICS FROM SECONDLIFE.COM**
>
> * 64% of members choose an avatar who looks different than the user
> * 45% choose a more attractive body
> * 37% want to look younger
> * 23% use a different nationality

Community websites also sometimes display a symbol or title next to a member's nickname that indicates a member's level of experience or activity or whether the member has a special status on the website. This helps other members know whom they can trust for advice and help, and it motivates members to stay active in the community, since, to a surprising degree, these status symbols are sought after within the online community.

Community websites give their members homepages or profile pages

On most community websites, each member has a personal page that summarizes information about him or her and that can be viewed by other members. This goes with the idea of giving each member an identity on the page apart from his or her individual actions. Frequently, the member's nickname, wherever it appears on the website, will be linked to this personal homepage, which might contain the member's photograph, biographical or contact information that the member wishes to make public, details about the person's membership (such as how long he or she has been a member), and links to content that this member has published on the website. Members are often given quite a lot of freedom to express themselves on these pages by adding text and even changing the color and look of the page itself.

Community websites give members a way to communicate one-on-one

To allow members to form relationships, a community website provides tools for members to contact each other outside the context of any activity. Sometimes the solution is as simple as giving members a place on their homepages to publish their personal email addresses. However, because many people are hesitant to make their contact details public on the Internet, most community websites offer options to keep the one-to-one conversation right there on the site, by means of internal email or message books on member homepages where other members can leave comments either privately or publicly.

TYPES OF ONLINE COMMUNITIES

So far, we've summarized the qualities and features that most online communities have in common and that distinguish them from other kinds of Web 2.0 sites such as wikis, message boards, and blogs. However, there are many different types of community websites, and each online community is its own unique social universe.

Open versus closed communities

Throughout most of this book, we are discussing online communities that accept an unlimited number of members. All of the best-known online communities fall into this category. If the business goal of a community is public relations or marketing for a brand, generating revenue through advertising or paid subscriptions, or increasing sales on an associated e-commerce site, then the more members join, the better. Some communities place restrictions on the *type* of member who can join. For example, in order to join BMW's exclusive M Power community, you have to provide the chassis number of your BMW M model car. If you don't own one, you're not allowed to join. However, within the population of BMW M model owners, anyone may join.

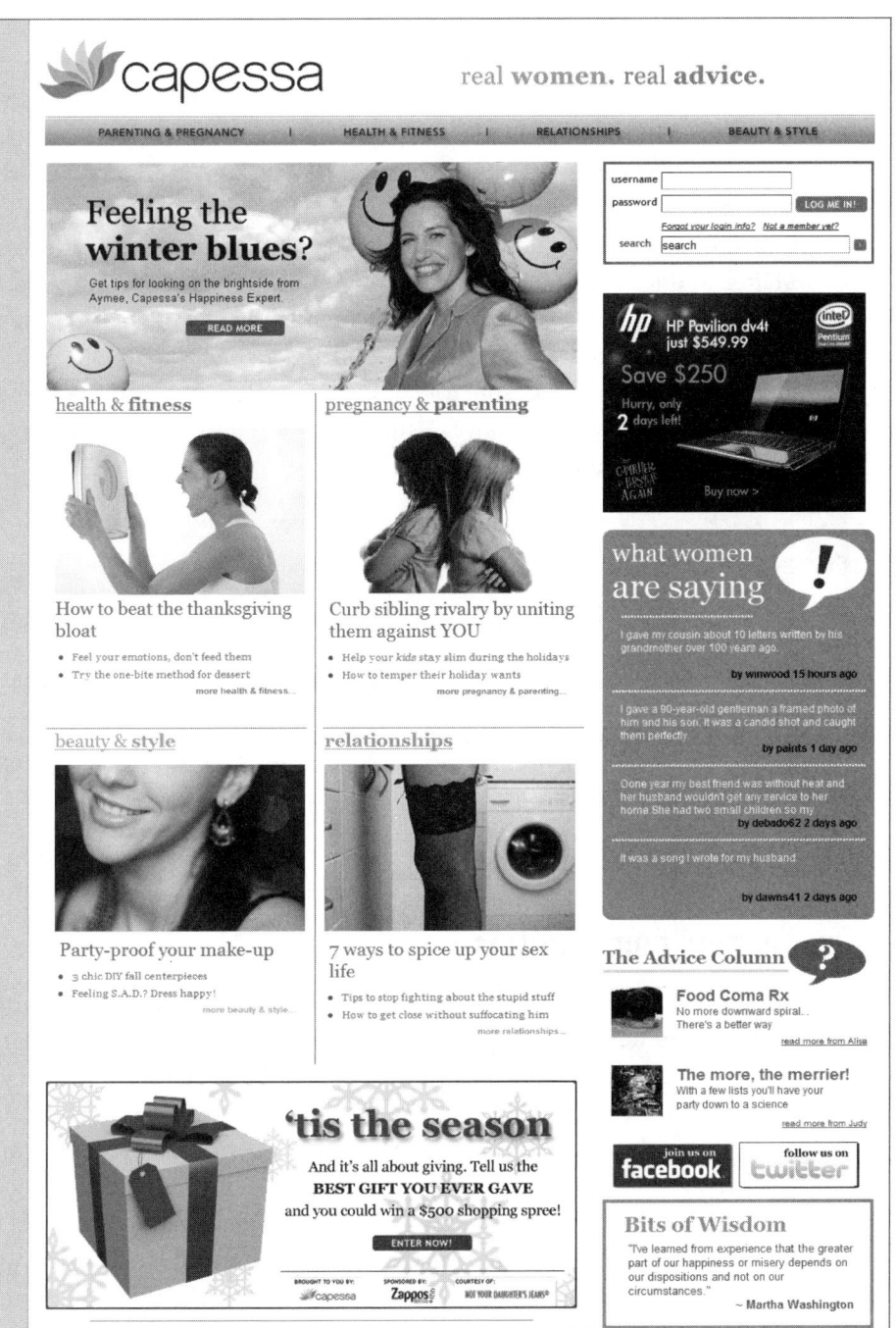

FIGURE 1.4 Capessa.com: A typical thematic community for women.

Other communities are still more exclusive. A number of companies are discovering the benefits of small, closed customer communities, which are often used for product testing and qualitative market research. Customers who fit a specific target group are invited to join these communities and participate in activities designed to generate input on products and marketing. Communispace is a company that creates and manages private brand communities for over 100 major companies and brands, including Hewlett Packard, Unilever, Mattel, and Kraft Foods. Communispace Vice President Debi Kleiman says they have found between 300 and 500 members to be the optimal size for communities aimed specifically at gathering customer insights. "We have identified this as a sweet spot for companies that want to engage with their customers in a meaningful way," she says. "When the community gets larger than that, you forgo some of the intimacy."

CAUTION
A **closed community** should not be confused with a **closed user group**, which is applied in a broader sense to a limited group of users with access to restricted areas of a website. Many websites include login-only areas where users can complete transactions, manage their personal details, access information or documents, interact with the company, and so on. Although some closed user groups can also be considered online communities, many others are not. Remember our main criterion for defining an online community: member-to-member relationships. Many closed user groups are just one-way communication channels that miss the opportunity to start a conversation.

Themed communities

Both open and closed communities are often focused around a certain topic or theme. Sometimes this is a topic of general interest such as travel, parenting, or health. In other cases, the topic is more obscure. Hamsterster.com is a community where members showcase photographs of their pet hamsters and create networks of virtual hamster friends for them. Lostzombies.com is a zombie-themed community. There are themed communities for professionals in a certain field, such as proteacher.net for the teaching profession. There are themed communities for aficionados of a certain hobby, such as the website scrapbookeronline.com for people who enjoy keeping scrapbooks. Think of any common interest that a group of people might share, and there is probably an online community based around it.

Many brands have their own themed communities that focus on the brand's products, as is the case with Lego.com and Barbiegirls.com. Others reinforce a key marketing message, such as campaignforrealbeauty.com, a themed community owned by the personal care brand Dove that focuses on self-esteem for women.

Other communities are centered on a specific activity, such as writing consumer reviews (e.g., ciao.com) or making predictions (e.g., ziitrend.com). Social shopping communities are a type of themed community based on shopping, or virtual window-shopping. On **social shopping** websites, members often share shopping wish-lists and recommendations, make friends with users who have similar shopping styles, publish photographs of themselves with products they've bought, and earn community privileges for shopping on the website. An example of a social shopping website is Threadless.com, where members design and photograph themselves with T-shirts that other members can purchase.

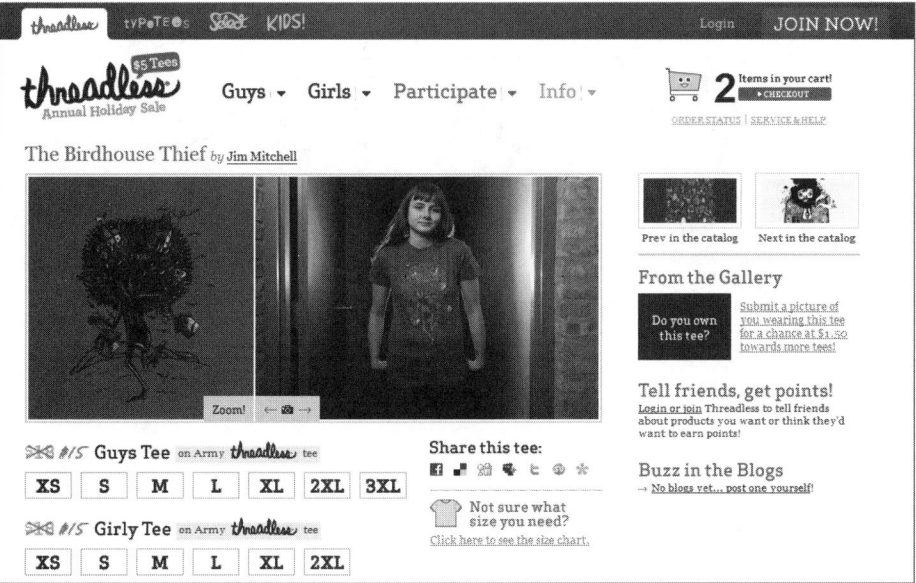

FIGURE 1.5 Threadless.com: A social shopping website whose members submit original T-shirt designs.

Social networks

We've defined online communities as websites where user relationships develop. By this definition, **social networks** are online communities in their purest form. On a social networking website, user relationships are the main focus and activity. Members introduce themselves with profile pages, create lists of their friends, meet their friends' friends, and communicate with each other in various ways. Facebook, MySpace, and Twitter are all examples of well-known social networks. An important subgroup of social networks is made up of business or professional networks such as LinkedIn and Xing. These communities are also focused on forming and managing relationships, but the main emphasis is on professional relationships rather than personal ones.

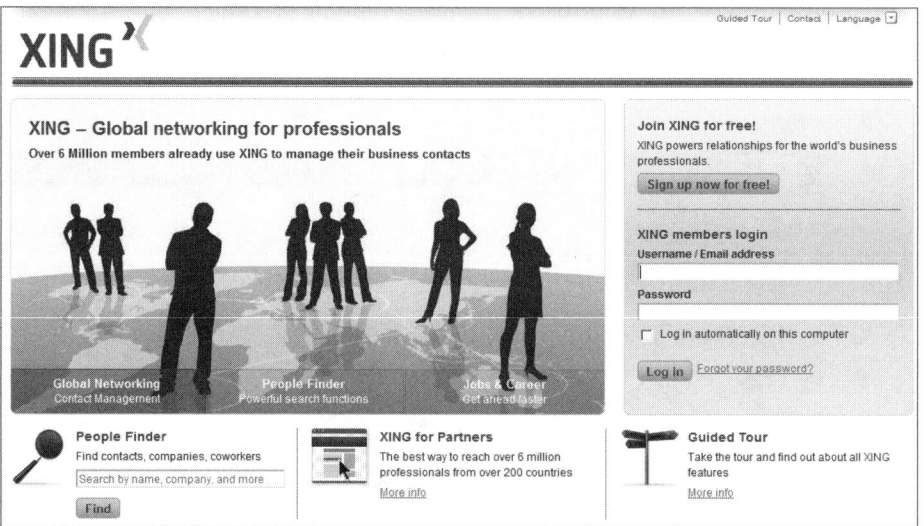

FIGURE 1.6 Xing: A business network that offers its services in sixteen languages.

Many social networks allow members to start their own themed micro-communities on the website, often called groups or clubs. The professional network Xing has over 22,000 such micro-communities created by members.

Ning.com is a kind of meta-community, a social network based around the creation of online communities.

THE POWER OF ONLINE COMMUNITIES

Not everyone is a member of an online community—yet—but the Internet community culture is already far too influential to be ignored, and increasing Internet penetration means that it will touch an ever-broader segment of the population. There's a huge, global conversation going on, and it's important to be aware of it and know what it might be saying about your brand. After reading this chapter, you have the necessary context to start doing that. The chapters that follow will explain, step-by-step, how you can harness the power of this phenomenon for your company's benefit, whether by listening to the global conversation, or by jumping in and starting a community of your own.

THE CHAPTER IN A NUTSHELL
What's an online community?

Online communities are an example of Web 2.0, a term that refers to an interactive use of the Internet, where visitors can publish content on a website.

The most important criterion for identifying an online community is the emphasis on member-to-member interaction. Community websites differ from wikis, blogs, and message boards in that they focus on helping users get to know each other and form relationships.

COMMON FEATURES OF COMMUNITY WEBSITES INCLUDE:
* An activity for members
* A nickname or online identity for each member
* A page summarizing information about each member
* A way for members to communicate one-on-one

SOME DIFFERENT TYPES OF ONLINE COMMUNITIES ARE:
* **Open versus closed communities:** Some allow anyone to join, some restrict membership based on certain criteria (e.g., M Power World is exclusively for BMW M model owners), and some are by invitation only (e.g. some private customer communities used for qualitative market research).

- **Themed communities:** These are centered around a common topic or activity. Some brands have themed communities that focus on specific products or on a theme related to key marketing messages. Examples: hamsterster.com, proteacher.net, lego.com, threadless.com

- **Social networks:** These are online communities in their purest form, where relationships between users are the main focus and activity. Examples: facebook.com, twitter.com, xing.com

TWO

WHAT CAN AN ONLINE COMMUNITY DO FOR YOUR COMPANY?

QUESTIONS ANSWERED IN THIS CHAPTER

* What are specific ways a community can benefit your brand?
* What are the business risks of a community and how can you address them?

BUSINESS BENEFITS OF AN ONLINE COMMUNITY

There's a global conversation going on in cyberspace. Here are just a few examples of what people are saying:

* About a printer/fax brand: "Just get a [brand name]. We've had three of them, and we've never had any problems."

* About a video game: "Isn't it time they put in some girl characters?"

* About a food brand: "Their products are totally artificial and full of toxic chemicals."

* About a cosmetics brand: "Personally, I love [brand name] even if their stuff's expensive, because they use quality ingredients."

What are they saying about your brand? What invaluable information can they give you? And what message do you want them to pass on to others? The online community trend can be a gold mine for companies that know how to tap into it. How can your company reap benefits of an online community? Let us count the ways.

1. Add value

Just by providing a community website to support and entertain your customers, you create a positive brand experience and offer value that differentiates you from your competitors.

2. Create loyalty

Just as people identify themselves with their community in the "real," offline world, members of your community website will feel like they're part of your brand. The result: a kind of loyalty that's hard to obtain by any other means. Your community members are investing in your brand every time they return to the website. They are building an identity in your community culture, a network of relationships with other members, and even a body of content that they have published there. Once customers are part of your community, it will be hard for competitors to lure them away.

> **CASE STUDY**
>
> Members of the business community Ecademy.com call themselves "Ecademists" and often display an Ecademy badge on their personal websites. "It's reputation by association," explains founder and CEO Penny Power. "The Ecademy brand says that this is a well-connected person who belongs to a high-quality group of people."

3. Get your message across

The focus you choose for building a thematic community can strongly associate certain qualities and values with your product. For example, the community website for a packaged food product might have either a healthy-living theme or a luxury-lifestyle theme, depending on its branding and market positioning. Whatever the key messages you want to send about your brand, your online community will listen to you carefully. An online community can also be an excellent forum for educating your customers about your company, your range of products, and new product lines. And your community members will educate each other about your brand: they're connected by a related interest and they're online to talk, so discussion of your product will emerge in a natural way.

4. Get your message out

What they say in the community won't stay in the community. It will get quoted on other websites; it will get called up on search engines; it might even get noticed by the press. And each of your community members is talking to a whole network of offline contacts and conveying an image of your brand.

5. Control your message

Your customers are already talking about your brand. Isn't it better to bring that conversation into your own territory, where you can listen, participate, and shape its direction? True, community members might tell you things that are uncomfortable to hear. But ignoring negative opinions doesn't make them go away, and if you don't provide a forum, there are plenty of other outlets where your customers can express themselves—maybe even an online community managed by competitors.

> **CASE STUDY**
>
> A disgruntled Dell computer customer wrote about his negative experiences with Dell on his blog (the popular buzzmachine.com). For a period of time, this was the top result on Google whenever someone searched for Dell. It's important to remember that customers will talk about your brand—whether you provide a forum or not.

6. Customer testimonials

Members will recommend your products to each other and share positive experiences of your brand. Keep in mind that many consumers do research on the Internet before making purchasing decisions. Your community members can convince them to buy your products. Internet users trust other Internet users more than they trust a company, so a happy online community can be a powerful marketing tool.

> **CASE STUDY**
>
> McDonald's used the social community MySpace as a platform for customer testimonials. They invited some MySpace members to learn more about McDonald's quality control procedures and ingredients. The resulting pictures, videos, and diary were then displayed as a brand profile page on MySpace. The focus was on the members: the page identified the members who had participated in the "Quality Tour" and used their photographs in the layout. So members saw that "Sweet Audrey" was on the Salad Tour, "Miss JC" took the Potato Tour, etc. This functioned as a member-to-member endorsement to increase trust in McDonald's quality.

7. Customer help desk

Community members love to advise other members. Giving advice is a way for them to make online friends and gain status in the community. It makes them feel like experts. And they *are* experts! You may be amazed to find that many seem to know more about your products than you do. Let them work for you. If your product is a printer, they can teach others how to use its features and even provide technical support. If you are selling a food product, they can offer recipes and preparation tips. As we've mentioned before, Internet users trust other users, so they are happy to receive advice from them. It's a win-win situation.

8. Viral marketing

Members of your website will bring their friends and family to the community. They will email links to their profile pages or to content they have published; they will talk about their community experiences, creating a buzz. Links to your community will start showing up on other websites and bringing new visitors. Everyone who visits your community website will learn something about your brand and message. A percentage of visitors will stay and join the community themselves, adding to this viral effect.

> **CASE STUDY**
>
> The business networking community Xing was launched with five-hundred members and doubled in size within twenty-four hours. "Seeing that the tool works makes you recommend it to all of your contacts," says Félix López Capel, business development manager for Xing Spain.
>
> To illustrate the potential of viral marketing, Anna looked at her own member account on Xing. She has ninety-five acquaintances in her Xing contact list. Imagine that she tells them something, and they pass it on to their own contact lists: 13,075 people will get the news. And if all those tell their contact lists, 587,930 Xing members will receive Anna's message.

9. Increase website traffic

A community will vastly increase traffic on your website. Your community members will come back again and again, creating an open line of communication between you and your customers. An important benefit to increasing traffic comes into play if you decide to monetize your website by incorporating advertising. The more visits to your pages, the more ad revenue you can earn.

> **CASE STUDY**
>
> The power of an online community to increase Web traffic is apparent if you compare Web statistics. One of the most successful German online newspapers, Spiegel Online, counted 394 million page impressions (page views) in December 2007. In the same month, the German social network studiVZ counted over 5,300 million impressions. This is surprising if you compare the number of users of these two sites: Spiegel Online had 4.5 million unique users, and studiVZ had 4 million. The difference in Web traffic is a result of studiVZ's online community format, which provides many more activities for members than the online magazine.

10. Generate content

As we discussed in the previous chapter, Web 2.0 is about users publishing content on a website. The bigger and more active your community, the more content the members will create for you. Here are some advantages of user-generated content versus content you create yourself.

* **Other users prefer it.** Internet users are more interested in what other users have to say then they are in content created by a company. Why not give the people what they want?

* **If they do it, you don't have to.** This advantage will be obvious to those of you in marketing or public relations departments. In addition to saving resources and time, there's another side to this that might be less obvious: you probably *couldn't* do it even if you tried. Of course, you or your company's copywriters or consultants are capable of writing perfectly good content for a Web 1.0 website. But imagine the staff resources that would

be required to reproduce the quantity of constantly renewed and updated content that's created by members on a successful community website.

* **Abundant and dynamic content.** Why is it a good thing to have new material continually being published on your website? Because a static website is only worth a single visit. No matter how talented and engaging your copywriter is, people don't generally want to keep coming back to read the same marketing blurb. Dynamic content gives users a reason to return repeatedly, even habitually, to your website, so that they are constantly reminded of your brand and it becomes part of their daily life.

11. Optimize for search engines

An online community can vastly improve your website's **search engine ranking**, meaning that when someone looks for information on a search engine such as Google, your website will appear higher up on the results list, where people are more likely to find it.

Search engine ranking depends on a number of factors, a fundamental one being the volume of website traffic. An online community multiplies the number of visits to your website, thereby boosting your search engine ranking. Another way that a community increases search engine ranking is through user-generated content. Such content generally contains a lot of key words that are relevant to search engines. And user-generated content grows organically. This is the best way to improve your search engine performance. Today's search engines monitor website development patterns because many companies hire Search Engine Optimization (SEO) experts and spend money to improve their search results. Search engines don't like this because it is seen as manipulation, and companies that artificially raise their results can be punished in the long term with lower rankings. So let your community members do your SEO the "honest" way.

> **CASE STUDY**
>
> The business community Ecademy allows members to keep blogs on the community website, which improves its search engine ranking. "We have a huge amount of constantly updating content, which optimizes our website for search engines," says CEO Penny Power. "Google checks us for new content every twenty-one minutes."

12. Product development

We've talked about several ways that you can put community members to work for you. They can create your website content, market your brand, recruit new customers, and provide customer support. What about involving them in product design? Okay, they're not going to design a spaceship. But why not a T-shirt, or a video game character?

13. Product testing

An online community provides a unique window into the minds of your customers. It allows you to eavesdrop on their conversations and learn what they really think about your products. And community members will care enough about your brand to give you specific feedback whenever you ask for it. If you are launching a new product, community members will be delighted to test it for you. You can invite volunteers to receive samples in their homes and report back. You can also send your members surveys, or run focus groups where a small number of people meet offline or in a chat room to discuss some aspect of your product.

> **CASE STUDY**
>
> The European community Toprural.com, which is focused on rural vacation homes, has used community feedback to make their website more useful to tourists. "Practically everything we do is based on user feedback," says founder/CEO François Derbaix. "During the last two years, we've run a survey on a panel of our users, and this has helped us to improve. For example, starting in July of 2008, we started including photographs in user opinions, because we saw that this was very important to users who are making travel plans."

FIGURE 2.1 Modo: The producer of 3D-modeling software offers a community to discuss the latest product versions and product features.

CASE STUDY

Communispace is a company that creates and manages private brand communities for over 100 major companies and brands. One of their clients, the investment firm Charles Schwab, created a community to understand the financial behavior of people in Generation X and learn how to enter their lives earlier. Traditionally, Charles Schwab had advertised retirement funds, but people in Generation X were not yet thinking about retirement. Their Communispace community helped them to come up with the answer—a high-yield checking account was the perfect product to attract Generation X to the firm and start building a relationship with them. The result of this exercise: a 55% increase in Generation X clients during the following year.

14. Data mining

The community will provide a huge amount of raw data about your customer base. What percentage of your community members are under thirty, like folk music, have children, and live in California? You can collect statistics and analyze a smaller sample of community members in great depth, learning everything about their everyday lives. You can encourage members to fill out profiles on their member pages, providing demographic information and detailing their interests and habits. If you give members room to express themselves freely, you can also get a level of insight into the minds of your customers not offered by traditional market research techniques. And by observing trends in your community, you can see how your customer base is evolving or shifting.

CASE STUDY

Campina, a Dutch dairy company with annual business of more than a billion dollars, launched a community for consumers of Optiwell, their yogurt drink intended as a weight loss aid. Optiwell's marketing manager Frank Müller believes that satisfied community members are "ambassadors of the brand." He adds, "And what's more, you can find out easily what customers want. That's the basis for marketing techniques in the future and helps us to make the brand more attractive."

CASE STUDY

Consumer products giant Unilever produces the personal care brand Axe, which is aimed at trendsetting young men. To understand their target customer better, Unilever hired Communispace to create and manage a community for these male style leaders between the ages of 18 and 22. "It's hard trying to get in the head set of this young guy when you're a 35-year-old female marketer," explains Debi Kleiman, Vice President of Communispace. "The community helps them to understand this guy, to get into his head. And as a result, they're able to design products and marketing messages that are really relevant to him, using his own language and style."

15. Press opportunities

You can convert your trend-watching into press releases. The theme of your community, any innovative features on it, the comments and content your members post, all of these can be shaped into stories that will interest the media and gain exposure for your brand.

16. Save money

The benefits that we've named so far can save your company money. You can spend less money on marketing if your community members market for you. You can save copywriting expenses if you have an online community working as a content-generation machine. And by listening to your community, you can avoid costly product and marketing mistakes.

17. Make money

Online communities can actually generate revenue—and a lot of it. Some of the ways an online community can earn money:

* display advertising
* email advertising
* affiliate marketing
* co-registration partners
* subscriber-only privileges
* links to buy products online

> **CASE STUDY**
>
> Livingathome.de, a cooking and lifestyle community, currently generates 20% of all magazine subscriptions for the German publishing house Gruner & Jahr.

FIGURE 2.2 Livingathome.de: One out of five subscriptions to magazines from the German publishing house Gruner & Jahr is purchased via this page.

In Chapter Seven, Monetizing Your Community, we'll discuss each of the revenue options offered by an online community, and strategies to take advantage of them without annoying your website users or compromising the image of your brand.

WHAT'S THE DOWNSIDE?

Writing this chapter was easy! We sat down to list the benefits of an online community for a brand or company and the list just grew by itself. So what's the catch? What's the downside of starting an online community of your own?

1. Development costs

Like a Web 1.0 site, a community website requires planning, technical infrastructure, and maintenance. The backend technology must also be much more reliable than when dealing with a Web 1.0 site. If user-generated content is lost in a system crash, you're in deep trouble. If thousands of community members can't log in because the system does not accept their password, then you're in trouble again. And it will be frustrating for your users if the system cannot cope with an unexpected rush of traffic. A reliable backend is essential to keeping a community running, building trust, and converting visitors into members.

However, there are ways to minimize development costs. Web 2.0 technology has become so common that a wide range of free or inexpensive software and tools are available. François Derbaix of Toprural.com suggests that using existing tools such as Ning or Drupal can be a better option than developing custom technology. "These tools allow you to customize, and they allow you to grow," he says. "You don't need your programmers to update the platform because these tools are constantly evolving. The main point isn't technical development—it's getting users who will participate."

2. Staffing costs

A community website will not manage itself. You will have to devote some staff resources to supervising the community, removing inappropriate content, and addressing member concerns. However, there are some tricks of the trade that can reduce this workload significantly. By putting experienced members in the role of moderators or guides, setting up a system for self-policing in the community, and including **FAQs** (Frequently Asked Questions) and other help texts on the site, you can take some of the burden off your staff. We will discuss all of these strategies in more detail in Chapter Six, Care and Feeding of Your Members.

3. Public criticism

The downside of open discussion is that it may take a direction you don't like. Your online community will give you feedback, and some of that feedback may be negative. Even if you appreciate constructive criticism, you might prefer not to see it published on the Internet where everyone can read it.

On the other hand, if you keep the discussion off your website, it's likely to surface somewhere else. In your own community, you can identify the author of negative opinions, and you have many options for responding. You can write a public comment, or you can engage the user in a private dialogue. If you treat the user with respect and care, you have a good chance of turning negative comments into a positive brand experience.

Providing a forum for your customers gives you the opportunity to answer their concerns. And, in the long term, open discussion is a way to create trust.

> **CASE STUDY**
>
> In our interview with 11870.com, a community that publishes reviews of services, they explained that business owners can actually benefit from critical reviews. They gave us an example of a restaurant that received a negative review from an 11870.com member. The restaurant owner responded by inviting the member to a free dinner and managed to change his opinion of the restaurant.

4. Undesirable content

Public criticism is not the only public relations risk that can arise with an online community. The tricky part of user-generated content is that you never know in advance what might end up on your website. Users will post offensive content, as well as material that is simply inconsistent with your branding strategy.

> **CASE STUDY**
>
> A popular German online magazine, Spiegel.de, quickly withdrew from a partnership agreement with the music community Last.fm after receiving complaints about Nazi songs on the community website. Spiegel.de didn't want this type of content associated with their brand.

KEYS TO DEALING WITH UNDESIRABLE CONTENT

* Always clearly indicate the origin of user-generated content, marking each piece of content with the author's user name.
* Offer website users an efficient way to report offensive content.
* Have staff and tools to censor content when there is a complaint. There are also tools that can be used to screen content before it goes online. We will discuss these points in more detail in Chapter Six, Care and Feeding of Your Members.

> **CASE STUDY**
>
> The business community Ecademy.com offers a button where members can anonymously report abusive content. CEO Penny Power explains, "If someone reports you, you receive a message explaining the error that the community feel you are making, however, you do not know the identity of the complainer—they remain anonymous to ensure witch hunts do not take place."

5. Legal exposure

In addition to publishing offensive or illegal content, abusive members may use your website to harass other members, insult other companies, or reproduce material protected by copyright. It is important to get a lawyer's help in reducing your legal exposure before you launch an online community. One way that community sites attempt to reduce their risks is with carefully worded Terms of Use agreements that members must sign at registration, in which they agree to abide by standards of conduct and assume responsibility for their actions. It is also important to have the infrastructure in place to react quickly when problems arise.

6. Information leaks

Another risk that comes with an online community of enthusiastic customers is that someone will post confidential information about your company.

> **EXAMPLES OF INFORMATION LEAKS**
>
> A member of a community sponsored by a home appliance brand described a new coffeemaker in the pipeline before the official launch of this product.
>
> A member of an online survey community posted information about a paid market research survey he took, including tips on getting past demographic filter questions.
>
> A community member who received a rude email from a company's customer service published the content of that email on their community website.

Let's examine the risk of information leaks by looking separately at each of the examples above. In the case of the coffeemaker, the first question to consider is how this fact reached the community member in the first place. If the information is in fact genuine, then perhaps the company needs to have stricter employee confidentiality policies or handle documents in a more secure manner.

Similarly, in the case of the online survey community, participants should be required to agree to a confidentiality statement created by a lawyer. A community member who violates this contract can be threatened with legal consequences. Either way, the company's first action should be to take the member's content offline. Open exchange may be the first value of the Internet, but the website belongs to a company, and there are times when it's in the company's greater interest to exert control.

With the customer service complaint, on the other hand, it is probably not advisable to remove the content, since censorship will likely create a worse public relations issue than the content in question. A better option might be to respond to the content, apologizing for the actions of the customer service representative and assuring the community of the company's commitment to high-quality customer service. And, of course, the company should actually take measures to address the apparent problem with their customer service department. Although the publication of the customer service email does not make the company look good, proper handling of the situation can actually improve the company's image in the long term.

7. Customer sense of entitlement

One of the wonderful aspects of an online community is the deep sense of connection that customers can develop with your brand. However, this intense relationship between brand and customer can have a negative side. In Chapter Five, Motivating Your Members, we will talk about how to engage members in your community and keep them coming back. Our techniques really work. The problem is that, strange as it may seem, some users will actually become dependent on the website. Downtime for maintenance? Expect some anxious or even angry emails from users who are missing their "fix." And if you decide to remove their favorite features, you may face a full-scale protest in the community. Telling them to "get a life" is not an option—these are your customers.

TRUE STORY
After a slight website redesign that involved moving important functionalities from the left to the right side of the page, a community manager from a shopping website says that members wrote to her complaining that they felt dizzy and disoriented.

Members who regularly contribute to a community often begin to view themselves as its real owners. "We made this website what it is today," they say, with some justification. If you involve members deeply in brand development, they may also begin to see themselves as owners of the brand and become angry when changes are made to product features without consulting them.

> **CASE STUDY**
>
> A TV channel has a vibrant community website with millions of regular users. Members of this community participate actively in product development. The same members also complain every time the TV channel changes anything, from the decoration of a set to a news anchor to the programming schedule. They send a huge number of emails to the TV channel, demanding detailed justifications of the decisions that have been made.

It is important to anticipate this problem and to walk the delicate line between making your customers feel important and letting them believe that they're in charge. The benefits of a loyal, passionate customer base are enormous, so don't be too frightened by the prospect of "customers who love too much." With careful management of the community relationship, you should be able to prevent it from turning into a fatal attraction.

8. Conflicts with your communication policy

Every company has rules for communication with press, customers, and partners, among others. A community can cause conflicts if your principles are too rigid, for example:

* Never comment on rumors
* Never respond to negative comments
* Never answer questions related to product development.

Imagine that a community member posts a negative comment about your product or writes about a rumor related to your company. How are you going to react? If you censor the content, another user might notice and start a blog discussion on the subject, creating a public relations fiasco.

Online community members are part of an Internet culture that values transparency and free expression. Before starting a community, make sure that your organization will be able to accommodate this. Work with your public relations department to develop a communication strategy adapted to the special needs and opportunities of an open conversation online.

PREPARING FOR SUCCESS

As we've seen, companies have a lot to gain from joining the online communities trend. The following chapters will guide you through the whole process of building, managing, and monetizing an online community. We will explain how to minimize your risks and solve problems that may arise, and how to take advantage of the many benefits an online community can offer.

THE CHAPTER IN A NUTSHELL
What can an online community do for your company?

BUSINESS BENEFITS OF AN ONLINE COMMUNITY

1. Build a website that adds value
2. Create brand loyalty
3. Communicate key messages about your brand
4. Project your message to the world
5. Respond to criticism on your own terms
6. Customers will recommend your products
7. Customers will help each other
8. Gain new customers through viral marketing
9. Increase website traffic
10. Generate dynamic website content
11. Improve your search engine ranking
12. Involve your customers in product development
13. Use your customers for product testing
14. Learn more about your customers
15. Get press exposure
16. Save money and resources
17. Generate revenue

THE RISKS THAT COME WITH AN ONLINE COMMUNITY, AND HOW TO DEAL WITH THEM

1. Technology costs: employ low-cost solutions that are widely available
2. Staffing costs: reduce them with community self-help strategies
3. Public criticism of your brand: use it as an opportunity to respond
4. Undesirable content: take measures to block it, disassociate yourself from it, and remove it
5. Legal risks: consult a lawyer to minimize your exposure
6. Information leaks: address the source of the problem
7. Customers who think they "own the brand": manage the relationship and benefit from their loyalty
8. Conflicts with your communication policy: agree on a workable strategy for your community

THREE

HOW TO SET UP YOUR COMMUNITY

QUESTIONS ANSWERED IN THIS CHAPTER

* What research will give you a head start on your community project?
* What is the most strategic way to choose your community's themes?
* What kind of activities should your community offer?
* How is the competitive landscape different online?
* What is the optimal level of brand visibility in your community?
* What features and functions should your website include?
* What infrastructure will your community require?

DEFINE YOUR COMMUNITY STRATEGY

Whether you are still unsure what kind of community to start or you have already settled on a plan, there are certain points you should keep in mind from the beginning to position your site for success. In this chapter, we'll walk you through the steps of defining a community model that will bring value to your brand, then planning the website and infrastructure to support it. If you are just starting out, you will be able to leave this chapter with a fully formed community plan. If you have a plan already, then you can use this chapter to develop and refine it and improve your results.

Begin with what you have

If you're planning a community for an established company, then you're never starting from zero. Your company's existing brand strategy, marketing material, and infrastructure are a foundation on which you can build. Even if your company is relatively new, you probably have some or all of the following to draw upon: market research information, branding documents, marketing plan, business plan, and initial demographic data on customers.

Have a look at your current company websites. The bigger your company, the more websites you likely already have: corporate sites, microsites, brand pages, product group pages, business to business (B2B) pages, business to consumer (B2C) pages, and so on. What do they tell you about your customers? Is there any content that could be relevant to a community? Maybe multiple websites could be combined into a portal that offers brand information and a community embedded within it.

Also look carefully at your company's current customer relationship management (CRM) program. There is probably a call center or an email help desk; perhaps your company includes postcards in its product packaging so that customers can register their purchases. Consider how your online community can work in sync with CRM. Customer mailing lists will become a source of website recruitment, while your website registration form can be designed for consistency with your data-collection postcards. Your help desk may be able to supply user-generated content that you can recycle in your community with the customers' permission.

TIP
As part of your community, you might decide to offer a forum for customer support, or Webinars (online seminars) with advice for using your products.

Take advantage of valuable sources of customer insight already available in your company. Your company's customer support staff probably have a deep familiarity with the concerns of your customers. They may even keep statistics on customer complaints and feedback. Web tracking statistics can also provide a wealth of relevant data. Find out where people spend the most time on your current websites and where they are coming from. If you are drawing visitors from Google, check which keywords are bringing them. Where are you losing traffic, and where does that traffic go? Look for trends in the number of visits and **page impressions** (pages viewed). If there are peaks, investigate the cause. Pay special attention to visitors who leave the website quickly after arriving, and try to figure out why they leave. They could represent a missed market opportunity and even a whole target group that hasn't yet been identified.

CAUTION
Web tracking results are easy to misinterpret. If you are not a Web tracking expert yourself, find one in your company to help you sort out the meaning behind the numbers.

Where are you headed?

Defining clear goals at the outset of your project is essential to choosing the right community model, presenting it effectively within your organization, and measuring success when it comes. Chapter Two, "What Can an Online Community Do for Your Company?," gave an overview of seventeen potential business benefits of online communities. Which ones are the most important to you? Think about how the answer to that question could impact your community model. If your priority is to increase traffic on your corporate website, you might want to focus on themes and activities that help with search engines and include plenty of viral elements. If you're primarily after press exposure, you could try to generate content related to current events and hot-button topics, or make your community innovative or groundbreaking in some way.

If you're looking for a source of product testing, your activities might include surveys, a product-related forum, chat-based focus groups, and online diaries related to the product use.

Based on your goals, there will be a target population that you want to participate in your community. In many cases, this will mirror your customer population or the visitors to your current corporate websites. Perhaps you want to appeal to the broadest range of users. Or you might want to focus on a specific customer demographic, for example, homemakers, teens, business people, or health care professionals. Maybe you intend to use your community to expand your market, appealing to a new kind of customer or gaining exposure in a foreign country. Take some time to define your target carefully based on your goals. This strategic decision has implications for every aspect of your community, from website colors and design, to tone and communication style, to the registration process, activities and benefits offered, and the kind of member management that will be required.

GET STARTED

Once you have a clear vision of your goals and target population, you are ready to start brainstorming to develop themes for your community. Here is an exercise to get you started.

THREE STEPS TO DEFINING YOUR THEMES

* *Step 1:* For a moment, try to forget about your products and the millions of statistics coming from your marketing department. What are the interests of your target users? What are their needs in their daily lives? What themes do these suggest? Write them all down.

* *Step 2:* Cluster the themes in bigger groups. Try to identify five to seven groups. These groups are a basis for navigation structure within the community, for example, to cluster discussion groups.

* *Step 3:* Write your company's name in the center of a piece of paper. Which themes are the nearest to your brand? Which themes are not so brand-related? The more brand-related a theme is, the more space you can dedicate to this theme in the community.

Keeping in mind the themes you've defined, you will have to plan some activities for your users. This is not Web 1.0; community members are not on your website to read, but to participate, and you should provide them with plenty to do there. Perhaps the best starting point for generating activity ideas is the exercise we suggested earlier, where you analyzed your target users, their interests, and their needs. In what ways could your website improve their lives? What tools can you offer to help them during a typical day? The more deeply you can integrate your community into the daily life of your members, the better. You will also want activities that keep your users coming back to the website again and again so you can maintain an ongoing relationship with them.

POPULAR ONLINE COMMUNITY ACTIVITIES

* Interactive diaries or blogs
* Publishing reviews
* Publishing original photos, video, and artwork
* Shopping wish-lists, shopping and product advice
* Rating or voting on something
* Simulations, fantasy lives or activities, or interactive games
* Message boards or discussion groups based around a specific theme
* Interfaces dealing with offline communities, such as excursions, sports, or dating
* Business or career networking opportunities for your members

What are the best activities for your community? In a few words: the activities best suited to your defined goals that will have the greatest long-term appeal to your target users.

FIGURE 3.1 MySpace: (Heading on top left means: "Change design.") Choosing an individual design is one activity to keep the members busy.

Principles of activity design

In thinking about whether an activity is right for your site, keep the following principles in mind:

* It should be something your user will actually want to do. Put yourself in the users' shoes. If there's nothing in it for them, they won't do it.

* It should have lasting power. Avoid activities that will get boring after a few repetitions. You want your user to spend time on the website.

* It should be open-ended. Keep activities and conversation topics open enough that the user will not run out of things to do or say. You want your user to keep coming back.

* It should be intuitive. Users do not want to read an instruction manual. They want to be able to understand activities right away.

ANALYZE YOUR COMPETITION

As you are developing your community plan, take some time to analyze your potential competitors. You may think that you already know your competition, but remember that the competitive landscape online is quite different from what you have been dealing with offline. For example, imagine that you are a pasta producer and want to start a cooking community. One of your competitors might even be an individual who owns a popular blog about Italian recipes. Or you might be competing against a women's magazine that offers successful discussion groups for users to talk about cooking pasta. A good tool to start identifying these new competitors is a search engine. Do searches on key words and phrases that your members will use to find websites that offer the same benefits as your community. Then analyze your new competitors. What do they offer? And what are they lacking? What are their strengths and weaknesses? What can you do better?

DEFINE THE ROLE OF YOUR BRAND

Another important strategic question is how visible the association should be between the community and your brand. You may have a fashionable brand that consumers already know and love. Nintendo, Apple, BMW, Lego, and

M&M's are examples of brands with a high level of established popularity. Most companies are in a different situation: people like their brands but do not love them. In this case, we recommend avoiding a strict separation between brand and community sites.

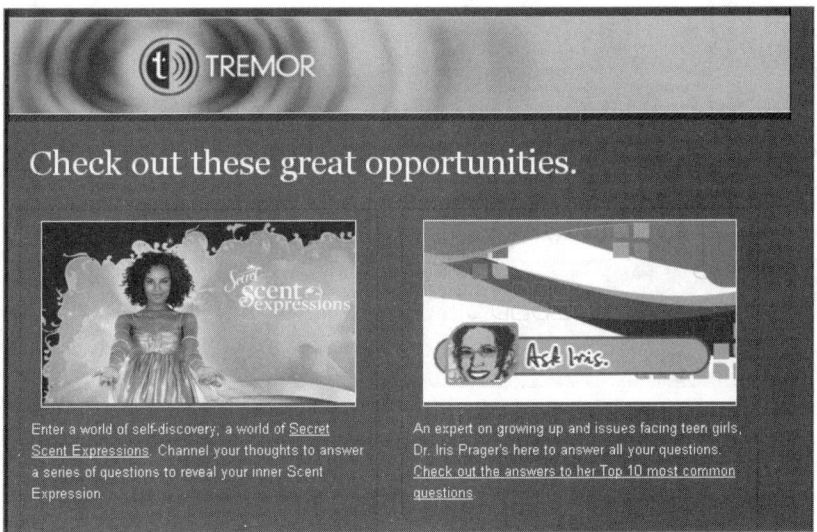

FIGURE 3.2 Tremor: A community where the brand is invisible.

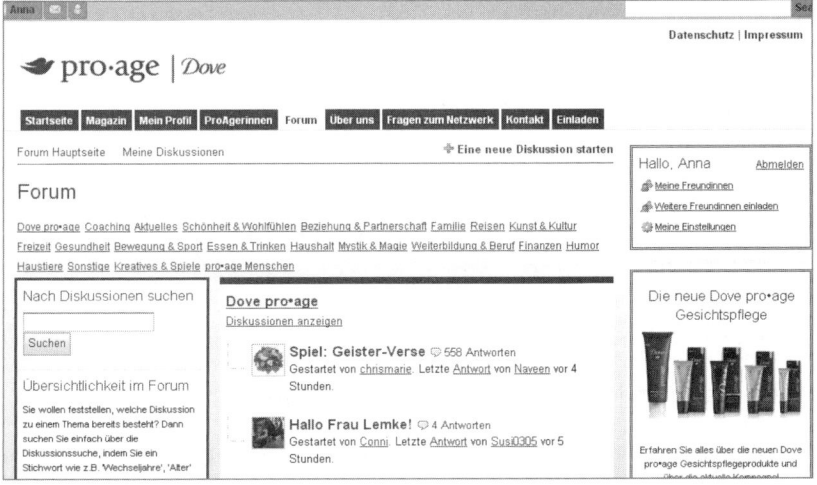

FIGURE 3.3 Pro•Age Network: The design makes it clear that this community is brand-related.

FIGURE 3.4 Homepage of Mini Space: The focus is not on the brand, but on the users' creativity.

IDEAS FOR INTEGRATING BRAND AND COMMUNITY

* Map different scenarios of how a customer might find his or her way from brand-related information to the community and from the community to the brand website. What are the **click paths**? The more that are available, the better!

* Choose brand-related themes for your community.

* We suggest mixing brand information with community content in a ratio of 1:3. In our experience, that is the best balance for introducing a brand without losing the perceived authenticity of the community.

* Keep your brand in the background as the website's sponsor but don't let it become intrusive. You want to run a community, not an online advertising channel.

* Let people in your company become active community members. Give their user profiles a special symbol to show that they are part of your company. For many customers, it is a positive experience to have such direct contact with company representatives.

* The brand-related content on your community website should include exclusive information. This is what will appeal to users the most. Offer them more details and news about products and services than they can find elsewhere on the Web. If you use the same content that you send out to the press, your members will be disappointed and will have no reason to come back.

> **CASE STUDY**
>
> BMW owns a community for drivers of the M sports models and makes a point of offering members brand information that they can't get elsewhere. "Our members are keen to read news about their beloved cars," says Helmut Bruendl, community manager. "From the very beginning, we took care to offer them exclusive magazine articles. In my opinion, this was one of the criteria for our community's success."

Even if a community is not 100% brand-focused, it is important to give something back to the user that is strictly brand-related. If content is too far away from the brand, people will go elsewhere on the Web. There should always be a reason for the user to come to your page rather than another company's. If you offer weather reports instead of exclusive product pictures, the user has no reason to stay on your page. No matter how closely weather reports are related to your brand, they are not ideal as content for your community page or as a central topic for your discussion forum. Why should a user choose your site? Weather reports can be found all over the Web.

PLAN YOUR WEBSITE

Your online community will need a website to house it. When planning this website, consider not only the theme and brand integration strategy you have chosen, but also everything you have learned about your target users. Are they knowledgeable about the Internet? If not, you should avoid tricky navigation, flashy website design, and complex functionalities. What are the circumstances in which they're likely to access the website? Are you dealing with an impatient user who makes frequent short visits, or a more relaxed user willing to spend some time surfing around? The second type of user likes **content navigation**, where one activity or piece of content leads organically to another, while users who are in a hurry prefer a well-structured **navigation bar** or menu of links. Elderly users generally prefer easy functionalities that do not require tricky button combinations; they often have trouble double-clicking and using long dropdown menus. What communication style is right for your users? Will they understand website terms such as "login," or will they require a different kind of language? What colors and images are most appropriate? A business community is quite different from a community for teenagers, or one for senior citizens.

Although content varies depending on the community websites' specific themes and activities, certain common elements can be found on most community sites.

COMMUNITY WEBSITE CHECKLIST

- Homepage
- Registration page
- Login
- Member profile pages
- Terms of use
- Help page
- Company information
- Features

Your homepage

The homepage is the first thing most users will see when they come to your website, so it should be attractive to your target user and tell new visitors at a glance what your community is about.

Show them where they are

The first task of the homepage is to identify your website with a logo and other branding elements so that visitors know they have come to the right place. Most community websites also include a very brief mission statement that summarizes the idea of the community in just a few words.

> **EXAMPLES OF COMMUNITY MISSION STATEMENTS**
>
> * Facebook helps you connect and share with the people in your life.
> * YouTube: Broadcast Yourself
> * TripAdvisor.com: Get the Truth. Then Go.

You will notice that these examples are extremely concise. Remember that Web 2.0 users are generally unwilling to spend time reading company-generated text on the website. When you need to post information there, consider ways to present it that allow the eye to take it in all at once. Think in terms of headlines, titles, graphics, and symbols, rather than sentences and paragraphs.

Besides the mission statement, many community websites feature examples of user-generated content on the homepage. Online communities are based around the contributions of their members. Whether these contributions take the form of recipes, videos, or consumer reviews, displaying some examples is an efficient way to give new users a taste of your community, while showing returning members the content that interests them most.

TIP
Programming your homepage to show the most recent contributions first will keep the content on the page fresh and changing.

Often selected members are displayed on the homepage in the form of profile photos, avatars, or another symbol that represents their online identity. Featuring members is a good way to give a community feeling to your homepage. The members might be shown at random on a rotating basis or chosen for the volume of their website contributions. Members generally appreciate being given this kind of exposure. It helps them meet other members and shows that they are part of your website.

Show them where to go

A homepage should make it easy for users to get to other pages on your website, either where *they* want to go or where *you* want them to go. Homepages generally display a menu, or several menus, of links to other site pages. Links to log in and register are often set apart from the menu to make these easier to find. The most important links and content get placed in a prominent position near the top of the page. Terms and conditions, company information, and similar pages are often linked to a separate menu at the bottom where they are less visible but can be found if a user looks for them.

People who work in website planning and design talk about **page real estate**. On a website, as in a city, there are prime locations, areas that have a higher level of visibility than others. The gaze of a website user will normally go first to the top part of the page. It is therefore a good idea to put your logo, mission statement, and most important links, including login and registration options, high up on the homepage. Content that falls below the middle of a viewer's computer screen is less visible, and if the viewer has to scroll down to reach a piece of content, there is a good chance that it won't be seen at all.

Registration page

Community websites normally require users to go through a formal registration process before adding content to the website. The easier you make it to register, the more users are likely to do it. This means displaying a registration link prominently on the homepage, keeping registration questions to a minimum, making the process as simple and clear as possible, and directly addressing user concerns about joining (for example, by mentioning that registration is free and that members' personal details will stay confidential).

You'll find more extensive advice on member recruitment and registration forms in Chapter Four, Member Recruitment.

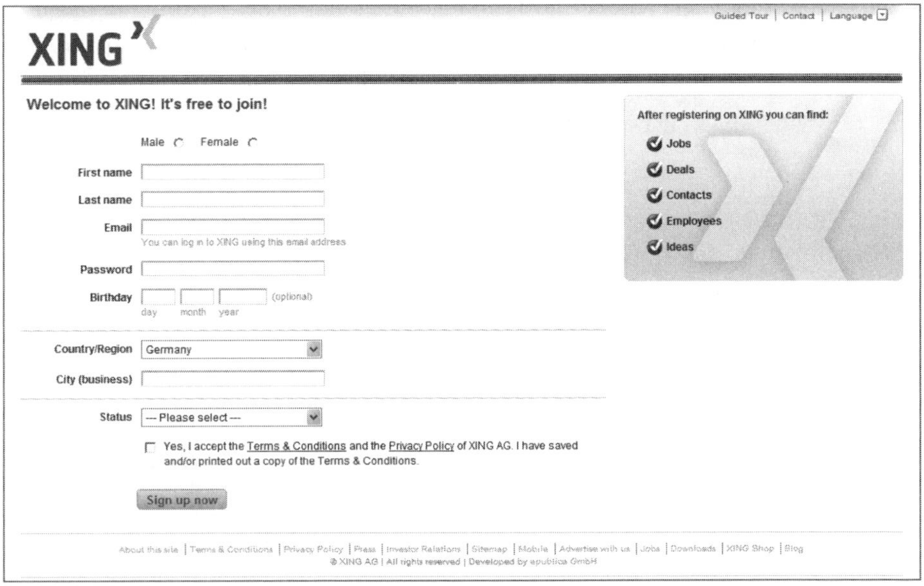

FIGURE 3.5 Xing registration page: Contains as few elements as possible and uses a very brief text to explain the benefits of membership.

Login link

Registered members are normally asked to identify themselves by entering a login name, email address, or nickname, and a password before participating in website activities. It's helpful to provide a password recovery link in the same place. You might also offer members the option of saving their website password in their computer.

TIP
Users who would like to participate on the website often attempt to log in even if they are not registered. You can help these users by placing registration and login options close together on the website and labeling them clearly to avoid confusion. When a login attempt fails, the user can be shown a registration link with a message saying, "If you haven't joined already, click here to do so now."

Member profile pages

On most community websites, there is a specific page dedicated to each member. This page will contain the member's name or website nickname and links to content created by that member, as well as a profile photo or avatar if one is available, and details that the member has chosen to make public such as hometown, age, and hobbies.

CAUTION
Inform members about which information provided by them will be displayed publicly.

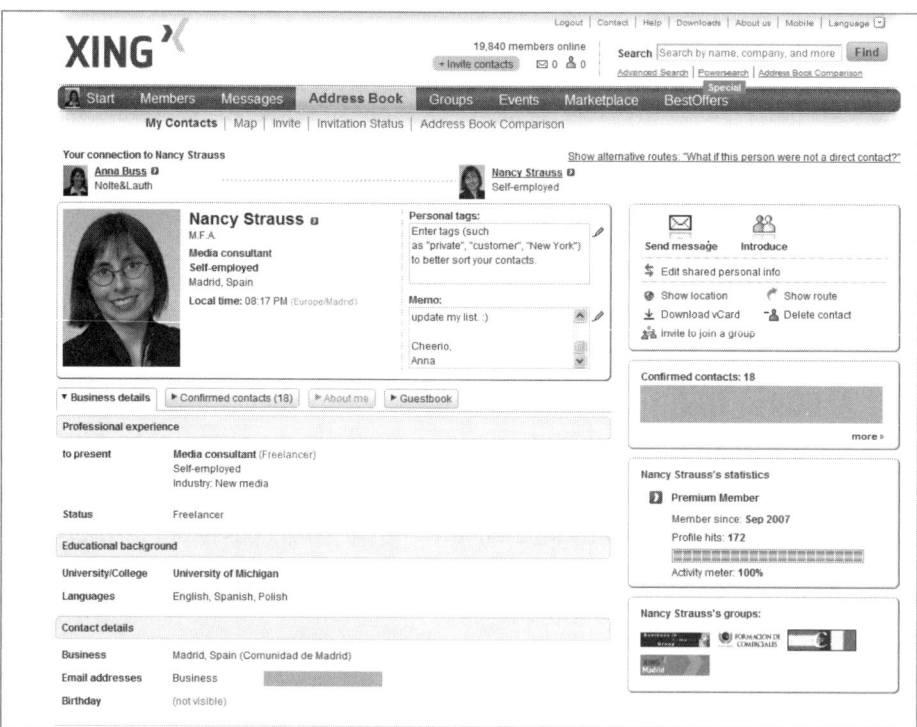

FIGURE 3.6 A Xing member profile: There are more than ten activities to do here. You can invite this member to join a group or write in her guestbook.

A member's profile page often includes statistics about the member's community participation and links to a message book or internal email account where he or she can be contacted personally. On many community websites, members can publish **friend lists** on their profile pages, showing the names or nicknames of their friends within the community. This feature is very good for community building as it encourages members to form relationships and to make new contacts through the friends lists of their friends. A member's profile page is normally linked to the member's nickname wherever it appears on the website. By clicking on the member's nickname, you are taken to that member's profile page.

There is usually a separate link to access your own profile page after logging in. Members can see functions on their profile pages that are not accessible to other members. They use their own profile pages as control panels to manage various aspects of their membership.

COMMON THINGS MEMBERS DO ON THEIR PROFILE PAGES

* Change their public information, including their member photo or avatar
* Update their registration details
* Change account email or password
* Change subscription status to newsletters, email alerts, direct marketing emails, and other optional or paid features
* Read messages from other members
* Check changes in their website activity statistics
* Unsubscribe

Many communities let members design and decorate their profile pages as another way to express themselves and feel at home on a website.

Terms of use

On every community website, it's important to post a Terms of Use or Terms and Conditions statement and require users to agree to it during the registration process. The specific content of this contract should be worked out with a lawyer.

WHY YOU NEED A TERMS OF USE CONTRACT

* To protect your company from legal responsibility for your users' content and actions

* To ensure your right to modify, reproduce, and remove user-generated content

* To ensure your right to cancel users' accounts when you deem suitable

* Depending on your country, you may be legally required to post one

Most websites also display data protection policies as part of, or separately from, the Terms of Use. You should also have your legal counsel advise you about legal requirements in your country related to data protection. Within the European Union, for example, data protection laws are quite strict and violations can result in heavy fines.

Help page

Community websites normally provide a way for users to contact the company if they have a problem, as well as a list of frequently asked questions (**FAQ**s) and answers. If you are anticipating a large amount of traffic on your website, we strongly advise posting an email address rather than a phone number for member support, unless you have a call center infrastructure already in place. Otherwise, the volume of phone calls can quickly become unmanageable. Another trick that can reduce the member support workload is posting the contact email at the bottom of the FAQ list so that users are forced to scroll down the FAQ page in order to find it. If you post the contact email at the top of the FAQ page, users will tend to send an unnecessary email before checking to see if their questions are already answered on the page.

Company information

For users who want to know about the company behind the community, you can post an About Us page or a link to your corporate website, as well as whatever publisher information is legally required in your country.

Features

This is the aspect of the website that will vary the most, depending on the activities you have chosen for your community. If your community is about photo sharing, then you will need a photo upload page and different ways to browse photos uploaded by other members. If your community is about online games, you will, of course, need the games. The features pages on your website will have two parts:

1. The functions that allow members to participate.

2. A display of other members' participation.

As much as possible, the website should be designed to allow members to participate autonomously. If your members will be contributing recipes, let them post the recipes on the website directly rather than sending them to you via email. If too much staff intervention is required in member activities, it will overburden your staff and keep your website from being as dynamic as it should be. Internet users accustomed to instant gratification will lose interest in your community if there is a lag time between making a contribution and seeing the result.

A display of member contributions is often ordered so that the most recent contributions are shown first or on top. This is a highly dynamic display option because it changes every time a new contribution is added. Sometimes viewers can choose to sort content lists in various ways; for example, by date or by popularity (if there is some kind of ranking or rating system incorporated). In many cases, the viewer can also use a search function to find contributions based on key words or other criteria. To see all content created by a specific member, you can normally click on the member's user name to be sent to his or her profile page.

Notes for the website developer

This book is not intended as a technical guide—there are plenty of technical resources out there if you need them—but here are a few points about community websites that should be kept in mind from the very beginning of technical development:

1. Anticipate a high volume of traffic and a potentially huge amount of user-generated data.

2. Website reliability is especially important for a community website; users will be upset if they can't log on.

3. Data backup is essential; you cannot afford to lose user-generated content or profile information.

4. Pages should load quickly; users will not want to spend time on the website if they have to wait between actions.

5. Search engines will be a major recruitment source, so search engine optimization (SEO) should be built into the website structure.

6. Automate processes such as password reminder and opt-out to reduce the potential for errors and give users instant results.

TIP
Find out if your website will eventually be translated into Asian languages or other languages with double-byte alphabets. Programming the website from the beginning to accommodate this can save a lot of trouble later on.

PLAN YOUR INFRASTRUCTURE

An online community will not manage itself. Someone has to provide support to members, answer their emails, resolve member disputes, block the accounts of abusers, remove inappropriate content, and transmit member feedback to the relevant departments. All of these tasks fall under the role we call **community manager**. Whether you need a part-time community manager or a dedicated team will depend on the size of your community and the degree of moderation desired. You might start with one part-time or full-time resource and have additional budget and resources lined up in order to expand the team quickly as the community grows. A more extensive discussion of community management can be found in Chapter Six, Care and Feeding of Your Members.

Community managers will need a way to access and manage member accounts and website content. At the same time you are planning the community website, you should plan an **admin (administration) panel** to manage it. The admin panel should allow community managers to:

* Search for a member by login name and email address (as a minimum) to access member account data

* View member registration information, registration date, membership status, and the content generated by each member

* Block or unsubscribe members

* Leave a note corresponding to each member account action in the member's record where it can be viewed by other community managers

* Censor user-generated content.

It might also be desirable to let them:

* View statistics about the community

* Send mass mailings to the community

* Export certain types of member data into an Excel file

* Screen images or video content before it goes online

* Manage rewards, payments, or fees if these are included in your community model (more on member reward programs can be found in Chapter Five, Motivating Your Members).

In addition to community management infrastructure, you will need a website domain and a Web server. A **domain name** is the Web address of your community, for example, www.yourcommunity.com. Perhaps you will be using the same domain name as an existing company website. Otherwise, you can check for and purchase an available domain name on any number of domain registration websites such as www.000domains.com and www.mydomain.com. Choose a name that will be easy for people to remember and spell correctly.

If you will be launching websites outside of the U.S., it's a good idea to reserve country domains (for instance, co.uk for the UK, .ca for Canada, .es for France) in addition to the .com domain.

TIP
To avoid losing visitors due to spelling or typing errors, you might want to buy possible misspellings of your domain (www.yourecommunity.com) and point these addresses to your main website.

A **Web server** is the computer that will host your website. You can rent a server or server space from a website hosting company, some of which offer 24-hour technical support. But for the long term, you will probably choose to have your own server in-house, in which case you will also need a systems administrator to take care of it.

A USER-CENTERED APPROACH

For your online community to function, your users have to come back over a period of time, allowing them to form relationships with each other and with your brand. Almost all of the benefits that can be derived from an online community increase in proportion to the amount of activity on your website. But users will only spend time on your website if they feel comfortable there and are getting something in return. It's therefore important to identify your target users according to your business goals, and then keep their needs and preferences at the center of your planning, rather than running the risk of building something they won't want to use. In the next chapter, we'll talk about how to find these target users and bring them to your website once you've designed the perfect community for them.

THE CHAPTER IN A NUTSHELL
How to set up your community

1. Do your research

    * Analyze your existing corporate websites and Web tracking statistics
    * Coordinate with your current CRM strategy

2. Define your goals

    * Based on your brand strategy, define what benefits you want to achieve from your community
    * Identify the target population that will allow you to achieve your goals

3. Generate ideas

    * Find themes that are important to your target population
    * Design activities relevant to your theme that add value for your target user

4. Analyze your competition

    * The competitive landscape is different online
    * Use search engines to research your community's competitors

5. Define the role of your brand

    * In general, use an integrated approach, where the brand has a background role in the community

6. Plan your website

    * Homepage
    * Registration page
    * Login
    * Member profile pages
    * Terms of use
    * Help page

- Company information
- Features

7. Plan your infrastructure
   - Community managers
   - Website admin panel
   - Web domain name
   - Web server and a hosting service or administrator

FOUR

MEMBER RECRUITMENT

QUESTIONS ANSWERED IN THIS CHAPTER

* How can you bring members to your community?
* How can you use search engines for recruitment?
* How can you make your website viral?
* What kind of registration questions should you avoid?
* What's the lowest-risk way to launch your new website?

RECRUITMENT STRATEGIES

With the millions of websites on the Internet, your target users are unlikely to land on yours unless you take steps to help them find it.

If you are building a closed community for research purposes, you might only need a few hundred users, combined with a high level of staff involvement. Your primary intention might be to have ongoing communication between your brand and a select group representative of your target customers. In this case, it is probably not your priority to maintain a constant level of activity in your community or to create a momentum for viral growth.

However, most other community models require a larger population to function. You will need to achieve a minimum level of activity and content in order to give members a reason to keep returning to your website. Then the more members and content you achieve, the more momentum you'll have to keep growing. You need a recruitment strategy, and the time to develop one is at the very beginning of your community planning. There are two types of recruitment: **passive recruitment**, where users come to the community by themselves, and **active recruitment**, where you go after them, by sending an email campaign or advertising, for example. In this chapter, we'll show you some ways that you can design your community and website to be user magnets, attracting traffic while you sit back and watch the population grow. We'll also explain how to run successful recruitment campaigns and how to convert casual website visitors into loyal members.

FIGURE 4.1 Bfriends: Nonmembers have many options for observing this online community of the German magazine Brigitte.de. On this screen, they can find active groups and upcoming offline events.

Recruit from your mailing list

An obvious source for active recruitment is your existing customer list. You can offer the website to your customers as a free value-added service: a gift to them from your company. Offline campaigns to promote your community can be effective, but there are obvious benefits to email campaigns, where people can visit your community directly with a click. Does your company send out a regular customer newsletter? Feature your community there. Also coordinate with your CRM team so that visitors are directed to your community when they register products online or contact your company.

GROUND RULES FOR DIRECT EMAIL CAMPAIGNS

* **Don't look "spammy."** These days, everyone uses spam filters to sift out **spam**, unwanted junk email. In your email subject line, avoid using dollar signs, exclamation marks, and all capital letters, since these are common spam filter triggers. Even if your email gets through the spam filter, there is a risk of the recipient deleting it at a glance if the subject line, text, or graphic elements give it the appearance of generic direct marketing.

* **Make it personal.** With any mass-mailing software, you can address the client by name. The more commercial and mass-produced your mailing looks, the more likely it is to end up in the trash. Consider taking a personal account-manager-to-client tone, and signing the email with your own name and title.

* **Keep it simple.** The recipient is likely to skim or even just glance at your email, so simplicity and clarity are essential.

* **Include a call to action.** What do you want the recipient to do? Click on a link to visit your community? Then focus your message on getting him or her to perform this task. Try to limit your focus to one recipient action per campaign to avoid diluting your message.

* **Be aware of the "fold line."** This is the imaginary point in an email where the viewer would have to scroll down in order to see the rest. A lot of recipients are not going to scroll. So everything important should be above the fold line, and the higher up, the better. If you want the recipient to click on a link, make sure the link is visible near the top of the message, and repeating the same link in multiple places never hurts.

Recruit from rented email lists

There are several specialized companies that maintain email records of millions of people. One of the easiest and fastest ways to get traffic to your site is by renting email lists for users matching your criteria. Companies like E-circle (ecircle.com) and Axiom (axiombpm.com/sales_marketing.html) have highly qualified data and can target almost all types of users. You can contact these companies and send out your carefully designed email to targeted users; this will generate responses almost immediately. Email lists are usually rented on the basis of cost per 1,000 emails sent. Therefore, you need to make sure your messaging is crafted to generate maximum impact for the email lists you are renting. If the messaging is not clear or attractive, using rented lists can be an expensive exercise.

Recruit from your corporate websites

Integrate your community into your corporate websites with links and tabs; put up banners to promote it. If your company runs e-commerce sites, you can route customers to your community on the purchase confirmation page, after they have finished shopping and would otherwise log off.

FIGURE 4.2 Brigitte.de: This is the website of a German women's magazine. The homepage explains the magazine's community Bfriends.

FIGURE 4.3 Kraft.de: This portal uses extra banners to promote the community. (Box on bottom right reads: "Become a member of our community" "Want to discuss hot topics with other people, find new friends or exchange cooking tips? Join the community. It's free and easy.")

FIGURE 4.4 BMW.de: The community for M drivers, M Power World, is integrated into the BMW website.

> **CASE STUDY**
>
> The consumer community Ciao.com converts new community members from visitors who come to use their shopping and price comparison portals. Managing Director Stephan Musikant told us, "There are different ways to attract members to a community, but, in the first place, it makes sense to convert regular users to community members. These are people who already have an interest in the website. This is much better than buying leads externally, which is the usual method."

Recruit with advertising

Where appropriate, give the address of your community website in your company's TV and print media campaigns and on product packaging. Choosing a catchy, easy-to-remember-and-spell Web address will make this strategy more effective. You can also buy banner space on other websites that appeal to your target population without directly competing against your community.

TYPICAL ONLINE ADVERTISING ARRANGEMENTS

* **PPI** (pay per impression) or **CPM** (cost per thousand impressions: you pay each time the page is displayed).

* **PPC** (pay per click: you pay only if someone actually clicks on the ad).

* **PPL** (pay per lead) or **CPA** (cost per acquisition: payment depends on the viewer performing a specific action such as completing a registration form).

You can also negotiate **coregistration** agreements with other websites. This means that when users register on the partner website, they will have the option to sign up for your website at the same time. For example, when customers buy plane tickets from an online travel agency, they might see a checkbox they can select if they want to join your travel community. The travel agency would then send you the details of the users who said yes and charge you on a PPL basis.

Recruit with Search Engine Marketing (SEM)

You can buy sponsored links on search engines so that people will see an advertisement for your community when they search for related topics. Google offers an option called AdWords, where you choose key words to trigger your advertisement and set a maximum PPC rate that you want to pay. This functions something like an auction; your ad will compete for ranking against other advertisers who have signed up for the same key words. Read more about Google AdWords at adwords.google.com. Before preparing your SEM ad, be sure to check the ad format guidelines of the search engine where you will be posting it; Google, Yahoo, and other search engines have very specific rules about ad length, content, and even punctuation.

CAUTION
Keep your key words and SEM ads relevant to your actual community content: you don't want to waste money on clicks from people who will be uninterested in participating in your community when they arrive.

Recruit with Search Engine Optimization (SEO)

If your website is attractive enough to search engines such as Google, then you won't have to pay for SEM because your website will come up naturally in the search results. Search engines like websites rich in text content, so you can improve the website's search engine performance by including activities where members are generating plenty of text content for you. You can also plan activities where members will be using frequently searched key words. Many community websites specifically ask members to label each content submission with several key words to help with online searches.

One important rule with search engines is not to cheat by including search terms out of context or creating an artificial density of key words. If users are being brought to your website on false pretenses, they are likely to leave as quickly as they come, and this can create a negative perception of your company. Search engines have also become quite sophisticated at detecting and penalizing manipulation.

Be sure to tell your webmaster right from the beginning that SEO is a priority so that basic optimization can be built into the code of the website. Some SEO tips for webmasters can be found at www.seomoz.org. Many companies hire a SEO consultant to improve their rankings. Before doing this, be aware that advanced SEO is a significant ongoing investment. Search engine behavior is constantly evolving, and staying on top of the changes is an around-the-clock job.

You can improve your SEO by sharing links with similarly themed sites. This increases your ranking for search engines within a certain category, and displays your links to potential visitors who might be interested in your community. Link sharing is a common practice, and you can write to webmasters of relevant sites to get your links inserted. There are also a number of services that sell links.

Whatever your strategy, be aware that optimizing your site for search engines takes around three to four months to start showing results, so some patience is required.

Viral and buzz marketing

Since your community website will have high-quality and relevant content, users will surely want to spread the news to others. You can encourage this viral effect by providing them with tools to do so.

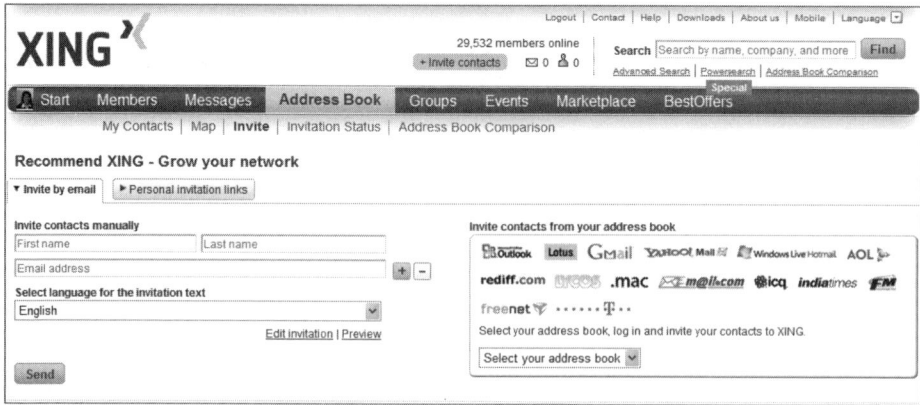

FIGURE 4.5 Business network Xing: Viral elements to invite friends and colleagues.

TOOLS FOR VIRAL MARKETING

* **Links to forward content.** A member clicks on an option to "Send this to a friend" or "Email this," which opens an email form where he or she can put the address of someone who might be interested in the particular piece of content. The email should send a link to the content, rather than the complete content itself. Why? Because you want to bring the friend to the website.

TIP
To facilitate viral and search engine marketing, program your website so that each piece of content has its own link.

* **Referral programs.** Community websites often include a feature where members can send emails to their friends containing a link to the registration page. Referral links normally contain a tracking code that identifies the new member with the referring member. Members can be given various incentives to refer others. More on member incentives in Chapter Five, Motivating Your Members.

* **RSS links.** RSS or **Really Simple Syndication** is code that people can use on their website to subscribe to content from yours. In this way, you can "feed" subscribers' websites with automatically updating links to your content. This is also great for search engine optimization.

* **Republishable content.** Offering branded content such as images, Web tools, and gadgets for republication is a way to spread the word about your community, especially if the content includes links back to your website.

* **Bookmarks.** A number of sites such as StumbleUpon and Digg provide small pieces of code that can be integrated into your website, allowing users to bookmark pages that interest them and bring your website to the attention of users who otherwise wouldn't find it. For example, when someone bookmarks a page using the StumbleUpon code, that makes your website more visible to other StumbleUpon users.

WAYS TO START A BUZZ

- **Humor.** Maybe your friends and family are already sending you joke emails that have been sent to them. And if you enjoy the jokes, maybe you pass the same emails on to others. You can use the same principle to create viral marketing. If you create content that's funny enough, people will want to pass it on. And if what's funny is an advertisement or contains one, people will distribute the ad for you.

- **Tell people what they want to hear.** The personal care brand Dove created very successful buzz marketing with a video that showed how the media uses makeup and photo editing to create standards of beauty that real women can't achieve. "You don't have to live up to this standard," "That beautiful model only looks like that because of photo editing": these are messages that women want to hear and send to other women.

- **Controversy.** This is the riskiest strategy. If you break a taboo, or publish controversial content, it can get your company a lot of attention including free media coverage, but you have to weigh the risks and benefits carefully.

- **Break new ground.** This is perhaps the hardest strategy. Invent new technology or a cutting edge concept that will attract attention and that people will want to see.

CASE STUDY

The directors of the Spanish travel community Minube.com decided to travel around the world, publishing their experiences in real time on the website and a blog. This viral marketing campaign, which they called "Around the World 2.0" was a huge success, generating a great deal of attention in the mass media and in blogs. They told us: "We were featured for a week on a Spanish television program, and it helped us get into places that would otherwise be hard to access and to meet people that would otherwise be difficult to meet."

TIP
Marketing expert Leesa Barnes explains that different target groups respond to social media differently, and stresses the importance of taking that into account when designing a viral campaign. She contrasts the online behavior of mothers, a group that enjoys sharing information, to the behavior of young men, who tend to prefer creative activities. "If you are launching a viral marketing campaign for say, young males, then you need to ensure that there is an element where they can create as well. So an example of that would be perhaps doing something on Facebook: perhaps you have a video that you are sharing, and then you invite your target market—who are young men—to contribute a video response."

REGISTRATION

Getting people on your website is nice, but you will probably want them to join your community through a registration process. This will allow you to contact them when needed. It also allows their community actions to be associated with a unique online identity, important for the formation of member-to-member relationships. And the member database that you develop through online registration will be valuable capital for your company.

FIGURE 4.6 Lego.com: A community for children needs a registration page that's very simple to use. A Lego figure is used here as a helper.

If your community is open to the public, you should put prominent registration links on the website with a clear, short message about the benefits of membership. Users will normally feel more motivated to sign up if they have a clear idea of what they are joining, so in most cases, it's better to allow unregistered users to read content in your community even if the ability to create content is reserved for members only.

Consider offering guest status to people who are interested in your community but not yet ready to register. Guest users might be allowed to read content but not to publish content of their own, create a profile page, or communicate with others. Try to define points of interaction where you can offer these users the option to register. For example, offer guest users the button to post a message, but when they click on it, instead of opening the message form, suggest that they register in order to send a message. This strategy is particularly relevant for communities that charge for membership, because you have to convince guests to become paying members. People naturally like to know what they're getting before they take out their credit cards. As guests, they can see how useful your community is and decide what membership is worth to them.

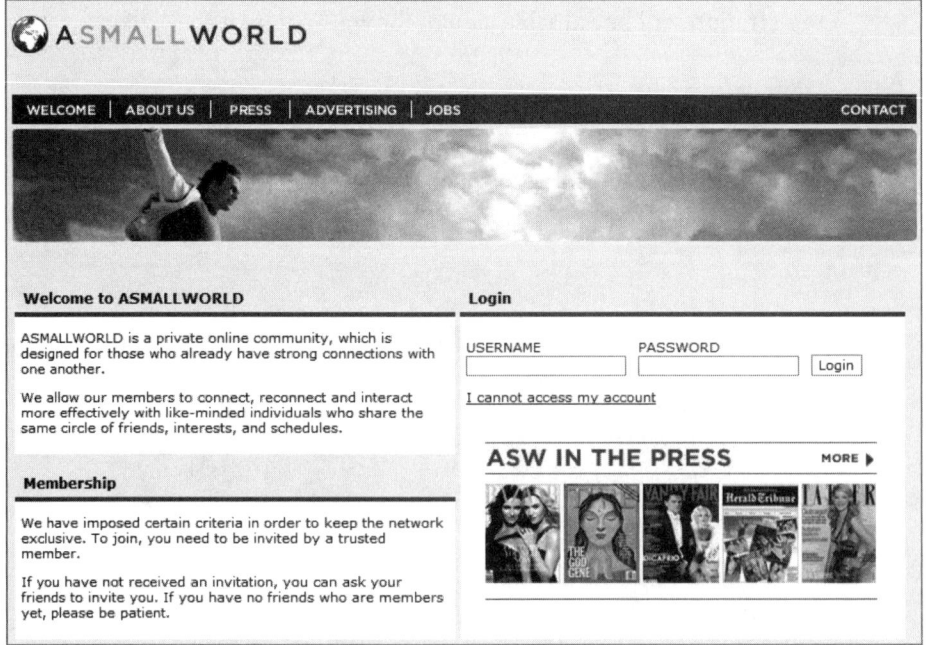

FIGURE 4.7 Asmallworld: This community is completely based on viral communication. If you're not a member, you can't explore this closed community until a member invites you.

> **CASE STUDY**
>
> Asmallworld.net is an example of a community that has opted for the opposite approach. None of their community content is visible to nonmembers, and membership is by invitation only. This is because they have a positioning strategy based on being highly exclusive.

The registration page

Your registration page should explicitly explain the benefits of membership. Maybe the first hundred registered members will receive a gift, a coupon, a free download, or special icons to decorate their profiles. Make it very clear to users why it is worth their time to join your community and what they'll get in return. Use the space on the registration page to explain this with a short text.

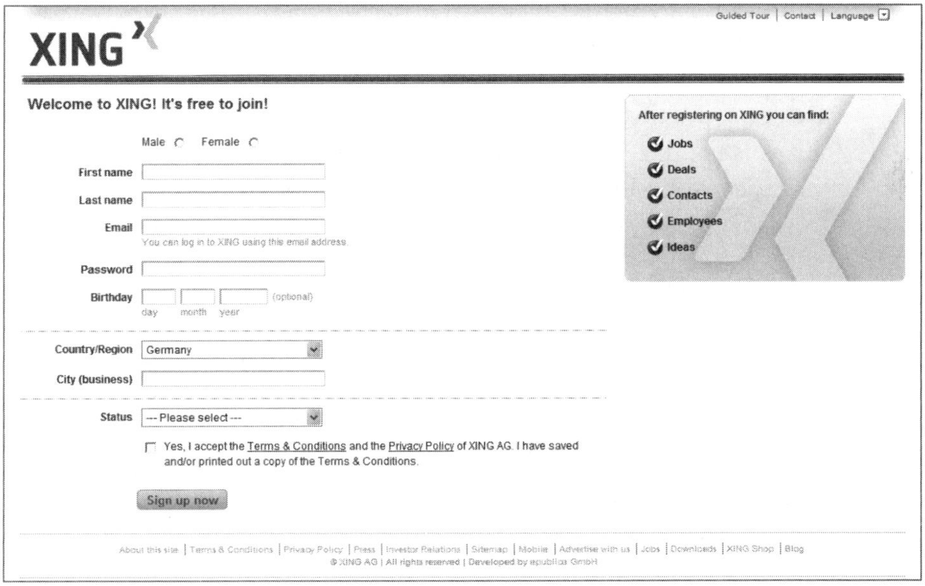

FIGURE 4.8 Business network Xing: Clean and simple registration page plus an extremely concise desciption of member benefits.

FIGURE 4.9 Lego.com: Even children can complete a registration process with an extra clear structure and simple explanations.

Don't misuse this page to ask a long list of questions. Filling out registration forms is not fun, so yours should be as short and painless as possible. Otherwise, people are likely to drop out partway through. And if your registration form looks long or complex, some won't even bother to start.

TIP
Registration pages often have legal importance. Most communities have lawyers review these pages to reduce legal risks. However, lawyers tend to be meticulous, and they often write huge amounts of text that users have to read before becoming a member. Try to avoid overwhelming users with too much legal content. Work with your lawyer to reduce the text to a minimum and ask a designer how to minimize the text display. Users prefer a one-minute registration process and do not like to read texts along the way. Large amounts of text will make your registration process seem burdensome and can turn off potential members.

People are also mistrustful when they are asked for a lot of personal information. Try to avoid sensitive questions about subjects such as income and health if this data is not essential to you right away. The important point is to capture the members you want. Once they have signed up, then you'll have many options for getting additional information from them.

REGISTRATION FORM CHECKLIST

1. **Nickname:** Do you want users to choose a nickname? Do you want it to be unique? Should the system suggest alternatives if users attempt to register with a login that is already taken?

2. **Password:** Let users choose their own, and make them enter it twice to avoid typing errors.

3. **Email:** You need to be able to contact the users. Make users type their email address twice. Do you want to confirm the validity of the email by sending them an activation link to finish their registration?

4. **First name, last name, and physical address:** This is required for legal reasons in some countries. Check with a lawyer to find out about the data you should store about members and the rules about how to store it.

5. **CAPTCHA image:** (Optional) This is a special image of letters or numbers that the user must type into a box as a security measure to avoid computer-generated registrations. (CAPTCHA is a trademark owned by Carnegie Mellon and means "Completely Automated Public Turing test to tell Computers and Humans Apart.")

6. **Direct mail opt-in:** Do you want to offer users the option to subscribe to a newsletter or marketing emails?

7. **Terms of Use acceptance:** Your registration form should include a checkbox to accept your website Terms of Use with a link to the legal document. This is normally the last question asked before submitting the registration form.

LAUNCH STRATEGY

How do you know when your website is really ready to open its doors to the public? Here is a three-step launch strategy that will reduce your risks and increase member loyalty.

Internal launch

As a first step, we suggest inviting, or coercing, your colleagues and friends to become members and create as much content as they can. This is a low-risk way to do some initial user testing and fix bugs before exposing your website to the public. And it is a way to get some early user content and avoid a website that looks too empty.

Soft launch

When you're ready to start bringing in "real" members, we suggest beginning with a **soft launch**. This means that you invite a small group of users to try out the website in **beta**, or test, mode. Many new websites explicitly include the word "beta" near their logo during their first months online. If you label your website as a beta product, users will be more tolerant when everything isn't working perfectly. You can create a communication strategy that gives these first users a sense that they are getting an exclusive advance opportunity to try out your website and makes them feel involved in the product development. Actively seek out their feedback and treat their comments with care. Not only will the users appreciate it, but you have a wonderful opportunity to test your product on your target population.

> **CASE STUDY**
>
> BMW M Power World is a community for drivers who own BMW M cars. The company started with a small group of users who were involved in the process of community development. With these first members as "seeds," the community was able to take root and grow.

Achieving critical mass

After you've implemented relevant feedback from your first group of users, you can start recruiting on a large scale. For most community models, you will need to achieve a critical mass of members and content just to get things off the ground. This rule is circular in the way of the saying "you need money to make money," or the idea that nobody wants to go to a party unless there are plenty of people there. A community with only intermittent activity is no fun for your users. And the possibilities of what you can do with it are much more limited. "On the Internet, it's not the volume of production that matters; it's the volume of users," explains François Derbaix of Toprural.com. "The more users you have, the better the service you can provide, and the stronger your position in the market."

Even if you hope to rely on passive recruitment in the long term, you may want to budget some money in the beginning to get things started. You can invest in advertising and coregistration campaigns and even pay members for desired actions such as referrals and content generation. In the next chapter, we'll talk more about member incentives. The more members and content you can get, the more you will be able to depend on viral recruitment and search engine traffic to give your community a momentum of its own.

THE CHAPTER IN A NUTSHELL
Member Recruitment

RECRUITMENT SOURCES

- Your company mailing list: Email campaigns should have a clear call to action and should avoid looking like junk mail

- Rented email lists: Target messaging carefully to get the most out of your investment

- Your corporate websites: Promote your community with links, banners, and tabs

- Advertising: If appropriate, include your community address in your current print and TV ad campaigns

- Search Engine Marketing (SEM): Buy key words to get featured on Google and other search engines

- Search Engine Optimization (SEO): Basic SEO should be built into the site, but advanced SEO will require an investment

- Viral and buzz marketing: Useful tools include referral and syndication links and links to email site content

RULES FOR REGISTRATION FORMS

* Briefly but clearly explain the benefits of membership
* Ask for essential data only (nickname, password, email address, Terms of Use agreement) and save the rest for later
* Avoid sensitive questions
* Avoid excessive legal texts

LAUNCH STRATEGY

1. Internal launch: Test the website on friends and colleagues and generate first content
2. Soft launch: Invite a small group of users to preview and test the website
3. General recruitment: An initial investment can bring your community needed momentum

FIVE

MOTIVATING YOUR MEMBERS

QUESTIONS ANSWERED IN THIS CHAPTER

* How can you capitalize on the enthusiasm of new members?
* How can you keep members on the website once you get them there?
* How can you create a member loyalty program without spending money?
* When should you pay members for participating?
* What do you need to know about the membership lifecycle?

GET THE MOST OUT OF YOUR MEMBERS

Once you've recruited the members, how can you keep them in your community? And how can you get the maximum mileage from your members, motivating them to participate as much as possible over the longest possible period of time?

Grab them when they're fresh

Newly registered members tend to be extremely motivated. They have gone to the trouble of filling out a registration form, and now they are eager to see the results. This is an opportunity for you to catch them and draw them into your community while their interest is at a high point.

Most registration processes include an email confirmation step, where members have to click on an activation link sent to them by email. Except in very specific cases, this email should always be sent automatically and instantly. Use the activation link to bring the member to a fun first activity on the website. This is key: get the member participating right away. And remember that logging in to a new website can be intimidating for many people. Make everything easy. Guide new members through their first steps with help texts where relevant.

> **CASE STUDY**
>
> In 2008, one of Anna's clients was a community for singles looking for partners. The community offers two types of memberships: a registered guest who has not paid for membership can read content, but not answer messages, and a premium member who has paid for the service has full user rights. The customer care department discovered that a short time window of just a few days was their only chance to convert guests into premium members.

The ideal first activity:

* Is simple to start and carry out without instructions
* Is enjoyable

- Shows an immediate result (for example, a photo appears on the page) for instant gratification

- Promises a long-term result (for example, other members will leave comments) to bring the member back to the website again.

Create stickiness

The term **sticky** is commonly used to describe website content that causes the user to spend more time on the site. Website stickiness is measured by the amount of time spent on the site by each user. While stickiness may not be desirable for an e-commerce website where the goal is to push the user through a purchase process, a community website depends on a high activity level, user content generation, and the formation of user relationships over time, so stickiness will be a key to your success.

One way to create stickiness is to organize the website so that one activity always leads to another. The user should never come to a dead end or be left without anything to do. A website is made stickier when each page offers a variety of ways to access new content; for example, a typical community Web page would include *all* of the following:

1. Navigation bars or link menus, sorted by activity type, subject category, and so on.

2. A search function to find content with certain key words.

3. A selection of popular tags—key words that members have used to label their content—and the option to view content by clicking on the tags.

4. A display of user-generated content such as comments, reviews, recipes, or poems, depending on the theme of the website. These are often presented in a vertical strip, ordered by publication date, popularity, and so on.

5. A link at the bottom of each vertical display to go to more content.

6. A subject link attached to each piece of content, leading to more content on the same subject.

7. An author link attached to each piece of user-generated content, leading to more content by the same author.

8. A comments link, leading to user comments on each piece of content.

9. An author link attached to each comment, leading to more content by the same author.

10. Links to add new content or comments.

On each page, you can suggest specific actions to the users to prevent them from getting lost in a sea of possibilities. New users, in particular, are often intimidated when they arrive on a website, and therefore require some guidance.

FIGURE 5.1 Brigitte.de: Even if users have a guest status, there are many elements that show how them how lively the community is. This is a strong motivator for new visitors to join. (Page title means "Find and start groups." Headlines include: "Bfriends presents: 'Groups of the Week,'" "New groups," "Find groups," "Favorite groups," "Group news," "Meetings in your area.")

Let's imagine we have a community website aimed at homemakers. A new user has clicked on the activation email to confirm her account. This link brings her to the website, where she sees a friendly welcome message. The page where she has landed also features some stain removal tips by other members and invites her to contribute her own. The new user types her tip in the online form and clicks on Submit. What could happen next to keep her from leaving the website after that?

1. She sees her comment published on the website with her user name (instant gratification).

2. She sees that other members will be able to rate and respond to her comment, giving her a reason to check back on the page later.

3. She is invited to choose a new discussion topic in order to browse and contribute more household tips.

Virtual rewards

Not only do you need users to spend time on the website, you need them to come back again and again. You should therefore aim for the right balance between instant and delayed gratification. On the one hand, users should see instant results from their actions, giving them a satisfying experience on the website. On the other hand, there should be benefits that build over time, enriching the experience the more time they spend in the community.

Users are at the peak of their natural interest in your community the first time they log onto the website. After that, to prevent interest from falling off, you will have to enrich and expand, rather than just maintain, their user experience.

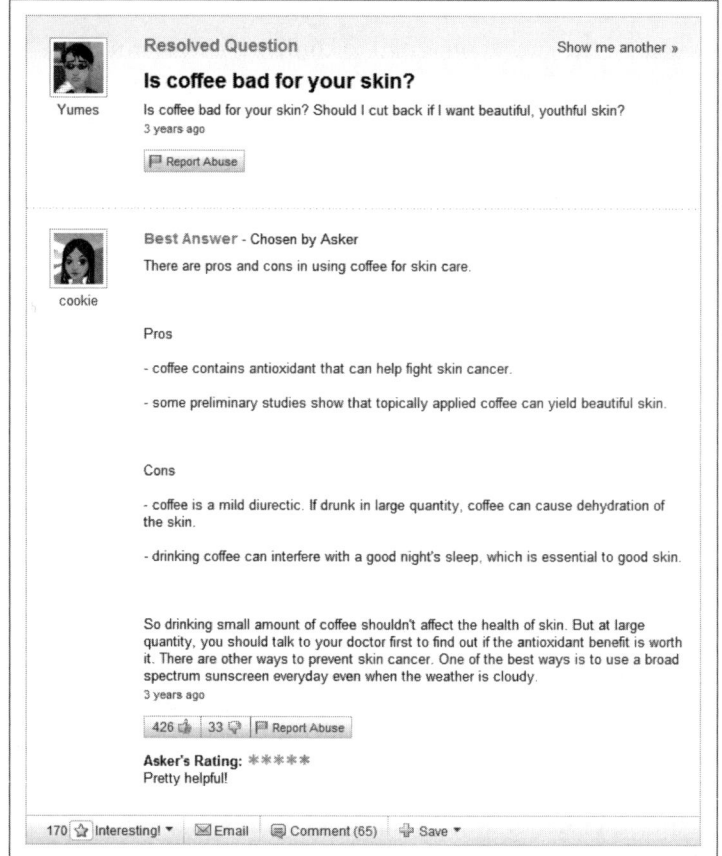

FIGURE 5.2 Yahoo Answers: "Best answer" is a virtual reward for users who write a lot of useful content. This user has collected another type of virtual reward: 170 stars.

Loyalty programs

One way to maintain interest is to create a kind of loyalty program. On some websites, users earn points for each website action or are shown an automatically calculated ranking of their activity level versus that of other members. This gives users a sense of progress toward a goal. Special privileges can be reserved for members with higher rankings or scores. Every time a user performs an action on the website, he or she sees an instant result (for example, points added or score improved) and is reminded of a longer-term objective (for example, a score of 200 points that means the user can access the website's video library).

Loyalty programs don't always have to cost money. Privileges associated with higher rankings could be access to certain features, anything from membership in an exclusive forum or business network, to the ability to publish comments in colored fonts, to a better-looking avatar.

The best approach for your website will obviously depend on your target demographic. Teenagers are not interested in a business card exchange feature, while business users may be less likely to crave virtual pets to keep on their personal homepages.

Symbolic rewards

Purely symbolic rewards can be oddly motivating. You might think that no one over twelve years old would be willing to spend hours on a website just to gain a little gold star by his or her user name. Well, we have seen adult community members lie, cheat, and fight for this type of prize. Some community websites have actually made a business out of selling virtual gifts and privileges in exchange for cash. For example, on Second Life, many people exchange real money for an imaginary currency, Linden dollars, in order to improve the appearance of their avatars (on Second Life, as in Hollywood, money can buy beauty) and to decorate their virtual houses.

> ### CASE STUDY
>
> The travel community Minube.com offers virtual medals and titles such as Explorer and Photographer to members who contribute certain amounts of content. They told us, "The idea is exactly like a video game where you earn points, which bring you to different phases. Visitors to the site see that a member has earned prizes and trust that person's content more. And the members who are earning the prizes are also getting visibility, recognition. They know that they're becoming popular in the community."

Social hierarchy

Social hierarchy in your community is a powerful tool. Just like offline communities, online ones quickly sort themselves into a hierarchical structure, normally with the most experienced members at the top. By encouraging hierarchy in your community and offering visible status symbols based on seniority and activity level, you can create an environment in which members feel as if they are working toward an objective: the next rung on the social ladder.

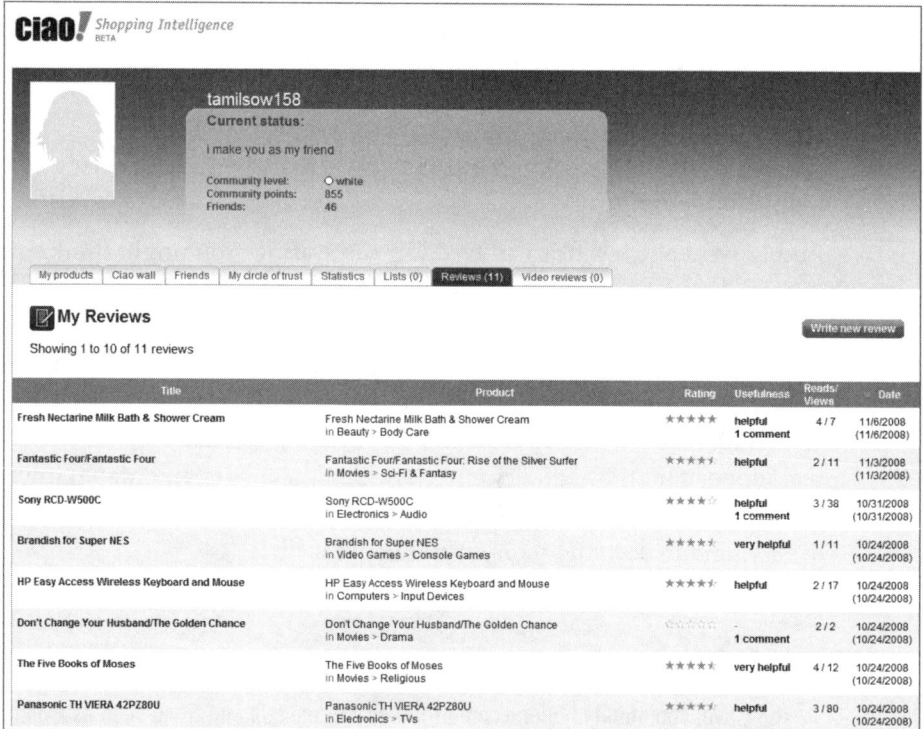

FIGURE 5.3 Ciao.com: This member page is all about status: level white, 855 community points, 46 friends. This creates an element of friendly competition—an additional reason to participate.

USES OF HIERARCHY IN A COMMUNITY

* Makes status symbols effective as nonmonetary rewards

* Gives members a feeling of personal investment in the website and creates a sense of progress over time

* Lets senior members take on a useful leadership role. You can offer them the possibility of moderating discussions, acting as liaisons between the community and your staff, leaving welcome messages for new members, running a member-to-member help desk—in other words, working for you for free! Many members love this.

> **CASE STUDY**
>
> The consumer community Ciao.com has a nonmonetary rewards system that uses colorful dots as a status symbol. Members can earn points to change the color of their dot by posting product reviews that other members rate as useful, or by performing other community actions. You can find many members who post messages on their profile pages related to this community points system. "Hooray, I'm finally red," they write. "Please read my product reviews and help me turn orange!"

IDEAS FOR VIRTUAL REWARDS

* Access to an exclusive forum, online club, or other group

* Access to exclusive online tools such as an interactive agenda or Web mail

* Access to exclusive features, such as the ability to form online clubs or invite members to chat rooms

* Improved tools for community activities: for example, if you have a website where users decorate virtual rooms, you could provide a limited color palette at first and let users earn additional color options over time

* Access to exclusive information, such as a premium recipe bank

* Points, rankings, titles (such as Top Member, Super User, or Veteran), or special symbols that appear next to the user's name

* Improved visibility on the website: member photo featured on the homepage, content published by the member given top rankings in lists

* Decorations or animations for the member's profile page

* The ability to give virtual gifts (for example, the image of a flower) to other members

* Downloads such as ringtones, screensavers, or whitepapers
* The ability to customize and improve the user's view of the website (for example, the user can choose the background color he or she wishes to see)
* Improved appearance of the member's avatar
* Added control over published content, for example, the use of different fonts or the ability to add background music

Product-related rewards

You can also motivate members and boost your brand by rewarding activity with benefits specifically related to your products. These may be aimed at adding value to products that the members already own: ringtone downloads for your cell phone brand, product accessories, special customer service options, or free upgrades, for example. Or, they may be exclusive discounts and offers associated with future purchases, such as a free meal in the hotel restaurant with each new reservation. You can also offer branded gifts such as T-shirts that provide viral marketing benefits for you while rewarding members. Product-related rewards may be used to complement another kind of incentive program.

CAUTION
If you are depending on product-related rewards to motivate your community, be sure that they are designed in a way that will be primarily perceived as beneficial to members rather than as advertising. Members will not want to participate in your community if they have the sense that it is aimed at selling them something.

Monetary rewards and gifts

Another option used by some websites is to pay members, literally, for their website participation, either by offering cash incentives, sweepstakes entries, or gifts. In some cases it is worth making a financial investment to offer attractive incentives to your members. If you need to quickly achieve a certain volume of activity or content in your community, you might consider spending some money to get things started; you might start by offering a dollar each to the first thousand contributors, or running a competition with a prize for the member who refers the most friends to the site. An obvious case where it might be worth paying for user activity is if that activity earns you revenue. If an advertising partner is paying you five dollars for each video your users create about their product, then you can pay cash incentives to the video authors and come out ahead.

TIP
In our interview with the consumer community Ciao.com, they emphasized that financial rewards are about more than just money. Members see financial rewards as a tangible recognition of their contributions, which adds a level of excitement to the community experience. "It's like when you play cards, the game is more interesting if you're playing for a few cents," says Stephan Musikant, Ciao's Managing Director.

If you are offering a fixed incentive per action in an area that is not directly producing revenue, then controlling your budget is obviously a concern; unless you set limits in advance, an unexpected volume of participation could lead to a big financial problem. Budget control is an advantage of offering sweepstakes entries or raffling off gifts versus offering individual incentives to each participant. There are companies that specialize in sweepstakes and can handle the administrative and legal aspects for you. If you decide to offer cash rewards, you will need to organize the infrastructure to process payments. Investigate whether your company can handle this in-house or if you're better off outsourcing to a third-party provider.

CASE STUDY

The management of the community 11870.com, which publishes reviews of services, have chosen not to offer members payment for their contributions. Instead, they have opted for a more personal touch. "We never say, 'Publish X contributions and get a prize'," they told us. "We don't want to buy users. Instead, we recognize their contributions afterwards. We might send a small gift, a real gift, but always after the fact, in a natural way. For example, one of our users was going on a trip, and we sent him a nice little book where he could take notes on the places he visited."

TIP
If your company owns an e-commerce website, you might be able to use this as a vehicle for your rewards program, offering store credit or vouchers, for example.

Any incentive program tends to attract abusers, who will cheat in an attempt to get the reward. You might be surprised at how many people there are in cyberspace who will commit elaborate fraud in order to obtain a few cents or a free tube of toothpaste.

TRUE STORY
In one online community, a member created a computer script that created automatic website registrations using his referral ID. Although the offered incentive was only about sixty cents per referral, this member managed to generate almost three thousand false registrations before he was caught.

Obviously, the last thing you want is to have members stealing money from you! In the next chapter, we will talk about community management and some ways to detect and deal with fraud in a community. But you should also set up your rewards program in a way that discourages and limits abuse. For example, instead of paying members for each referral who signs up, you might pay for each referral who contributes a useful piece of content or who achieves a certain activity level. It is easy to create false registrations, but requires more effort to participate on the website under multiple identities.

TRUE STORY
An online community member created a total of fourteen member accounts which he used to give positive evaluations of his own content. His motivation in this case was not economic: he was trying to improve his ranking in a "Best Rated Members" list!

Many websites that regularly pay their members use a system where earnings are credited to online accounts. Members can accumulate earnings in these accounts and then request a payment in the form of a check, PayPal payment, shopping voucher, or whatever method is offered by the particular website. One advantage of this system is that it separates the crediting of incentives from payment processing: while the member has the instant gratification of seeing a reward credited immediately in his or her online account, there is still time for your company to do a fraud check before actually paying out. Some websites also require members to accumulate a minimum earnings balance before requesting a payment. This can be a way of encouraging members to continue participating over time. In all cases, to avoid an accounting nightmare, your reward program should pre-establish time limits on payment claims, after which unclaimed incentives expire.

Charging your members

It is not common for an online community to charge members for registration, but many charge for value-added service or premium accounts. For example, the business networking website LinkedIn allows paying members to do more extensive searches of the member database and to contact other members through internal email. Stardoll, the virtual paper doll community, sells a Superstar status that includes first access to new designs and the ability to broadcast messages to the entire community. One advantage for charging for certain services is that this allows you to incentivize members with free membership upgrades or access to features that otherwise cost money. The fact that you charge for a feature can increase its perceived value when you give it as a gift. Another advantage is, of course, that you could generate revenue. However, be aware that people are used to doing things for free on the Internet and are often unwilling to pay to participate on a website.

CASE STUDY

Google launched a website, Google Answers, where users could pay to ask questions of researchers. This community failed and eventually shut down. Yahoo launched a similar community, Yahoo Answers, where users could ask questions to other users for free. Yahoo Answers has been extremely successful.

MANAGING THE MEMBERSHIP LIFECYCLE

Membership in an online community has a natural lifecycle, and an understanding of its phases will help you get the most out of your community.

Integrating new members

New members, as we've said, start out with a high level of interest, but they are also skeptical. They have not yet built up any loyalty toward your website, and they can leave as easily as they've come. The first website experience of new users is therefore critical. Their natural enthusiasm has to be satisfied right away. The new user also needs to feel welcome and reassured. It is intimidating for many people to try to use a new website, and far more so when their actions are visible to other members.

There is also a kind of social intimidation that can take place. The new member is entering an established social structure where other members are more experienced and have already formed relationships. Many websites offer Flash or video introductions to new members, giving them a tour of the website and showing them what to do. A welcome message at first login is nice, and it is common to give new members welcome gifts such as reward points, a product discount, or temporary access to features that normally have to be purchased or earned.

Experienced members can be enlisted, encouraged, or even paid small amounts of money to serve as new member guides, welcoming and helping new members, inviting them into online discussions, and giving positive feedback on their contributions.

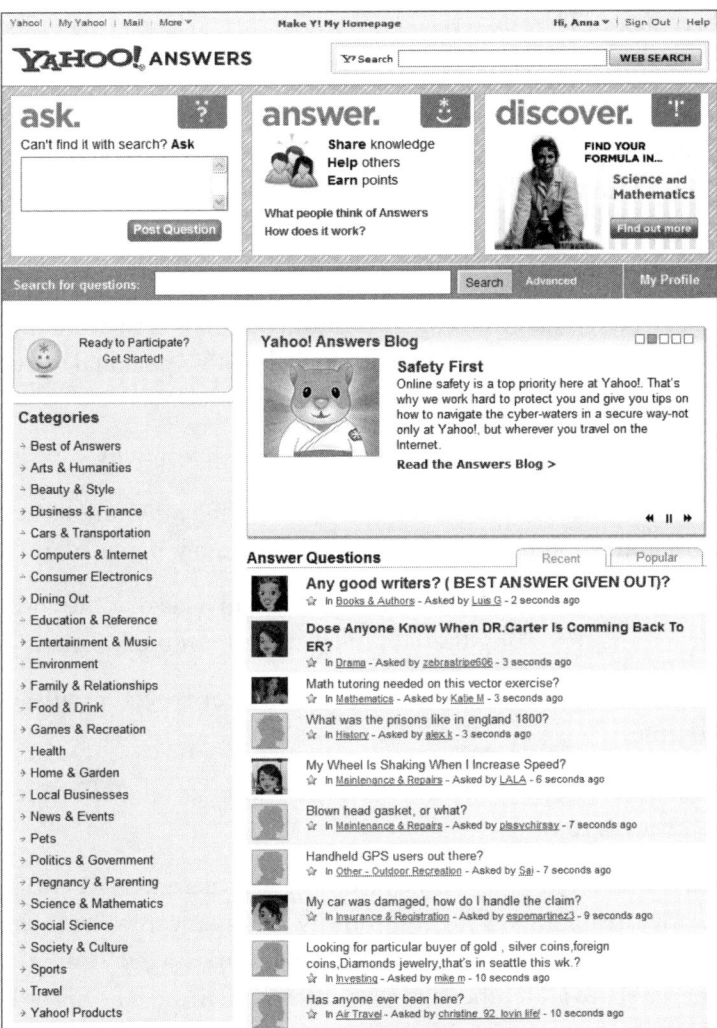

FIGURE 5.4 Yahoo Answers: The homepage offers many suggestions for getting started. A new visitor is very likely to find an interesting question.

Activating passive members

To keep the community lively, you want members to come back as often as possible and spend a lot of time participating in community activities. But some members will show a different behavior pattern. Some register and never return. There are even paying premium members who will stop coming to the community after their first week. Others return, but leave the site again after visiting three pages. They do not add anyone to their friends lists or use the other community features.

To make the most of your community database, you will need a special strategy for passive members. What can you do to make them come back and start using the community regularly?

IDEAS FOR ENGAGING PASSIVE MEMBERS

* Send a personal email from the community manager, inviting them to participate and offering them assistance. The more personal the communication, the better.

* Run a fun competition based around a community activity.

* Alert them to changes on the website that might be relevant to them based on their public profile information. Again, the more personal, the better.

* Send a regular email newsletter that gives them a taste of the community. Include teasers that bring them to the website for more information.

* Offer them a free premium membership or other special privileges for a limited time.

* If you have a monetary or nonmonetary rewards system, offer them free points toward a reward.

* Get active members involved in the effort. Ask them to leave messages for passive members. Then your community manager can write to the passive members to let them know they have new messages. (Important: You must never share a member's private information, such as his or her email address. But if a member wishes to contact another member, your community manager might do so on that member's behalf.)

* On an active member's login page, you could reference some of the passive member's public profile details: "This user has a birthday today," or "Lives in your city," or "Has similar interests."

The goal is to show passive members that you care about them and that other members are visiting their profiles, sending them messages, and adding them to friends lists. Just as in an offline community, some online users need a little extra help to get involved and feel like part of the group, but if you reach out to them, you can often draw them into the circle.

Maintaining active members

As members spend more time on the website, there is a tendency for them to lose interest. Using the types of incentives that we've been discussing to reward continuing participation will help to keep members active longer.

> **CASE STUDY**
>
> A community focused around reviews of services, 11870.com, has discovered that 5-10% of their users contribute 90% of their content. They use a system of virtual prizes to keep this core group motivated.

It is also important to design the community's activities broadly enough that they don't get "used up" by a member. You can generate some additional excitement by running website competitions and challenges, and publishing lists of winners or even offering real prizes.

> **EXAMPLES OF WEBSITE CHALLENGES**
> * Become our Travel Reviewer of the Month
> * Write a breakfast cereal haiku
> * Test your celebrity knowledge
> * Win a deluxe breadmaker for the best baking tip of the week!
> * Are you millionaire material? Play our virtual stock market game!

Adding new features to the community from time to time can keep things fresh and provides an excuse to send members an announcement email and remind them that your website exists. Stay in touch with your members. Allow them to sign up for a member newsletter, which should be interesting enough that they'll actually want to read it and should be full of links back to the website. Many sites offer **RSS** feeds, which send real-time updates that users can receive using online tools or software. Community websites also frequently provide an alert service, where members can sign up to be notified by email when certain kinds of content are posted on the website. Rather than sending website content to the member's inbox, email alerts should contain content links to bring the member back to your website.

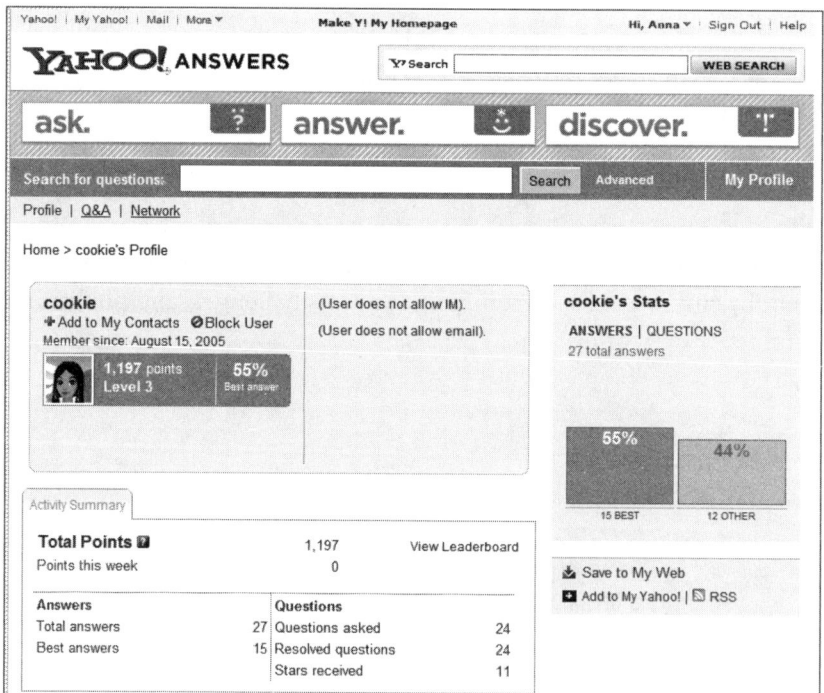

FIGURE 5.5 Yahoo Answers: Users like to compare themselves with others. Pages that show statistics are very popular and motivate users to participate actively in the community.

> **TYPICAL EMAIL ALERT OPTIONS**
> * Notify me when someone visits my profile page
> * Notify me when someone leaves me a personal message
> * Notify me of new articles by my favorite authors
> * Notify me of new articles about my favorite subjects

Reactivating fading members

Nothing lasts forever, and eventually members do drift away. But don't say goodbye too soon. Inactive members can often be reactivated with a little effort. Send targeted emails to members who haven't logged in for a long time, telling them about new content or features or offering a special promotion, competition, or incentive for becoming active on the website again. Sometimes it's enough to send them a personal-sounding note to say that they're missed and invite them to participate in upcoming community events.

THE CHAPTER IN A NUTSHELL
Motivating Your Members

GET THE MOST OUT OF YOUR MEMBERS

1. Give them something to do as soon as they arrive

2. Keep them on the website with sticky navigation

3. Get them hooked by creating a balance between instant and delayed gratification

MOTIVATE MEMBERS TO KEEP PARTICIPATING

1. Give virtual rewards

    * Show immediate results from activity (such as points or ranking) for instant gratification

    * Get members working toward longer-range goals such as:

        * Access to exclusive features and tools

        * Rankings, titles, social status in the community

2. Provide incentives related to your company's products

    * Value-adds for products they've purchased

    * Discounts on future purchases

    * Branded gifts

3. Offer monetary rewards, sweepstakes, and gifts

MANAGE THE MEMBER LIFECYCLE

1. Welcome and reassure new members

2. Activate passive members

3. Maintain contact with active members and keep their experience fresh

4. Reactivate fading members

SIX

CARE AND FEEDING OF YOUR MEMBERS

QUESTIONS ANSWERED IN THIS CHAPTER

* What is community management and why is it fundamental to your project's success?

* What's the ideal community management setup?

* How can the community help to manage itself?

COMMUNITY MANAGEMENT

An active community requires some maintenance. Your members will have questions and problems; they might get into public arguments or even abuse the website. There needs to be someone keeping an eye on things and intervening when necessary to guide a lost member, lay down ground rules, or remove offensive content. This person's job is known as **community management**.

Effective community management is fundamental to the success of your community project. Your **community managers** will become, for your members, the human face of your brand, and their decisions will influence the content that every visitor sees on your website. At the same time, the community manager will be the person best placed in your organization to gather information on the needs and desires of your community members.

CAUTION
"One misconception with communities—it doesn't happen with ours—is that the company will build it and then think it can take care of itself. But communities need care and feeding; otherwise, they languish," explains Debi Kleiman of Communispace, a company that builds and manages private brand communities.

WHO CAN BE A COMMUNITY MANAGER

The community manager's role is typically a mix of help desk, ambassador, company spokesperson, parent, camp counselor, and police officer. In a community focused on qualitative market research, you might want researchers in this role. Otherwise, it is a role that you may be able to fill initially by training existing CRM staff in your company. The community management workload is closely related to the volume of activity in a community, so a single manager, or even a part-time manager, should be sufficient in the beginning. But be prepared to add resources as your community grows.

The amount of community management needed obviously depends on your target population and the community model that you have chosen, as well as the quality of tools at the community manager's disposal. Later in this chapter, we will talk about how to optimize the efficiency of community management and make your community as low-maintenance as possible. As a *very* rough guideline, we'd say that one full-time staff person can manage a population of 50,000 for a community with a low-maintenance model and a single language.

QUALITIES OF A SUCCESSFUL COMMUNITY MANAGER

* Communicates clearly, effectively, and sympathetically in writing

* Has good organization and time management skills and knows how to prioritize

* Keeps an eye on the company's global goals and makes judgment calls about the community accordingly

* Cooperates with the rest of the organization to solve problems and reports information learned from the community

TIP
Debi Kleiman of Communispace says it's often beneficial to choose community managers with backgrounds or experiences similar to those of the members. Finding a common ground among members—and between members and facilitator—works as a "social glue," she explains. "For a community of early stage cancer patients, you might have more success with a facilitator who really understands what that's like—someone who's been a caregiver, for example. Or if the community's for avid runners—or moms—facilitators who understand and have been there will be able to communicate more effectively with the members to help them feel comfortable, encouraging them to participate more."

WHAT A COMMUNITY MANAGER DOES
Member support

Your community members will want to contact your company. They will have registration problems and login troubles; they will want to know why they haven't received a reward, or to report a technical problem or abusive content; they will want to talk about your products; they will have ideas and feedback for you.

> **EXAMPLES OF REAL EMAILS RECEIVED BY COMMUNITY MANAGERS**
>
> * "Unfortunately, my cat stepped on my keyboard when I was submitting my recipe to your competition and now it's lost. Can you find it?"
> * "I forget my user name. Love, Fuzzy74"
> * "A new member called Maybell is giving Useful ratings to all my reviews. I have worked hard on those reviews and deserve Very Useful ratings. Please rectify this."

Community managers respond to members' questions, complaints, and feedback, normally by email or by another electronic means. This is often the main task in a community manager's workday. With some emails, the community manager can just answer from a set of standard reply templates, choosing the one that fits the member's situation. In other cases, there is an actual problem that has to be solved. As much as possible, community managers should have the tools and the authority to solve problems themselves, as well as clear, efficient escalation procedures for problems that need to be solved by another department, such as Accounting or Technology. Prompt and effective response to member communications ensures that members can join and participate in your community and creates a positive brand experience.

Facilitating activity

In addition to responding to members who contact the company, community managers can add value by proactively communicating with the community. They can optimize the member lifecycle by welcoming new members, providing recognition to active members, and offering special attention and assistance to inactive and dormant members. They can maintain ongoing contact with members with a community newsletter or blog, and organize competitions and other special events to keep the community fresh.

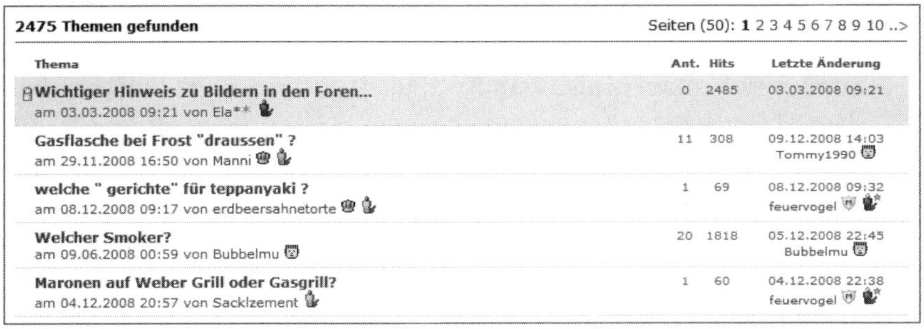

FIGURE 6.1 Chefkoch.de: This cooking community uses a special symbol—a crest with an M—to mark content that comes from a community manager (in this case feuervogel, the last entry).

If your community is mainly aimed at qualitative market research, your community managers might also have the role of facilitators in structured discussions.

Liaising between members and the company

As staff people who are in constant, direct contact with your community, community managers serve as a filter, speaking to the members on behalf of the company and making sure that member feedback gets to the right ears. Some community managers actively participate in the community and use their website accounts to make announcements or address community concerns. Community members generally appreciate the chance to mingle with staff in this direct, peer-to-peer way.

CAUTION
Resist the temptation to manipulate the community by creating false members or injecting disguised advertising into website discussions, and so forth. Members have a good nose for this and several major brands have harmed themselves by attempting it.

The community manager is normally the first person in a company to hear when anything goes wrong on the website. In a lively community, members will generally write to the community manager within minutes of noticing anything irregular. By providing community managers with clear lines of escalation for issues they can't address themselves, you can get problems solved before they are experienced by more than a handful of website visitors.

Censoring content

Community managers also remove abusive content from a website before it can be widely seen or have a negative impact on your brand image. It is important to set clear ground rules for members ahead of time and take care only to suppress content that is clearly abusive. Community members believe they have a right to free speech online, and anything seen as an attempt by the company to suppress or control website discourse can have terrible consequences. It is normally far better for public relations to leave a criticism of your company on the website than to be seen censoring it. On the other hand, community members understand that communities have standards of conduct, and they are glad to see abusive content removed. Abusive content is normally reported very quickly by the community.

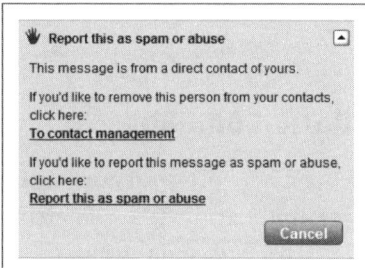

FIGURE 6.2 Xing: When a user on this business network receives a message on the site, there's always the option to report it as spam or abuse.

COMMON TYPES OF ABUSIVE CONTENT

* Nonsense: for example, a member types "adafjajfaf" over and over and publishes it all over your website

* Aggressive content: members publish attacks on other members

* Copyright violations: members plagiarize content by other authors

* Offensive content: racist or pornographic material, for example

* Spam or unauthorized advertising

* Off-topic content: someone publishes romantic poetry instead of cooking tips on your culinary website

* Libel, defamation, or other content that could leave your company open to a lawsuit

TIP
The European community Toprural.com reduces abuse by making members feel accountable for the content they publish. "We don't check the content published by users; we allow free expression, except in the case of insults," CEO François Derbaix explains. "Instead, we focus on identifying the users. When they create a new account, we send them an email confirmation, and we require them to provide personal details—not in order to publish this information, which is for internal use only, but to establish their identity and create a sense of responsibility for the content they publish."

Policing the website

In addition to removing abusive content, a certain amount of website policing normally is necessary. The Internet encourages aggressive and antisocial behavior even from people who are much milder offline. Many community websites are overtaken by cliques, battles, and power struggles among the most active members, with mischievous adolescents—or perhaps adult psychopaths (online, who really knows?)—stirring up trouble from the margins. Members who join websites specifically to cause trouble are known as **trolls**. You need community managers to set limits, and they should be able to enforce their authority by banning problem members from the site. Even cliques and infighting among legitimate members should be nipped in the bud to avoid annoying or scaring away other users. Otherwise, all of your relevant website content can get drowned out by a soap opera created by a few drama queens and kings.

WHAT A COMMUNITY MANAGER NEEDS
Clear objectives

Community managers represent the company to the members. Their workday is full of judgment calls—how to explain a problem to the community, whether to block or tolerate a misbehaving member, which content to censor. Community members can be needy, and there are a lot of them. Your community manager may end up getting a hundred emails a day from members, all of them wanting fast, personalized attention, and possibly making conflicting demands, particularly in the case of a website dispute. Community managers need clear objectives in order to make the right decisions and prioritize their time. It is important for them to be able to see their work in the context of your company's goals.

In many organizations, community managers are left out of strategic discussions and decisions about the community, and are simply tasked with cleaning out the email inbox. We believe that this is a mistake. Involving community managers at a higher level will not only make them more motivated in their job, it will allow them to perform their job intelligently in a way that furthers your objectives. Community managers left in a vacuum will tend to take cues about priorities where they are getting the most feedback—from the community. This is a real danger: community managers getting managed by the members, whose priorities might not be the same as yours.

We have seen cases where community managers are given numerical targets based on the number of emails answered and the response time for each one. This is a waste of resources. If community managers are copying and pasting empty standard replies in order to meet a target of two emails per minute, they are not adding to your brand image. Members who are not satisfied with the response that they receive are likely to write again or, alternatively, to leave the community: you have gained nothing either way. On the other hand, you will also create a negative public relations situation if nine hundred emails wait unanswered while the community manager spends five hours writing a thoughtful reply to a single upset member. Worse: you have nine hundred and one emails waiting unanswered while the community manager seeks help from someone authorized to make a decision or with access to the necessary information.

Training community managers should involve setting out priorities in explicit terms, for example:

* Deal first with problems that affect a large number of members or could compromise the image of your company.

* Encourage website activity, and give priority to problems that block members from joining or participating.

* Optimize member satisfaction in the community as a whole, with an eye on the big picture. (It is impossible to satisfy everyone. If three high-maintenance members are demanding twenty percent of the community manager's time, then keeping them satisfied is probably not cost effective to the community. The community manager has to set limits and focus on the highest possible level of general satisfaction.)

Authority to make decisions

You can set objectives and priorities for your community managers. You can provide guidelines for how to respond and act in specific foreseeable scenarios. You can even supply a complete library of standard email replies along with instructions on how to use them. All of this can be extremely helpful, but it is not sufficient.

The community managers will face situations that do not fall clearly into one category or another. They will need to reply to emails not covered by the template library or to adapt standard replies to the tone and situation of a member. There are situations that demand exceptions to the rules. A community manager's global goal might be member retention, but he or she will also need the authority to enforce website rules by banning members who break them. You can set a policy that no customer email goes unanswered, but what happens when a banned member starts harassing your poor community manager with fifty emails a day?

In some companies, community managers are required to escalate all matters requiring judgment calls. We see three possible outcomes to this setup:

* Two people are doing the work (community manager plus supervisor: not very efficient).

* The supervisor doesn't have time, and the work doesn't get done.

* Community manager tries to avoid inefficient escalation by applying standard rules in nonstandard situations: work isn't done properly.

We therefore recommend that you choose community managers you trust to make day-to-day decisions and empower them to do so.

Necessary tools

In the Chapter Three, How to Set Up Your Community, we describe an **admin panel** that should be developed along with the community website. Community managers need a way to interact with the member and content database in order to identify members who write in, to answer member account questions, to block and unsubscribe members, and to control website content. In other words, community managers cannot do their job without an admin panel, and the community website should not be launched to the public until this software is ready for use.

In addition to the admin panel, you need to offer a means for communicating with members. We strongly recommend that member contact be managed via email or an online CRM tool rather than by telephone, unless you already have call center infrastructure in place that can handle it. Fielding a single phone call from an irate member can require twenty minutes; responding to an email with a standard reply takes thirty seconds. Although some websites offer support by means of a live chat, anything involving real-time communication is likely to vastly increase your staffing needs.

If, as we suggest, you offer an email address or online form to members, there are a number of options for managing this at the back end. Your company may already have an email support infrastructure that can be adapted perfectly for community management.

KEY POINTS FOR A COMMUNITY MANAGEMENT EMAIL/CRM SOLUTION

* It should be easy to track the complete email history of each member even if emails have been dealt with by multiple community managers.

* If multiple community managers are answering emails for the same community, there should be a way to avoid duplicated work and responses.

* There should be a way to manage spam. Any website community email account is going to get attacked by spammers.

* There should be a good search functionality.

* You should be able to back up everything regularly.

* If you will need regular reports on email volume and type, look for a CRM solution with built-in reporting functionalities.

Starting out with a single community manager and a relatively small community, almost any email system will do, provided that you have the option to export the emails and import them into a new system as your community grows. There are many out-of-the-box CRM solutions, which are often organized around trouble tickets: when a member fills out your website contact form, this opens a ticket, and all replies to the ticket get automatically grouped together, making it easy to keep track of the history of a particular situation.

> **CASE STUDY**
>
> In one company, multiple community managers were answering emails to the same address using Outlook and Microsoft Exchange server. Unfortunately, their system was set up in a way that made it very hard for any community manager to see the replies that had been sent by the others. As a result, each time a member wrote to the company to follow up on an issue, the community manager would have no idea what the member was talking about and would either guess or ask the member for an explanation. The member would send the explanation and get a different community manager who, again, would be unsure what was being explained. Another problem: the community managers were sending members standard replies to common questions; if a member was unsatisfied with the standard reply, she or he would write again, often reaching a different community manager who again sent this member the exact same standard reply!

A network in your company

A strong network of collaborators in your organization is not needed for everyday community management. But it is essential as a long-term strategy if you want to establish your community as a useful marketing tool and help it grow successfully.

Who should be a part of your network? First, the network should include product managers who can support your community management team when users have product-related questions and ensure that users get fast and accurate responses to these questions. These product managers can also join the community and answer product questions directly on the platform. There might be other communities online that focus on your product or company, but your community can offer users a unique opportunity to talk directly with experts in your organization.

> **CASE STUDY**
>
> The German community on a major business networking website offers a forum called "Senseo—The Cool Coffee Machine." The members of this forum are interested in coffee machines and discuss advantages or disadvantages of coffee brewing techniques. But the four hundred members do not include any employees of Philips, the company that produces Senseo. Philips could take advantage of this gap and offer staff presence as a unique benefit on the Senseo website.

Your network should also include your market research department. Earlier, we talked about how useful a community can be as a market research tool. But this will only work if your market research colleagues know that the community exists, what you have planned for it, and the possibilities it offers them. Depending on your organization, there might not be much natural information flow between departments and you will have to make a point of getting them involved.

> **CASE STUDY**
>
> One of Anna's German clients has a brand-related community for retailers. By pure chance, an IT person mentioned during an in-house training for content managers that it is very easy to implement online surveys on the community interface. No one had been aware of this—not even the community manager.

Tell your market research department who your community members are and keep them informed about community activities and discussions as well as specific measures you can implement to support market research efforts. For example, you can add forums for users to discuss a new product. You can invite market research colleagues to offline community events—where else will they have the chance to talk to customers face to face? Of course, in this setting, they will only talk to a few customers, who may not be a representative sample. But such encounters complement traditional market research surveys by allowing discussion in great depth and detail. You can also provide Web analytics and publish website polls about the usage of a new product.

Your network should also include brand communication. This is important because you need brand-related content for your community that is both detailed and exclusive. If the only content you get is standard press material, your members will be disappointed and look elsewhere on the Web. Offering exclusive information is an easy but effective way to give something back to community members who have a genuine interest in your products and brand.

TIP
Helmut Bruendl, community manager of BMW's M Power World, says that a strong network within the organization is critical to the success of every community manager. "Explain to market research people what a powerful instrument a community is. Yes, go around and advertise your community!", he recommends. "If nobody knows what you are doing and what possibilities there are to ask your members product-related questions, your community will be isolated from the company. But if you are able to integrate your community actively, the community will reveal its usefulness, and lots of people will listen to your members."

EFFICIENT COMMUNITY MANAGEMENT

There are many ways to reduce your community manager's workload and help the community run more efficiently. The better designed your website is, the more user-friendly the processes, and the more activities and actions the members can handle autonomously, the happier everyone will be. Use technology to handle any situation where the community manager is not adding value. For example, a community manager should not have to generate passwords and email them back to members: a computer can do that. The same applies for unsubscribing to a newsletter.

Try to anticipate member questions as much as possible; preventing a problem is always preferable to solving one. For example, if seventy users are writing every week asking how to upload an image, pasting seventy standard replies into their emails is not an adequate response. Consider:

1. If no one knows how to upload images, the function may not be designed well. Fix it.

2. Post clearer instructions on the upload page.

3. Route users who want to send you an email through a Frequently Asked Questions (**FAQ**) page, which they have to scroll down before filling out your email form.

The best community management systems are a layered mix of member self-help and peer help, automation, semi-automation, and community manager attention, organized so that problems get escalated to the community manager when they cannot be dealt with as effectively in another way.

How can a system be set up to direct a user's problem to the appropriate level of escalation? Let's consider the example of a user with login problems:

1. The user tries to login and gets an error message *that includes login tips and a link to recall a password.*

2. The user receives an automatic password reminder and tries to login with the password he or she has just received. Another error.

3. The user clicks on the Help link to send an email. Instead of being shown an email form directly, the user is shown a list of frequently asked questions and answers about login.

4. At the bottom of the list, the user is asked, "Did you find the answer to your question?" The user clicks on the option "No." This opens up an email form. The question is now escalated to the community manager.

This principle can also be used for managing website content. Many websites use "bad word filters," which automatically censor rude or offensive language, replacing it with the substitute of your choice, such as "bleep" or "%!@=$)!" or "(Please keep it clean!)" There are also filters that recognize and censor images and video content that is likely to be pornographic. You can allow members to censor comments that have been sent directly to them. You can also create an **ignore button**, so that they can choose not to see content posted by certain users. This helps to prevent problems between members from turning into public feuds and alerts the community management to potential problems—if multiple members are ignoring the same user, the community manager knows to investigate the situation. Almost all communities include buttons to let users report inappropriate content. This option can even be programmed so that content reported by multiple users is taken offline temporarily until a community manager has approved it.

The better organized your member management infrastructure, the easier it will be to collect statistics and data about what is going on in your community. If users are navigating a self-help menu, or filling out contact forms that require them to select a category for their emails, this not only makes community management more efficient, it also provides an opportunity to track the volume and type of user concerns.

TIPS

A good FAQ page goes a long way. Make sure members have to pass through it before sending an email.

Supply community managers with a library of prepared reply templates. Instead of writing a new email each time, community managers can start with the most relevant template and then customize it for the specific member/question. If the community manager is working in Outlook, these templates can be stored as email signatures and quickly inserted into email replies.

Keep adding to the FAQ resources and template library as the community manager identifies new topics that are generating frequent emails.

Have members presort their emails by topic. If you don't have a contact form set up where the member can classify the email, you can easily set up different addresses or aliases by theme: suggestion@, login@, abuse@, competitions@, and so on. It is always faster to deal with groups of similar emails at once.

PEER MANAGEMENT

As we mentioned in the previous chapter, helping members to help each other is not only efficient but also highly motivating to the community. Giving members a leadership role creates a sense that they are a part of your website and, by extension, your brand.

ROLES MEMBERS CAN PLAY

* New member guides or welcomers
* Advisors on a member-to-member help desk

* Discussion moderators: Members can be given the power to initiate and direct discussions, censor content temporarily until it can be permanently removed or approved by staff, and close discussions that are getting out of hand.

* Community representatives or spokespeople

ROLES MEMBERS MUST NOT PLAY

* Members should not have direct control over other members. This can create conflict, abusive behavior, and bad feelings.

* Members must never have access to other members' data.

* Members should not have power that would allow them to change the overall direction of the community.

* Members should not be able to perform any actions that are not reversible.

* Members should not be allowed to publish or communicate anything that might be construed by anyone—even a casual visitor—as an official action in the name of your company.

CAUTION
If you are debating whether to put something in the hands of your members, it's better to err on the side of caution. Once a power is given to users, they will resent it being taken away.

A WELL-MANAGED COMMUNITY

If you've ever spent time on a badly managed community, you probably saw a certain amount of chaos: junk content, fighting members, and quite possibly public complaints from the members about the lack of community management. A well-managed community, on the other hand, is an asset to your brand. The members feel welcomed and cared for; the activities run smoothly; user-created content is relevant and appropriate. Successful community management doesn't necessarily cost more money. By providing a staff person with the necessary training and resources, and helping that person use time effectively, you can create a community to be proud of.

THE CHAPTER IN A NUTSHELL
Care and Feeding of Your Members

WHAT A COMMUNITY MANAGER DOES

- Respond to member questions and feedback, normally by email
- Interface between members and the community
- Facilitate community activity
- Censor abusive content
- Police the website

WHAT A COMMUNITY MANAGER NEEDS

1. Clear objectives
2. Authority to make decisions
3. Necessary tools:
   - Admin panel to access the member and content database in order to diagnose and solve problems
   - Tools for communicating with members (preferably email or another method that does not require answers in real time)
4. A network in the organization

EFFICIENT COMMUNITY MANAGEMENT

- When possible, prevent problems instead of solving them
- Provide automated or self-help solutions wherever possible
- Create a layered system that escalates problems that the user can't solve alone

PEER MANAGEMENT

1. Users can help each other as moderators and guides
2. Users must not be given power over other users or your brand

SEVEN

MONETIZING YOUR COMMUNITY

QUESTIONS ANSWERED IN THIS CHAPTER

- How can you get members to pay for premium features?
- How can your community boost your e-commerce site?
- How does online advertising work?
- How can you turn advertisements into gifts for your community?
- How can you send marketing emails without annoying your members?

PROFITING FROM YOUR COMMUNITY

Online communities can make money. According to an article in eMarketer, Fox Interactive Media (FIM), owner of social networking giant MySpace and a number of other Web properties, generated $856 million in revenues in 2008. The same article says that the social network Facebook reported $210 million in U.S. ad spending in 2008. Online advertising is by far the largest revenue source for most online communities, although there are exceptions such as the business network Ecademy, which has decided to focus instead on paid subscriptions.

> **CASE STUDY**
>
> The professional networking website Xing has a successful business model with three income streams: advertising, e-commerce, and paid subscription. In 2007, Xing generated around $28 million in revenue.

Even if you make the decision not to sell advertising to third parties, your community website is ideal for your own online marketing. It allows you to advertise on a perfectly targeted platform that is fully under your control, while saving the expense of renting advertising space on someone else's less ideal platform.

Studies about social networking show that users in Europe and the U.S. don't mind advertising if community membership is free. If you display advertising that matches the interests of your community members, users accept it, and will even click on it. The more relevant the advertising is to your target group, the more likely it is to get their attention.

In addition to keeping ad content relevant, it's important to choose the right advertising format. The German study "Community Effects 2008" asked more than 1,500 teens and twenty-somethings about their attitudes toward advertising on their favorite social networks. Teenagers said they liked viral video campaigns and sponsored music downloads. Young people between the ages of 20 and 29 like advertisements that contain product information, such as product-related discussion groups organized by the company. What both of these user groups like the most are interactive formats. Among their favorites are sponsored games and in-game advertising. If games fit well with your community concept, you can integrate advertising into opportunities for users to have fun and communicate with each other.

Another reason for using interactive formats is that Internet users are no longer passive viewers. If you display simple banner or text ads, there's a risk that users won't pay attention because they are busy with community-related activities: checking their mailbox, answering a message, starting a discussion group, or making new friends. In a study of 1,000 European users, nearly 50 percent said, "I do not pay any attention to online advertising in my community," and 13 percent incorrectly believed that their community didn't contain any advertising at all.

Whether you plan to convert your community into a new revenue source or just use it to save on advertising costs, you have to be careful not to compromise your credibility with website users. *Community members want to feel that the community belongs to them and that the website exists for their benefit, not in order to manipulate them or sell them something.* This doesn't mean that you can't turn the website into a cash machine. You will just have to do it sensitively and intelligently.

CAUTION
Usability expert Jakob Nielsen compiled a list of the most-hated advertising techniques based on research presented at one of his conferences. Some of the techniques that elicited the most negative reactions: "Tries to trick you into clicking on it" (94% of the users studied responded negatively); "Covers what you are trying to see" (93% responded negatively); "Occupies most of the page" (90% responded negatively); "Blinks on and off" (87% responded negatively); and "Floats across the screen" (79% responded negatively).

From a usability perspective, it's especially important never to interrupt a user who is involved in a process with multiple steps, such as writing and submitting a discussion post. The more steps in the process, the more critical the interruption.

SAVING MONEY WITH YOUR COMMUNITY

If you have planned your community properly around clear goals, it should naturally bring in indirect revenue through greater visibility, increased customer loyalty, and the other benefits we outlined in Chapter Two, "What Can an Online Community Do for Your Company?" Your community also gives you direct access to a targeted database of your customers and potential customers. If you take advantage of its potential, it can mean vast savings for your company in terms of advertising and market research costs. It can help you design better products and campaigns for your target market and avoid costly mistakes.

> **CASE STUDY**
>
> Communispace is a company that creates and manages private brand communities for over 100 major companies and brands. Debi Kleiman, Vice President of Product Marketing, says that customer insights from online communities have helped many Communispace clients such as Unilever, Hewlett Packard, and Charles Schwab to increase revenue and capture new markets. "We know communities drive growth," she explains. "They allow companies to be very nimble. When our clients want to test an idea, they go directly to the community for instant feedback. This means they are faster to market with new products and more relevant, effective marketing, and that they are creating the products that consumers really want to buy."

With your community, you have an audience predisposed to listen to what you have to say, and you have the space and time for a sustained conversation. You can use all this as an opportunity to give your members information they actually want, to educate them about products that are relevant to their discussions, to solve their problems. Instead of simply advertising to your members, engage in dialogue with them, talk to them in a way that offers them value, and they will appreciate it. When it comes to research, you can be more direct. Community members want to feel involved in your brand and your community, and generally will be glad when you ask their opinion—especially if you let them know that their feedback will have an influence.

EARNING MONEY WITH PAID SUBSCRIPTIONS

In the previous chapter, we talked about charging members for access to premium features and services. To make this successful, keep two points in mind:

1. The free features on your community should be sufficiently interesting to keep members engaged and make them want more. As we have mentioned, Internet users are often unwilling to pay for basic website

participation. But if your free website features are good enough, they will be willing to pay for more and better. Therefore, it is important to give people a taste of what they'll be getting for their money. For example, the professional network Xing does this in many ways. As a nonpaying member, you can have a profile page and a guestbook, send invitations to contacts, manage your contacts, and invite a limited number of people to events. However, paying premium members can also send private messages, see who has visited their profile, invite an unlimited number of people to events, and use a more powerful search feature. On the photo-sharing community Flickr.com, even nonpaying members can upload 100 MB per month on the website and use all community features. This allows them to get accustomed to using Flickr and even to become dependent on it. Then when they reach a point where they need more than 100 MB, they are willing to pay for a membership upgrade.

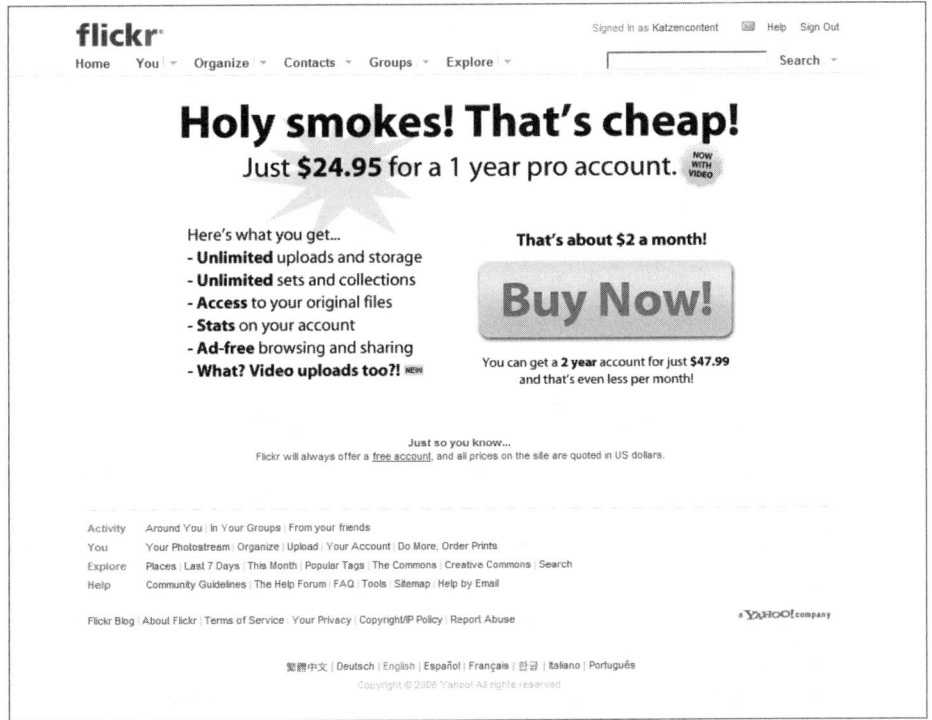

FIGURE 7.1 Flickr: Basic functions on this photo community site are free, but users have to pay if they want to upload an unlimited number of photos.

2. The premium features should either add enough value that it's worth paying for them or be inexpensive enough that members don't mind. On Facebook, for example, a member can pay $1 to give a virtual gift, such as the cartoon of a cupcake, to another member. It's not really useful, but it's fun, and it only costs $1. Depending on the projected size of your community, you can charge amounts of money that will seem symbolic to many members, while adding up to real profits. For example, if you get 100,000 members subscribing to a $5 service, you've already paid back your initial investment for the community project. Members are less likely to resent your charging for website services if you occasionally offer them for free or allow members to earn them through website activities. In fact, by sometimes charging for these services, you increase the perceived value of such gifts or incentives.

	Free membership	Premium membership
PARSHIP test and results	✓	✓
Your own profile with a description of yourself and a photo	✓	✓
Send/receive an Icebreaker	✓	✓
Receive Contact Requests	✓	✓
Send Contact Requests		✓
Secure sharing of photos		✓
Detailed Personality Analysis (c60 pages) (6 month and 3 month subscriptions only)		✓
Contact guarantee (6 month subscription only)		✓

FIGURE 7.2 Parship: This singles community page shows at a glance what members can use for free and what they have to pay for.

EARNING MONEY WITH E-COMMERCE

If you already have an e-commerce website, your community can be a way to drive traffic there. Discussion of specific products in the community can be linked to purchase pages. You can feature a "Shop" tab on the community website and announce special promotions to the community. If your community website motivates members through virtual incentives and prizes as described in Chapter Five, Motivating Your Members, or includes premium membership features, you can have members redeem or purchase them through the e-commerce site. In addition to bringing potential customers to the site, this will also increase the perceived value of virtual incentives by treating them as physical products.

Another way to link e-commerce and community is by encouraging community members to write product reviews. You can run review competitions about a particular product as a way of drawing attention to it. And the reviews can then be integrated into the shopping website as customer testimonials.

EARNING MONEY WITH ADVERTISING

Advertising arrangements

In Internet marketing, the term **publisher** refers to a website that displays advertising for third parties. By becoming a publisher, your community website can generate significant income. There are different ways for publishers to earn money, depending on the type of advertising and the agreement with the advertiser. A pay-per-impression (**PPI**) arrangement means that the publisher is paid according to how many times an ad is displayed to users. Pay-per-click (**PPC**) means that the publisher earns money only when a user clicks on an ad banner or link. Pay-per-action (**PPA**) means that payment depends on a specific action on the part of the user such as filling out a registration form on the advertiser's website. Pay-per-sale (**PPS**) means that the advertiser pays only when a purchase is completed.

Incentivized advertising

In incentivized advertising, you reward your users when they perform an action for your advertiser. For example, you might offer users a free e-book when they sign up for the advertiser's newsletter. It is the advertiser who bears the cost of the incentive, so incentivized advertising can be a way to offer gifts to your members. If you arrange interesting incentives for your community, you can present this type of advertisement as an added value to membership. For example, you might have a separate page on your website for Special Members-Only Offers from Our Partners.

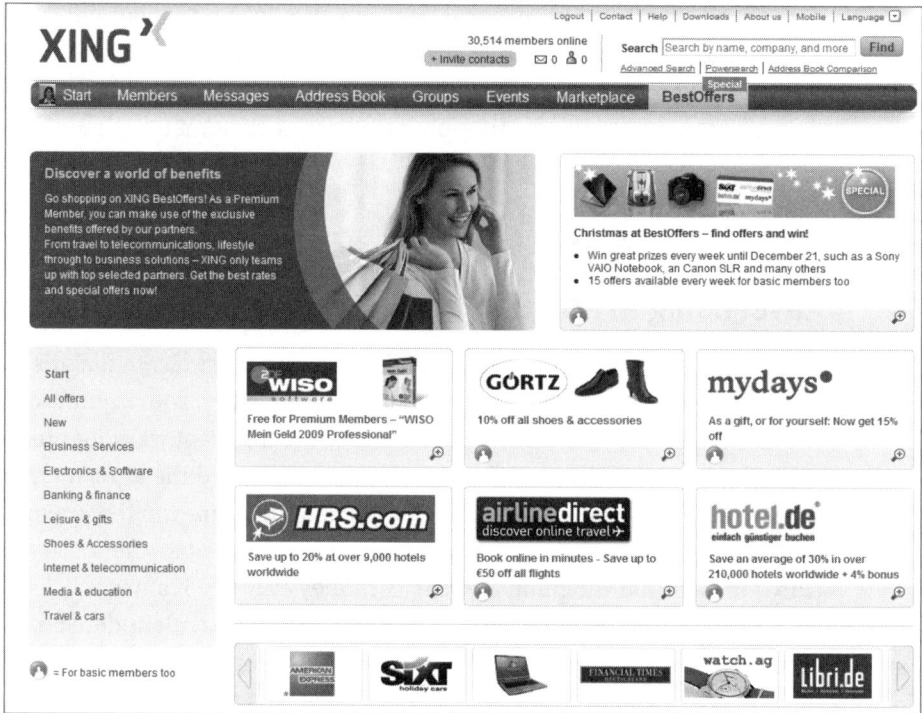

FIGURE 7.3 Xing: The navigation bar on this business network site includes an extra option, BestOffers, which contains content from partner brands.

You can even incorporate partner offers into your rewards system, allowing members to earn "shopping points" that they can redeem on your Special Offers page. In this case, the promotion should involve something that is free and does not require a purchase, such as a product sample or a newsletter subscription. In all cases, member sign-up for partner offers must be voluntary.

Display advertising

You can dedicate space on your website for banner and text advertisements, and then sell advertising to companies with products that are relevant to your community. For example, if your breakfast cereal brand has developed a community around a healthy lifestyle theme, you might not want to advertise other breakfast cereals, but you could display ads about spa vacations or natural cosmetics.

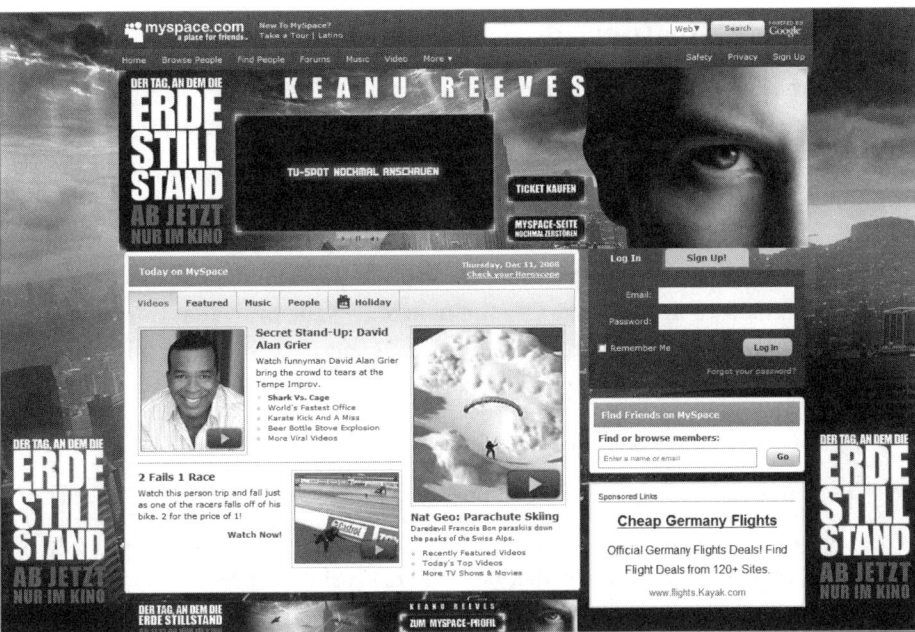

FIGURE 7.4 MySpace: Nearly 70 percent of this social network's homepage space is devoted to advertising.

 CAUTION
Be careful not to let advertising on your website become too abundant or intrusive, or it will drive visitors away.

Some communities that offer several membership levels show banner ads to nonpaying members, while allowing paying members to enjoy an ad-free website as a benefit of premium membership.

You can also sign up for a service such as Google AdSense, which uses technology to feed your website with advertisements related to the content on each page—what is called **context-sensitive advertising**. Google AdSense is very easy and convenient to use. The disadvantage is that you lose some control over the specific advertisements that appear on your website. This is a public relations risk if you end up with ads that offend your customers or don't match the image your brand is trying to project.

Coregistration

Another option is to make **coregistration** offers on behalf of compatible websites and mailing lists. When users register for your community or confirm their membership, you can offer them the option to sign up for the partner website and list at the same time. For example, you can a present a checkbox next to the option, "Also sign me up for BrandName's recipe website, www.brandnamerecipewebsite.com." Or you can display a page with multiple coregistration offers and let the user select the ones that interest him or her. The user only has to register once, and then his or her data is transmitted to the partner, who will pay you per coregistered member.

CAUTION
Make sure that communication about coregistration offers is very clear. Users should actively choose to sign up for the partner list (no preselected boxes) and should be aware of what they are joining. Otherwise, you risk losing member trust when they sign up for your website and suddenly receive emails from other companies!

Email advertising

Obviously, your community members will not appreciate being sent unsolicited direct marketing emails. But you can give them the option when they register to receive offers about certain types of products that interest them. If they agree, you will be able to send them offers from your company and from partners. Even better, you can send a monthly website newsletter with content relevant to your members and devote some space on it to advertising.

Another option is to offer an alert service, where members sign up for email notifications about new content published in the community. You can then put advertising links at the bottom of each email.

TIP
Nancy owns a global translation and content writing company called William Victor, which can take care of all of the writing, editing, and translation work for your newsletter and other mailings. You can request a free consultation at info@williamvictor.net.

Whatever your email strategy, be sure to follow applicable laws related to mass emailing and the handling of members' addresses. You can find some useful information about U.S. legislation at www.ftc.gov/bcp/edu/pubs/business/ecommerce/bus61.shtm. Apart from legal factors, it will be disastrous for your website and your brand if you get a reputation as a spammer. *If you're going to send mass emails, do it right.* Most community websites have published policies stating that they will never pass on a member's personal details to third parties; any emails that go out are sent by the company that owns the website. The main part of each email should be content that the member has requested or is likely to want, such as news about other members or special community competitions. And always make it easy to unsubscribe from mailings when desired.

A PROJECT THAT PAYS FOR ITSELF

If you are setting up a community for an existing brand, chances are that your main motive is not to build a new revenue source. Still, the savings and earning potential of communities are important to calculating your potential return on investment (ROI). Allocating a budget for your community project seems less risky if you keep in mind the project's potential to pay for itself. And if you can bring in additional revenue for your company without hurting your objectives, that's a wonderful bonus.

THE CHAPTER IN A NUTSHELL
Monetizing your community

WAYS TO MONETIZE YOUR COMMUNITY

1. Charge for premium membership

    * Free features should be engaging enough to make members want more

    * Paid features should add clear value or be very inexpensive

2. Use your community to drive traffic to your e-commerce website

    * Include shopping links on community pages
    * Incorporate product reviews into the community

3. Display advertising: Choose banner or text ads that are relevant to your community. Do not allow advertising to become excessive or invasive.

4. Coregistration: Give users the option at registration to sign up simultaneously for partner websites or mailing lists

5. E-mail advertising

    * Integrate ads into emails the members actually want, such as newsletters and alerts
    * Always make subscription to mailings voluntary
    * Comply with anti-spam regulations

EIGHT

GROWING YOUR ONLINE COMMUNITY

QUESTIONS ANSWERED IN THIS CHAPTER

* How can you measure your community's success?
* How can you keep your community fresh and relevant over time?
* How can you tell when you've outgrown your infrastructure?
* How can you adapt your community to promote your brand globally?

MEASURING SUCCESS

As your community grows and blossoms, you will want to quantify its success. Although the definition of success will depend on the goals you have set, you have many options for measuring the progress of your community and its impact on your brand.

Community success metrics

- **Website activity:** Your company probably has infrastructure already in place to track such metrics as website traffic and activity. If not, this type of tracking can easily be outsourced to a company specializing in website analytics.

- **Community membership and participation:** Configure your community admin panel to make it easy to see community statistics, such as registration rates, unsubscribe rates, content publication rates, member-to-member referral rates, and the amount and type of content forwarded from the website.

- **Email campaign success rates:** If your company does not already have infrastructure to track how many recipients are opening email campaigns and clicking on links, you can outsource this to an email marketing company.

- **Traffic from community to e-commerce and corporate pages:** Use tracking links to count visitors who originate from the community site.

- **Community-generated sales leads:** Use codes, promotions, and other measures to identify sales leads that are coming from the community.

- **Press attention:** Watch for increased references to your brand.

- **Search engine ranking:** Watch for improvements in the ranking of your corporate and e-commerce websites as well as your community website.

- **Customer feedback:** Your company's CRM department can provide anecdotal data on changes in overall customer satisfaction. You can also run surveys within your community.

- **Changes in public awareness and perception of your company:** Run tracking surveys to measure brand recognition and perception among your target customer population.

KEEPING YOUR WEBSITE FRESH

To maintain your success over time, you need to keep things fresh and relevant for your members. Even superficial changes on the website, such as holiday decorations or new colors and design elements, help to create a sense that the website is alive and fresh. Check related and similar sites regularly to see what is changing there. The competition may have interesting ideas that you can borrow or that will inspire new ones. It's important to keep on top of online trends. Internet culture is constantly evolving, and you don't want to miss out on new features or design developments on other sites that make your site look passé. If you have a trendy brand, the last thing that you want is an outdated website.

Ideally, your community should offer members a constantly improving experience. Fortunately, you don't have to rely on guesswork to figure out what changes and new features will work for your community; you have all the data you need right in your hands. Analyze website statistics—if possible, with the help of someone knowledgeable about Web tracking:

* Which of your current activities are the most successful?

* What topics are your members discussing feverishly?

* Can you expand or shift your focus to cover the areas of greatest interest to your members?

* Can you give members more of what they like the most?

Your community manager will have a clear idea of member preferences and the types of requests and suggestions members are making. Run surveys on your website to get member feedback. Your community manager can also point you to leaders at the top of the member hierarchy, who will be delighted to take part in brainstorming sessions. The best predictor of what will appeal to members is what has appealed to them in the past. And members will be more enthusiastic about website changes if they feel that they have been involved in the decision process.

> **CASE STUDY**
>
> The rural tourism community Toprural.com told us that user feedback is the basis for almost everything they do. "During the last two years, we've run a survey on a panel of our users, and this has helped us to improve," said François Derbaix, CEO. "For example, starting in July of this year, we have started including photographs in user opinions, because we saw that this was very important to users who are making travel plans."

KEEPING COMMUNITY MANAGEMENT FRESH

Over time, community managers become true experts on your community. They know the overall mood of the community at any moment, what members are discussing, member likes and dislikes. They know which members are conflictive and which ones to contact when you need input or a product testimonial. Their intimate knowledge of the community can be a valuable asset, but there are also some dangers to watch out for.

HAZARDS OF LONG-TERM COMMUNITY MANAGEMENT

* **Overidentification with the members:** It is easy for community managers to get excessively involved in the community, to take website politics personally, and to start receiving their priorities from the community rather than from the company.

* **"Functionary" mindset:** In any job, habits form. This can be a problem for community management as the scale of the community grows. If your community managers developed work processes based on seven emails a day, they need to be able to adapt when these turn into seventy.

Take preventive measures to head off these problems from the beginning. Train your community managers to distinguish between community demands and company priorities; empower them not to be bullied by members; and teach them how to develop efficient working methods. Giving your community managers regular feedback on their work and involving them in higher-level community planning will help them keep things in perspective.

ADAPTING YOUR INFRASTRUCTURE

As your community grows, one intern and a computer with Microsoft Outlook may no longer be enough to manage your member support. If your community managers are overloaded, we recommend looking first to technological and process solutions to optimize efficiency, and then adding human resources as needed to do the work that cannot be automated.

Signs that you need to improve technology or processes

You'll know it's time to upgrade software or streamline work flows when you find that community managers are repeating each other's work or spending a significant amount of their day on the following:

* Sorting or clearing out emails
* Performing tasks that require no thought or decision-making, such as responding to members' requests to unsubscribe
* Compiling statistics on incoming emails or membership trends (CRM tools can do the former, admin tools the latter)
* Dealing with problems with existing community features, leaving less and less time to work on new features and improvements.

Signs that you need to hire more human resources

After you've optimized processes and technology to reduce the workload as much as possible, consider hiring additional community managers if you still notice:

* A backlog in work that is growing daily
* A problematic backlog or delay in work after a staff vacation or sick day
* Inundation during peak periods, for example, activity spikes resulting from promotions or product releases
* A significant number of emails received in a language that the community manager doesn't speak.

RECRUITING MORE MEMBERS

In general, the bigger and better known your website is, the easier it is to attract members through passive recruitment. Once you have achieved a certain level of success, you can adapt your recruitment strategy accordingly. You may be able to stop spending money on recruitment altogether and rely solely on viral methods, press relations, member-to-member referrals, and search engine traffic. All of these tactics become exponentially more effective in proportion to the size of your community. Or you can focus your recruitment efforts on expanding the scope of your community to reach new target groups according to your company's sales and marketing needs.

INTERNATIONALIZING

One way to increase the scope of your community is to make it more international. The Internet is inherently a global medium: a website can be accessed from anywhere in the world. You can take advantage of the global power of the Internet to promote your brand in foreign markets. Let's say you have a website mainly oriented toward U.S. customers, and you would like to encourage traffic from the U.K. as well. It may be enough to make small adaptations such as prices listed in multiple currencies, slight changes in the copy to neutralize linguistic differences, new discussion threads for products that are available only in the U.K., and links to your U.K. e-commerce site as well as the U.S. one. On the other hand, if there are major differences in your branding or products between one country and another, you may decide to set up separate sites for each country.

If your current Web address is www.samplewebsite.com, you might set up a similar address with a local country domain (e.g., www.samplewebsite.co.uk for the United Kingdom). You can either have a separate website at this address or have it point to the same site you use for other countries.

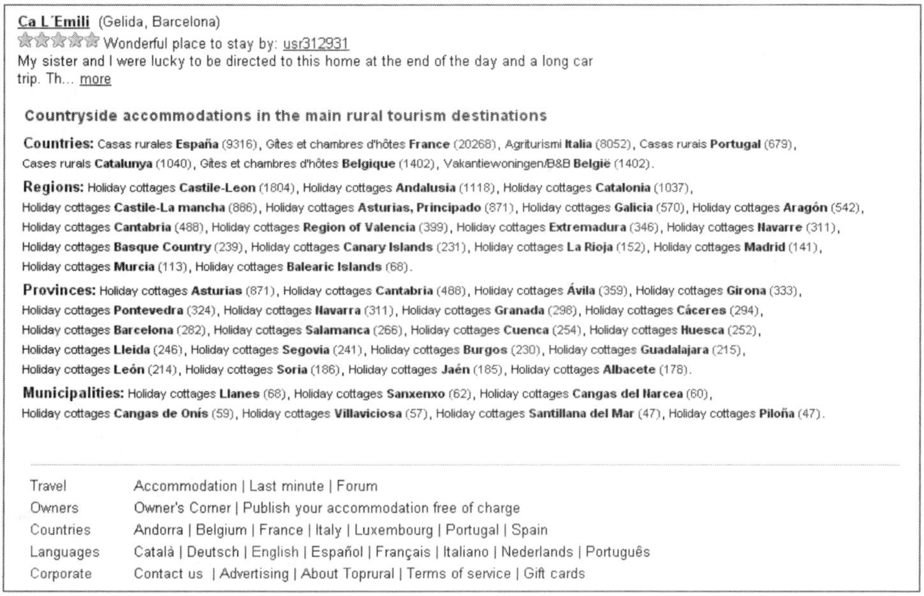

Ca L'Emili (Gelida, Barcelona)
Wonderful place to stay by: usr312931
My sister and I were lucky to be directed to this home at the end of the day and a long car trip. Th... more

Countryside accommodations in the main rural tourism destinations

Countries: Casas rurales **España** (9316), Gîtes et chambres d'hôtes **France** (20268), Agriturismi **Italia** (8052), Casas rurais **Portugal** (679), Cases rurals **Catalunya** (1040), Gîtes et chambres d'hôtes **Belgique** (1402), Vakantiewoningen/B&B **België** (1402).

Regions: Holiday cottages **Castile-Leon** (1804), Holiday cottages **Andalusia** (1118), Holiday cottages **Catalonia** (1037), Holiday cottages **Castile-La mancha** (886), Holiday cottages **Asturias, Principado** (871), Holiday cottages **Galicia** (570), Holiday cottages **Aragón** (542), Holiday cottages **Cantabria** (488), Holiday cottages **Region of Valencia** (399), Holiday cottages **Extremadura** (346), Holiday cottages **Navarre** (311), Holiday cottages **Basque Country** (239), Holiday cottages **Canary Islands** (231), Holiday cottages **La Rioja** (152), Holiday cottages **Madrid** (141), Holiday cottages **Murcia** (113), Holiday cottages **Balearic Islands** (68).

Provinces: Holiday cottages **Asturias** (871), Holiday cottages **Cantabria** (488), Holiday cottages **Ávila** (359), Holiday cottages **Girona** (333), Holiday cottages **Pontevedra** (324), Holiday cottages **Navarra** (311), Holiday cottages **Granada** (298), Holiday cottages **Cáceres** (294), Holiday cottages **Barcelona** (282), Holiday cottages **Salamanca** (266), Holiday cottages **Cuenca** (254), Holiday cottages **Huesca** (252), Holiday cottages **Lleida** (246), Holiday cottages **Segovia** (241), Holiday cottages **Burgos** (230), Holiday cottages **Guadalajara** (215), Holiday cottages **León** (214), Holiday cottages **Soria** (186), Holiday cottages **Jaén** (185), Holiday cottages **Albacete** (178).

Municipalities: Holiday cottages **Llanes** (68), Holiday cottages **Sanxenxo** (62), Holiday cottages **Cangas del Narcea** (60), Holiday cottages **Cangas de Onís** (59), Holiday cottages **Villaviciosa** (57), Holiday cottages **Santillana del Mar** (47), Holiday cottages **Piloña** (47).

Travel	Accommodation | Last minute | Forum
Owners	Owner's Corner | Publish your accommodation free of charge
Countries	Andorra | Belgium | France | Italy | Luxembourg | Portugal | Spain
Languages	Català | Deutsch | English | Español | Français | Italiano | Nederlands | Português
Corporate	Contact us | Advertising | About Toprural | Terms of service | Gift cards

FIGURE 8.1 Toprural: The homepage of this rural travel community automatically analyzes the user's IP address to determine which country the user is in and opens the corresponding version of the site. If this is not the right choice, the user can change languages with a single click.

Many brand websites have an international **start page**, where the user selects his or her location from a menu and is routed to the corresponding country page. There is also technology available that can guess at a user's location. Each individual country page then includes links to change countries in case someone ends up in the wrong place. A user's country selection is saved for the future by means of a **cookie**, a temporary Internet file.

Adding languages to your community

If you are targeting multiple countries where different languages are spoken, then you will probably need to translate the content of your website. Some online communities such as Xing and 11870.com offer multiple languages on the same platform. If you click on the option to view the Xing page in French instead of English, you will see the same users as before, but the fields labeling their profile information now appear in French. Similarly, on 11870.com, if you choose to view the website in English instead of Spanish, you will see the same user reviews as before in their original language, but the page around them will be translated. By maintaining everything on a single platform, these communities are able to maximize the volume of content and activity that users see. This is important for a business networking site such as Xing because the usefulness of the platform is directly related to the number of people in the network—and many Xing users will be looking for international contacts.

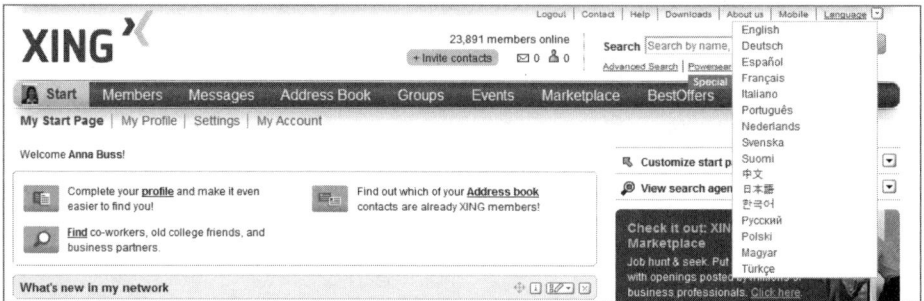

FIGURE 8.2 Xing: The content on this business network site is available in sixteen languages.

CASE STUDY

Xing uses a common information structure to permit users to understand content that has been submitted in a foreign language. For example, users can complete an online form to share professional details about themselves. Their responses are displayed to users all over the world, but with field names in the user's own language. If I share the fact that I graduated from Oberlin College, English speakers will see "University/college: Oberlin College," Spanish speakers will see "Universidad: Oberlin College," and Polish speakers will see "Uczelnia: Oberlin College."

Other communities such as Ciao.com have separate websites for each country. If you go to the Ciao U.K. website, you will only see content by users from the U.K. This makes Ciao more useful as a shopping portal, since products and pricing are different in different countries. Users can find what they're looking for without being distracted by information irrelevant to their location or in a language they can't read.

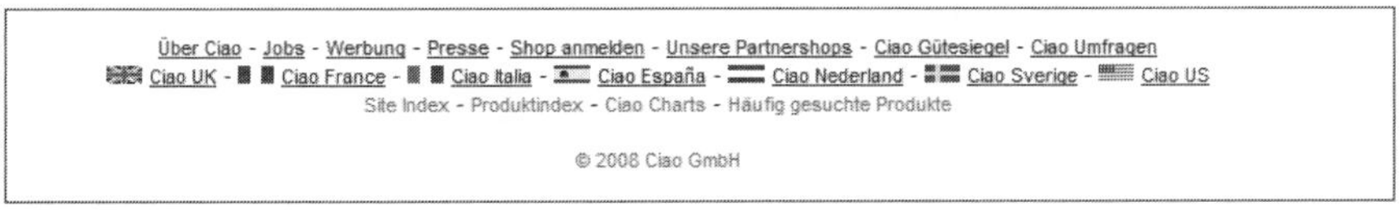

FIGURE 8.3 Ciao: This shopping community offers eight versions of its website.

As illustrated in the case of Ciao, language is not the only issue to consider when globalizing a website. People in different countries often use different products and have different customs, habits, and cultural norms. And, of course, if you have very different brand strategies or product lines in two markets, it may not be possible to address them both on the same site. Whether you decide to consolidate content by globalizing on single platform or accommodate differences by launching separate country sites, the decision to globalize a community entails some development and staffing costs, so you will need to determine whether a potential market is important enough to justify the investment required.

CASE STUDY

Adapting website texts for another culture can be more complicated than it seems! Several years ago, Anna had to translate some English texts into German for a children's community. It might seem easy to translate short sentences for kindergarteners, but the job was more complex than Anna had expected. "Do you see the red bus?" one sentence read. But buses in Germany aren't red. Cars are on the other side of the road. Police look different. And a small child will notice every single mistake you make. So the translation work was time-consuming, requiring many adaptations and careful review.

Another globalization project of Anna's was a different story. This time, her client was a community for singles, and the task was to create country-specific versions for a large number of countries from Switzerland to Mexico. Everyone thought this would be difficult and time-consuming. But it wasn't. Anna's client did a usability study that showed the use of the community didn't differ from country to country. The only points requiring special attention were the payment options and the Terms of Use.

Key points on translation

* The translator should be a native speaker of the target language; that is, if your translation is from English to French, the translator should be a native French speaker rather than a native English one. Studying French in college or having lived in France for several years does not qualify a native English speaker to translate a website to French. Even if you can't tell the difference, your French customers can! Just think of it the other way around. Have you ever seen an instruction manual or a website that was not written by a native speaker? That's not the public image of your company you want to project!

* Look at the translator's nationality too. The Spanish spoken in Spain is not the same as Mexican Spanish, the Portuguese spoken in Brazil is quite different from that spoken in Europe, and so forth.

* Not everyone who speaks a language can translate. Translation is a specific skill, and there are many mistakes that untrained translators commonly make which can lead to undesirable results. Also, not all people write well even in their own language, and the finished translation will reflect any limitations in the writing skills of your translator. So you might not want to trust the presentation of your website to your French sister-in-law. A good translation agency has translators who have been screened for the necessary skill sets. In addition, they should have experience with translating websites and software that will make the work more efficient and consistent.

Foreign-language support

When planning the budget and infrastructure for a Web page in a new language, keep in mind that when you build a site in Bulgarian, you are inviting your customers to speak Bulgarian with you. If you build a Bulgarian community, someone needs to be able to screen Bulgarian user-generated content and to answer emails in Bulgarian. The language skills required for community management are lower than those needed for translation. Your Bulgarian community manager doesn't necessarily have to be a native speaker, but he or she does need to be fluent enough in Bulgarian to handle member emails diplomatically, to distinguish between an appropriate and inappropriate joke posted by a member, and so on. You will also probably want to set up separate email addresses or an automated workflow system to direct emails in different languages to the right staff person.

Internationalization checklist

* Make sure that the language is appropriate for your target population.

* Check that address and phone fields in your registration form work for all countries.

* Ensure that currency and measurements are correct for all countries.

* Check that valid payment options are offered for each country. Your company may accept a different type of credit card in Spain than in Canada.

* If possible, optimize the look of the website for the target culture. Keep in mind that aesthetics and the meaning of colors and symbols differ from country to country.

* Use appropriate images. If you are launching a website in India, you might want to use photos of Indians instead of Americans.

* Check for cultural appropriateness of topics, taking into account differences in such areas as cuisine, holidays, religion, pop culture, even seasons.

* Some things cannot be translated. Humor often doesn't translate well, and the best option may be to remove jokes and wordplay from your Web copy or to replace them with new jokes. With marketing copy, the same text may not resonate in the same way in different languages. Instead of simply translating, it may be best to hire copywriters in the target culture to come up with new copy.

* Have a lawyer investigate legal differences in the target culture that may become important. Areas to look at include minimum age restrictions; laws governing sweepstakes, competitions, and remuneration; and data protection laws.

TIP
Nancy owns a global translation and content-writing company called William Victor that delivers high-quality translations in major world languages. William Victor also has native writers in many countries who can create content for your websites and email newsletters. Such an option saves internal resources and produces more culturally appropriate content for international websites. You're welcome to contact William Victor at info@williamvictor.net for a free consultation. More information is available at www.williamvictor.net.

AN ASSET FOR YOUR COMPANY

If you've followed the advice throughout this book, at some point, you will likely have a vibrant community full of enthusiastic members. You will have built a valuable asset for your company—a competitive advantage, a source of real-time data about your customers, a powerful marketing and public relations tool. You will have strengthened brand loyalty and expanded brand recognition. You may have even opened the door to new market sectors or turned the community into an important revenue source of its own. Congratulations in advance!

THE CHAPTER IN A NUTSHELL
Growing Your Online Community

METRICS FOR TRACKING SUCCESS

- Website activity
- Community membership and participation
- Email campaign success rates
- Traffic from community to e-commerce and corporate pages
- Community-generated sales leads
- Press attention
- Search engine ranking
- Customer feedback
- Changes in public awareness and perception of your company

KEEPING YOUR COMMUNITY FRESH

- Even superficial website changes help
- Look at the competition to stay on top of online trends
- Analyze your community's preferences to keep the website relevant for members

ADAPTING YOUR INFRASTRUCTURE

* Use technology and optimized processes to minimize repetitive tasks
* Signs that you need more human resources:
    1. Regular work backlogs occur even after you've optimized processes
    2. Your site receives a significant number of incoming emails in a language your community managers don't speak

INTERNATIONALIZING

* To encourage traffic in foreign countries where the language and branding are similar to your main site:
    1. Purchase country Web domains and redirect them to your main site
    2. Adapt site content for differences in currency, measurements, and cultural references
* To encourage traffic in foreign countries where the language and branding are different from your main site:
    1. Develop separate country pages if needed
    2. Get content professionally translated or adapted for the new culture
    3. Hire community managers who speak the website languages

NINE

SOCIAL NETWORKS AS A PLATFORM FOR YOUR BRAND

QUESTIONS ANSWERED IN THIS CHAPTER

* What's a social network?
* Why market on social networks?
* What can your brand do on a social network?
* Are social networks right for your brand?

WHAT'S A SOCIAL NETWORK?

Earlier, we defined an online community as a group of people who regularly interact with each other on a website. By this definition, social networking websites are online communities in their purest form. In other types of communities, member interaction is focused around a specific theme such as cars or travel reviews, but in a social network, member interactions themselves are the main focus and activity. Members use these websites to socialize. They create profile pages to represent themselves, and they visit the profiles of other members to see who shares their interests and who lives in their city, to find friends, and to learn about their friends' friends. Each member adds contacts to a personal network or friends list, which is generally visible to other members. Popular activities on social networking sites include leaving status updates on your profile (for example, "I am in Hamburg today"), reading and commenting on news from your personal network, and other activities based around the question, "What are members I know doing?" A large network and a popular profile page are important status symbols on social networking sites.

Social networks often allow members to start their own micro-communities. For example, Xing has more than 12,000 micro-communities created by members in the German language alone. No idea is too obscure to attract members. You can find, for instance, discussion groups like these:

* Table hockey, a visionary sport
* Barbecue in Cologne
* Friends of biomass
* Anatolian rock music
* Name Storm: How to create a name for your brand

Social networking is becoming more and more popular. The Nielsen Company published statistics in 2008 about the growth rates of the most popular social networks. LinkedIn grew from 4 million unique vistors in September of 2007 to nearly 12 million visitors in September of 2008, with a growth rate of 193 percent. Facebook, which had 18 million visitors in September of 2007, grew to more than 39 million visitors in September of 2008, a growth rate of 116 percent.

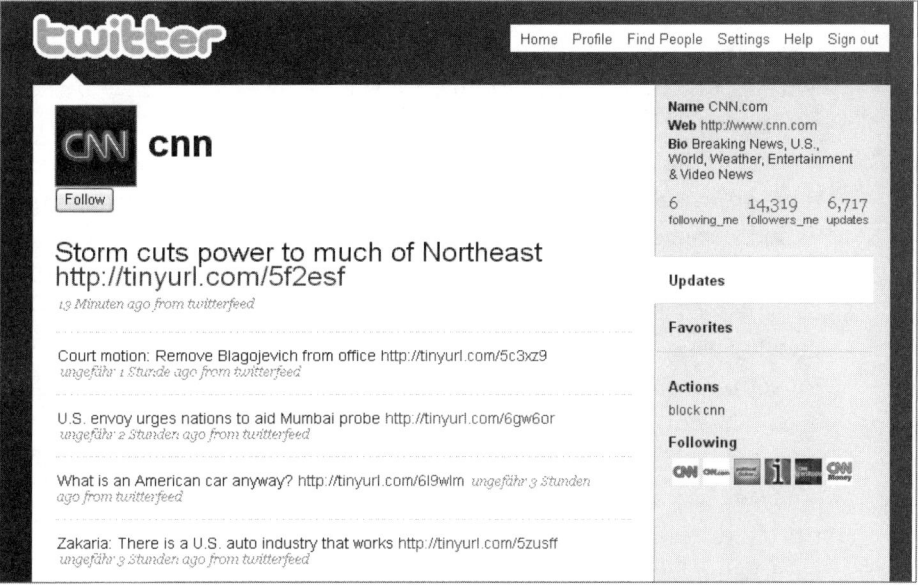

FIGURE 9.1 CNN's Twitter page: Twitter provides a new kind of news channel.

Twitter grew from 533,000 unique visitors in September of 2007 to 2.35 million visitors in September of 2008, outpacing the others with an extraordinary growth rate of 343 percent. Twitter offers fewer services than Facebook and other major social networks. As a member of Twitter, you have exactly 140 characters to answer the question, "What are you doing?" Other members can become your "followers" and receive constant updates online or on their cell phones about what you and their other friends are doing. You can also post comments or publish a picture on a simple profile page. That's all. But it's a service that many people seem to find useful and enjoyable, and one that marketers are now discovering as well.

WHY MARKET ON SOCIAL NETWORKS?
Get past banner blindness

When's the last time you clicked on an advertising banner? Very likely you can't remember because you always ignore ads online. If that's the case, then your behavior is typical of the vast majority of website users. Most people don't pay attention to anything that looks like an ad. This phenomenon is known as

banner blindness. Web users are often looking for specific information, which they want to find quickly. Advertising banners are distracting to someone who is trying to complete a task online. For this reason, users have learned to ignore advertisements. A study by Nielsen Norman Group revealed that users not only ignore ads, but they also ignore all website elements that look like ads—whether these are actually banners or not. 86 percent of users in a test situation failed to find a specific piece of Web content when the information's format included typical elements of advertisements. Ignoring or overlooking online ads has become second nature to experienced Internet users, a group that is rapidly growing every year. At the same time, companies are spending more and more money on online ads. During the first 6 months of 2008, $3,800 million was spent on online display advertising in the U.S. alone, up from $3,200 million reported for the same period in 2007, according to a PricewaterhouseCoopers study sponsored by the Interactive Advertising Bureau (IAB). To overcome banner blindness, advertising agencies have developed a wide range of elaborate new advertising formats that are less easy to identify as an ad. But it is still a problem to get the attention of users who are being flooded with huge amounts of competing information. Social networks can offer a solution.

Reach Generation Y

If you are marketing to teenagers and twenty-somethings, then you know the difficulty of coming up with a good media mix to get their attention. This target group—people who were born between 1977 and 1995—is often called Generation Y. The young people in this group have radically different media consumption habits than the generations before them. A survey of over 7,700 Generation Y students in the U.S. discovered:

* 97% own a computer
* 94% own a cell phone
* 76% use instant messaging
* 34% use websites as their primary source of news
* 28% author blogs and 44% read blogs
* 75% have a Facebook account
* 60% own some type of portable music and/or video device such as an iPod.

Members of Generation Y are not attached to "old-fashioned" scheduled TV like the generation before them. They prefer to watch a DVR-recorded program at a time of their choosing or an online version with substantially fewer commercials. Even when watching a live program on a TV screen, they don't pay full attention to it because at the same time they need to update their Facebook page, chat with three friends on Instant Messenger, or read Twitter messages on their mobile phones. All of these communication channels reduce the attention span. To reach this target group via newspapers is "mission impossible"—Generation Y won't buy a newspaper that is only published once a day. Wait until morning for news? Out of the question. Sure, news is important. But Generation Y gets it in real time from online publications or blogs. The same with radio. Why wait to hear a favorite song? Young people download their music and pay (if record companies are lucky) to hear it when and where it fits into their world.

Companies have to adjust their advertising strategies to the media consumption habits of this generation. TV, newspapers, and radio are overshadowed by cell phones, personal Web pages, and social networks. Peer-to-peer or customer-to-customer communication is essential for reaching this young target group.

Other advantages

Marketing on social networks can bring many of the benefits we described in Chapter Two, "What Can an Online Community Do for Your Company?" Like a brand community, social networks offer opportunities to establish a dialogue between brand and customer, to engage in emotional marketing, to gain important insights about your target market, as well as numerous other advantages:

* **Savings:** Publishing a brand on a social networking site costs much less than an advertising campaign that would reach the same number of consumers. It is also, of course, much less expensive than developing your own community platform.

* **Viral recommendations:** A member who adds your product to his or her friends list has a strong attachment to your brand. If that member recommends your product to his or her network, other members will add it to their own friends lists. Peer-to-peer communication has much more credibility than brand-to-customer communication.

- **Long-term customer relationships:** 70 percent of social network members say they want to remain in their social network forever. The contacts you make on these networks are likely to stick around. And once your brand is added to their friends lists, it will stay there.

- **Shorter sale cycle:** Your presence on social networks allows potential customers to get to know your brand over time, so when they visit your e-commerce site or see your products in the stores, they can make a purchasing decision more quickly.

- **Community recruitment:** If you build your own community, you can use social networks to market it and to recruit new members. For example, the rural tourism website Toprural.com has pages on Facebook and LinkedIn, publishes photographs on Flickr and videos on YouTube, maintains a blog, and posts on Twitter.

- **Targeted advertising:** You can do more on social networks than creating a member profile. You can also advertise, taking advantage of new hyper-targeting techniques that group users according to their interests as well as sociodemographic data. For example, MySpace clusters users into categories based on interests such as sports and fashion. They can then subdivide these groups into hundreds of specific selections for targeting ad campaigns. The results make sense because of the large number of members on these social networks.

Marketing on social networks is a good way to support a brand community or to help launch a new one. On the other hand, you might decide to use these networks as an alternative to developing a proprietary community platform. The cost is much lower, and you can get faster results in the short term. Building a new community takes time. There is always a high-risk period after the launch when you need to generate enough activity so that members will have a reason to stay. When you market on social networks, you can skip this phase. The users are already there, visiting the platform each day, and all you have to do is engage with them.

WHAT CAN YOUR BRAND DO ON A SOCIAL NETWORK?

Create a profile

On many social networking sites, you can have a profile page for your brand that looks similar to an ordinary member profile, including the same basic functionalities, such as:

* Add this member as a friend
* Add this member as a favorite
* Forward this to a friend
* Leave a comment
* View a video or photo gallery.

Your brand is seen as a person and interacts with the community like another member. For example, when users add your brand to their friends lists, they might receive a message that says, "Thanks so much for adding me as your friend."

TIP
Leesa Barnes, an expert in marketing on social media and author of the book *Podcasting for Profit*, emphasizes the importance of a detailed and transparent profile page. Her advice: "Complete your profile as much as possible—include your URL because that helps to make you look transparent, and if you are the CMO or the VP of Marketing or Marketing Director with a big name brand company, make sure you identify that in your profile. It is all about transparency and that is what people are looking for."

Get involved

Once you've filled out a profile, it's time to start interacting with the community. But remember that social networks are part of Web 2.0—this means that they are not a one-way channel for brand communication. If you start out in a social network by pushing your product promotions, this is not likely to win you a lot of friends, just as it would not be appropriate behavior at a cocktail party. First, it's polite to show an interest in the other person and engage him or her in a conversation. The product discussion can come later.

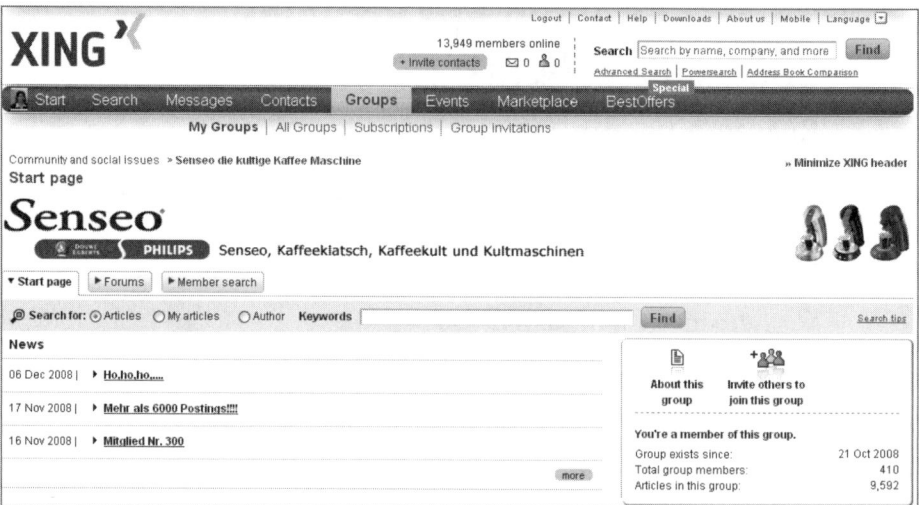

FIGURE 9.2 A Xing discussion group focused on a coffee machine: This social network lets users create micro-communities to discuss a wide range of topics—which might include your brand or your products. (Group description means "Senseo, coffee break, the cult of coffee, and classic coffee machines.")

The more opportunities you offer users to communicate actively with your brand, the better. Marketing expert Leesa Barnes suggests starting out with a survey. You can use the survey to test your marketing ideas and find out the best way to communicate with your social network.

Invite users to upload photos or videos on your profile, post product-related comments and questions, contribute their ideas, express themselves in different ways. Respond to them, and you've started a dialogue between customer and brand.

Isn't there a risk that a social network member will write a negative comment on your brand's profile page? Sure, this can happen, and everyone in the network will be able to read it. On the other hand, you will have the chance to react quickly. If you provide a specific and respectful answer, you can turn a negative comment into a positive public relations opportunity.

Give something back

When members visit your profile page or add your brand as a friend, you should give them something back. The U.S. survey "Never-ending friending" asked 2,600 people between the ages of fourteen and forty about the reasons why they added a brand as a friend in a social network. Two top reasons were, "For exclusive offerings," and "For discounts, coupons, free samples, and other free stuff from them." Popular gifts in social networks include icons, wallpapers, or other digital design elements. Offer these as free downloads. Members who are fans of your brand will use them to decorate their own profile pages. Icons and labels are a signal to other members: "Look, I am a fan of Apple computers, Adidas shoes, or Burger King."

Offer emotional brand experiences

Studies show that emotional brand experiences such as concerts and competitions are more and more appealing to customers. These customers are not interested in lists of product features and rational arguments about why they should buy. Engaging them emotionally is a way to distinguish your brand from others. Brands that touch people's emotions have a competitive advantage. The Adidas Streetball Challenge is a good example of this strategy. In Germany, Adidas started this sports competition with 300 teams in Berlin in August 1992. A year later, Adidas organized the "German Tour 1993" with six events in major German cities; more than 20,000 players and 400,000 visitors participated. The most effective way to increase brand visibility and awareness is through a combination of offline and online activities.

FOUR OPTIONS FOR COMBINING OFFLINE AND ONLINE ACTIVITIES

* Attend offline mega events such as the FIFA World Cup or the Olympic Games. Although these events are not organized by your brand, they attract a huge amount of attention. You can offer news of the events on your profile page, along with pictures, games, raffles, and other items in combination with your product information.

* Attend offline events for a young target group. You can offer a calendar of these events on your profile page, or a cool photo gallery that shows social network members at the events.

* Organize an offline event with visible brand sponsorship. Use your online network to generate interest in the event and even to manage invitations. Afterward, you can publish photos of the event on your profile page and encourage post-event discussions.

* Use a media mix that combines multiple communication channels. For example, you might start a video contest and use your profile page on a social network as a platform for uploading videos. The winning videos could then be converted into a television ad on MTV.

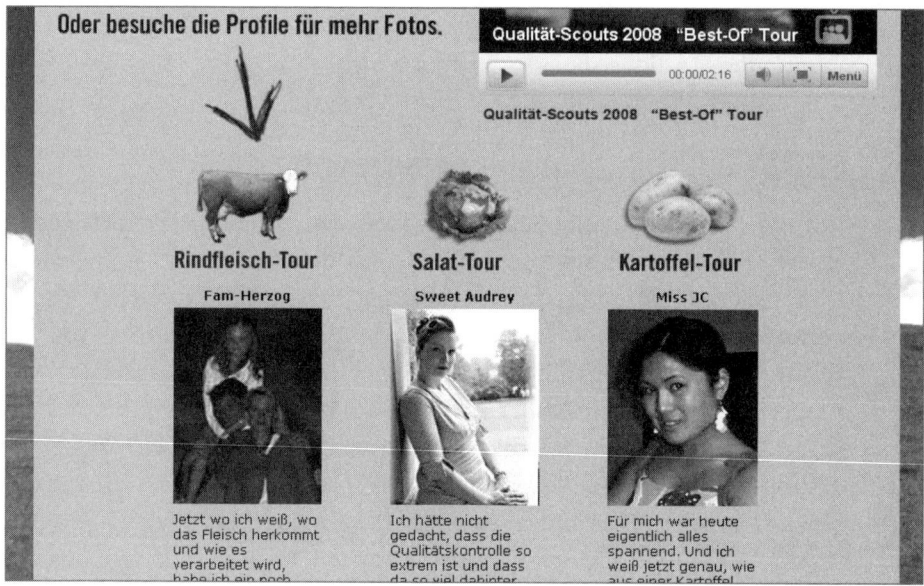

FIGURE 9.3 MySpace: McDonald's built a marketing campaign around user-generated content to increase users' trust in the brand. (Members Fam-Herzog, Sweet Audrey, and Miss JC are discussing the "Beef Tour," "Salad Tour," and "Potato Tour.")

ARE SOCIAL NETWORKS RIGHT FOR YOUR BRAND?

Not every brand can be supported successfully by a social network. If you are selling an expensive, complex B2B product that needs a lot of explanation and has a ten-year product lifecycle and a very small, highly specialized target group of five hundred experts worldwide (drilling towers, robots, or high-tech medical equipment, for example), a social network like MySpace is not the ideal platform to increase sales volume. So let's have a look at some criteria that can help you decide if a social network is the right marketing tool for your company.

First, consider your target group. Social networks are great for targeting young people; baby boomers are also increasingly using these platforms. You're likely to have less luck if your target population is older, or, of course, if it is a group with a small online presence.

Another important factor is the type of product you have. Do you have a brand with which customers can identify and develop a strong emotional relationship? Kevin Roberts, CEO of Saatchi & Saatchi, coined the term "lovemarks" for products that achieve this. Typical lovemarks often come from the high-tech, fashion, music, sports, and automotive sectors. These products increase the customer's heart rate. The relationship between product and customer is as emotional as a love story: a sensible "trustmark" becomes a hot lovemark. To use a lovemark is to express your social identity, who you are, the group to which you belong or want to belong, your place in a community. This is what makes social networks the ideal platform for a lovemark. If such a product is on your friends list, it is a signal to others that says, "I love this brand because I am cool, sexy, modern, or high tech"—or whatever the brand's image represents. On a social network, you can connect with other people who like the same brand and have added it to their own friends lists. You can use the social network to stay in touch with your favorite brand and share your passion for it with others.

The majority of products do not achieve true lovemark status. But social networks work better for products that can become a part of the user's everyday life and that awaken desire and other strong emotions. Expensive lifestyle products are more successful on social networks than low-cost products such as chocolate or chewing gum. For example, Wrigley's Airwaves chewing gum had its own profile pages on social networks and didn't manage to attract many users.

Success story: Puma v1.08 The Speed Boot

One product that has its own profile page on a social network is the Puma athletic shoe v1.08 The Speed Boot. For the product launch, Puma created a MySpace profile page for the shoe that offered a range of typical activities to other MySpace members:

* Watch the TV commercial and see how it was produced
* Download wallpaper images, MySpace skins, buddy icons, or profile pictures that show famous athletes such as Mario Gómez, Alexander Frei, or Peter Crouch
* Add Puma to your friends list
* Write a comment.

FIGURE 9.4 MySpace brand profile: This Puma athletic shoe has attracted 2,000 friends on the MySpace network.

In December 2008, the shoe had collected nearly 2,000 friends. This may not seem such a large number—Justin Timberlake, a MySpace member since May 2006, has more than 1 million friends. But every MySpace member who has added the shoe as a friend is likely to be a loyal customer and a powerful source of viral marketing. Keep in mind that 80 percent of all members use the same social network as their offline friends do. With just one click, 2,000 friends of the Puma shoe can forward the shoe's profile link to their other friends.

Why is an athletic shoe an ideal product for a social network? Puma is a brand that is well-established as a lovemark. Customers have an emotional relationship to this type of athletic shoe because the brand is exclusive and not part of the athletic shoe mass market. Here's how Puma describes its brand strategy: "By maintaining a connection with our core values of inclusiveness, innovative design, sophistication, and individuality, Puma will consistently set the bar for what it means to be the most desirable Sportlifestyle brand in the world."

CHAPTER IN A NUTSHELL
Social Networks as a platform for your brand

Social networks such as Facebook or MySpace offer a way to market to Generation Y—people born between 1977 and 1995—a group that cannot be reached effectively by traditional media. Social networks also offer a solution to the problem of banner blindness: the more people use the Internet, the more they learn to ignore everything that looks like advertising. A brand profile on a social network website is not seen as a boring advertisement, and it's able to attract people's attention.

Social networks are not useful for every brand. They work best for products aimed at a fairly broad user group. The product should inspire emotions such as empathy and desire, and should stand for a way of life. If a member adds your brand as a friend, this should make a clear statement about the person who adds it. Social networks are often a particularly effective marketing platform for products in the high-tech, fashion, music, sports, or automotive sectors.

Marketing on social networks is most effective when it combines online and offline events. Events such as competitions, concerts, or games can engage customers on an emotional level that is far more powerful than rational arguments for why they should buy.

Don't forget that social networks are not platforms for one-way communication, but belong to Web 2.0, which is all about dialogue. Users will expect the opportunity to talk to your brand and get answers.

PART TWO
REAL WORLD LESSONS

TEN
CIAO.COM

> "Give it the time it takes to establish a real community... The key is to focus on quality and long-term sustainable thinking."
>
> —Stephan Musikant, Managing Director, Ciao.com

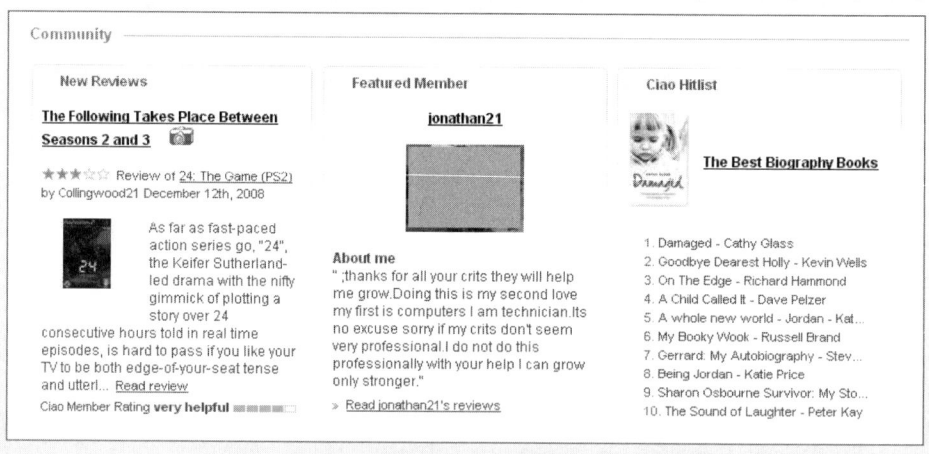

Ciao.com: Members have published over 5 million consumer reviews on their websites.

Ciao is Europe's leading consumer and price-comparison portal, with shopping communities in seven European countries and a new one in the U.S. Ciao community members can publish consumer reviews in both written and video formats, and they can create private or public lists of their favorite products and services. In 2008, there were over 5 million member reviews on the Ciao websites. Ciao community members also create profile pages, rate each other's reviews for usefulness, leave comments on reviews and on other members' profiles, and build networks of members whose opinions they trust. Ciao offers members two parallel rewards programs to motivate participation: monetary rewards as well as "community points" that increase a member's ranking in the community hierarchy (symbolized by a colored dot next to the member's user name).

The content created by Ciao's members adds to the usefulness of their huge catalogue of product information and comparison pricing. The Media Metrix Report from comScore, Inc. found that Ciao had 18.12 million unique visitors on their websites during February 2008.

We spoke with Stephan Musikant, Ciao's Managing Director.

Ciao.com product page: Users who are not logged in see a balanced mix of product information and community elements. Interactive features such as the "Click if you like this product" link require registration and thus recruit new members to the community.

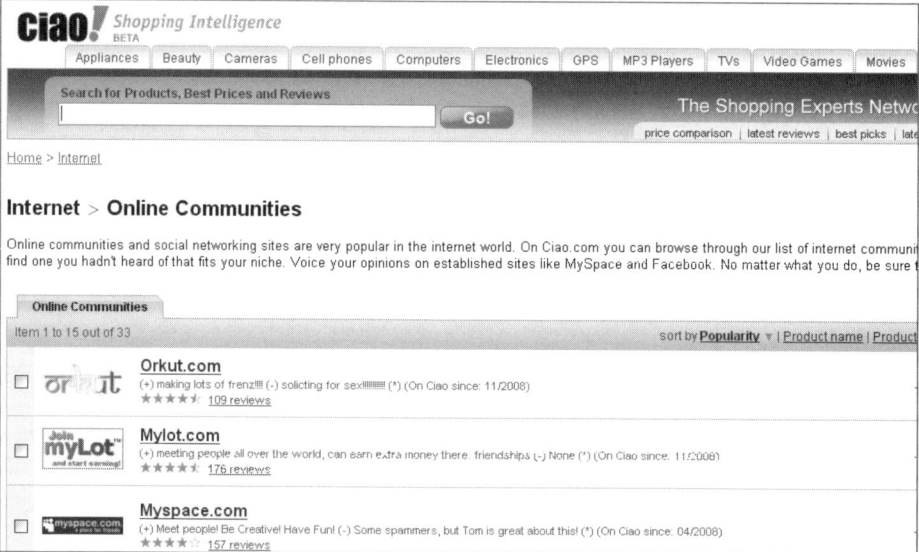

Ciao.com category page: The catalogue contains millions of products. Users even post reviews of other online communities.

INTERVIEW

The Ciao websites have two main offerings for users: a comparison shopping portal and a consumer community. Could you talk about how these two aspects of Ciao feed each other?

In the beginning, Ciao was founded as a pure opinion portal. The idea was that everyone could help each other and give advice by writing consumer reviews. From that existing structure, a detailed product catalogue evolved. Around 2001, it became clear that a pure community model would not be profitable, and so we added the price comparison component. There were two reasons for doing so. First, it was a way to bring in revenue. And second, it was a service that people already expected; someone searching for a product on Ciao would also naturally want to find the lowest price. It was the next step in the whole purchase cycle. First, you search for the product to buy. Then, you read reviews and learn more about the product. After that, you make up your mind and look for the best price. And finally, you make a purchase.

What advice would you offer to a company that is interested in adding a community element to an existing e-commerce website?

To define what you expect to get out of the community. To separate yourself from marketing trends and identify a specific goal. It's hip and trendy to have a community these days, but you need to define what you expect to accomplish over the next two to three years, and, based on this definition, you should work to establish your individual community. Based on this definition, you also need to define how much space to give community features on your website.

In the case of Ciao, the community is important and therefore has more space. We try to find a balance between general interest topics and community topics. The website is designed so that non-logged-in users can still find the community, and logged-in users can customize the site according to their needs. It's important to accommodate both kinds of users by having a different view of the website before and after login. A logged-in user is likely to come to the site to write a review and interact with other members. A non-logged-in user is there looking for product information and the best prices; this user has different goals and should not be distracted by member photos and community information.

How does Ciao recruit new members?

There are different ways to attract members to a community, but, in the first place, it makes sense to convert regular users to community members. These are people who already have an interest in the website. This is much better than buying leads externally, which is the usual method. What we figured out was that the community is all about the core members, and we need people with a real interest in giving advice and helping others. When we worked with lead generation in the past, we could claim that we had 50,000 more members in our community for example, but it turned out to be more trouble than it was worth. Recruitment in-house brings the best results, the friends-recruiting-friends program and members recommending us to people they know.

Ciao has two parallel remuneration systems to reward members for participation. You offer monetary rewards, and at the same time, you offer nonmonetary recognition through a points system that shows a member's level of experience in the community. Could you discuss these two systems and how they work to motivate members?

Both programs are important for growing the community. It's important to remember that there's a difference between remuneration and spending a lot of money. The people on Ciao are not here to make money. There are a lot of websites on the Internet for people who are interested mainly in making money. Of course, we get some users like that, but we've found that they're generally temporary. The core community members are looking more for exposure and interaction. For them, the money represents real appreciation of their activity in the community, and it's a kind of scorecard. It's like when you play cards, the game is more interesting if you're playing for a few cents. But at the end of the day, what people on Ciao care about is the exposure they get, the appreciation, reaching the next level in the community, earning superstar status, engaging in a group of people.

What community points do is give people an instant reward. When people do something, they want feedback. They want to see some kind of reaction and to feel appreciation and recognition for what they did. If you ever read letters to the editor in newspapers, you might be astounded at how emotional people get in reaction to something in the news, but they normally never get feedback on their comments. So you can imagine the same kind of situation, but where the writers get feedback and it starts a conversation.

What is your strategy for managing an international community in multiple languages?

We've chosen a centralized approach because it's important to share learning. But it's also important to think locally, which is why we have native speakers managing every community. This is essential. Imagine a user in Madrid and another in the North of England: these are totally different cultures. They have different holidays, different languages and behavior, and use different products and services. For example, UPS is something relatively new in Spain, but mail order has been popular in the U.K. for years. There are hundreds of things that you can't know if everything's centralized, and you need people who know these tiny differences to make sure everything's localized.

What other advice would you give to someone interested in starting a community to support a product or brand?

Give it the time it takes to establish a real community, rather than a fake community brought in by lead generation. We've figured out over the years that members may come and go, but the really important core community members are there for years. It's easy to spend money on marketing and build up a community, but most of that is going to be fake. You can spend money initially on lead generation to reach the size you need to get started, but the real community needs to be built over time and is not something you can do quickly on the run. You need a mid-term and a long-term plan. So if you're a marketing manager starting a community project, you need to get a mid-term commitment from your organization. People need to differentiate between setting up a group quickly for a promotion versus building a real community.

How can companies use Ciao's platform to promote their products or brands?

Retail shops should make sure that their products can be found on Ciao. Many people put a lot of effort into providing good services and attractive products, and if you do good things, Ciao helps to spread the news around. You can do some special promotions to make sure that your best customers are letting people know about their good experience by writing reviews on Ciao.

For example, you could offer a free pen to everyone who writes a Ciao review. The more people talk about your products, the more people will learn about them, and people on Ciao are looking for this information.

What is the secret of Ciao's success?

Four years ago, we changed our strategy. We were tempted to go for quicker, artificial results and push for money, but based on our community, this would have been the wrong approach. Slow and steady is the way to go. You have to focus on your goals and build up a quality experience. We're adding to the website every day, making thousands and thousands of small improvements. The key is to focus on quality and long-term sustainable thinking. There are always short-term marketing trends that come and go. For example, a couple of years ago companies were all rushing to invest in marketing on SecondLife, and now no one is paying attention to SecondLife anymore. Our approach is to concentrate on building up real assets instead of following popular trends.

LESSONS LEARNED

Ciao.com is a community that has made quality a part of its strategy. They have taken a long-term approach to building a solid community.

It is interesting to look at Ciao's decision to add price comparison to what was originally an opinion portal. Price comparison made the website more profitable but, importantly, it was also a service that met an existing user need and a natural extension of the way people were already using the Ciao website.

Ciao has also recognized two different uses of the website and accommodated these with two slightly different interfaces, using login to distinguish users who are interested in the community from users who may only want to see product reviews and price information.

Our interview with Managing Director Stephan Musikant offers many valuable lessons for anyone embarking on a community project. Some key points:

* Define your goals for the community, and use these to determine the space it will get on your website.

* Don't be distracted by marketing fads. Focus on quality and creating value that will last.

* Building a real community takes time. You need a two- to three-year plan and a mid-term commitment from your organization.

* Lead generation can help your community reach a minimum volume of activity when you are first starting out, but it brings in lower-quality members than other recruitment strategies. Converting your existing users to community members and member-to-member referrals are two ways to generate higher-quality members.

* Monetary incentives for members don't have to be expensive. For the members, it's not only about the money—it's about recognition.

* For an international community, a centralized approach can be combined with the use of native community managers who have important cultural knowledge about specific countries.

ELEVEN
11870.COM

> "The center of what we do isn't technology; it's humanity."
>
> —11870.com

11870.com: This community is based around reviews of services, from restaurants to housepainters to accountants.

The website 11870.com is a community based around reviews of services, from restaurants to housepainters to accountants. It is like an online telephone directory transformed into a lively and attractive community platform. Members can add new services to the site, post reviews (including photos and video), and "follow" certain members or places that interest them. In addition, 11870.com offers a number of other tools to make the site more fun and useful, such as the ability to find other members with similar interests, and the option to download information from the website to a GPS device. Companies can also use 11870.com to promote their services and communicate with potential customers.

The design of 11870.com was specifically intended to be useful even for new users who do not yet have a network of contacts in the community. In this respect, it is different from many pure social networking sites such as Facebook or Twitter, which are entirely focused on interaction within a group of contacts. The idea of 11870.com is to encourage users to start creating content right away, before they are necessarily aware of the site's social side.

Although the 11870.com website is available in English and its content is international in scope, the company is based in Spain, and the majority of its current members are Spanish. When the community was launched in 2007, it immediately generated a great deal of attention, achieving a number one ranking on Technorati, the leading blog search engine, during its first week. 11870.com reported the following statistics for December 3, 2008: "11,383 registered users, 70,654 services, 89,228 reviews, 105 countries, 3,864 cities, 252,880 pictures, 2,673 videos, 8,862 categories, 38,280 tags."

The 11870.com spokesperson is Nacho Puell, cofounder and design director of the community.

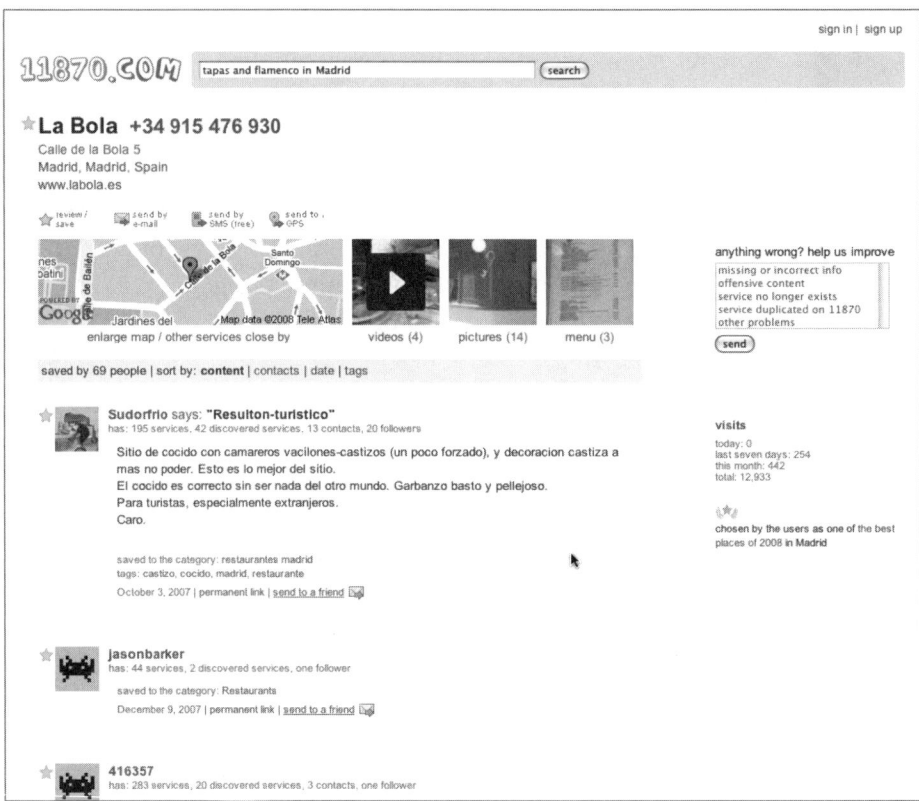

11870.com: Looking for a restaurant in Madrid? Videos, pictures, and comments from the community result in a page which is much more useful than a simple Yellow Pages entry.

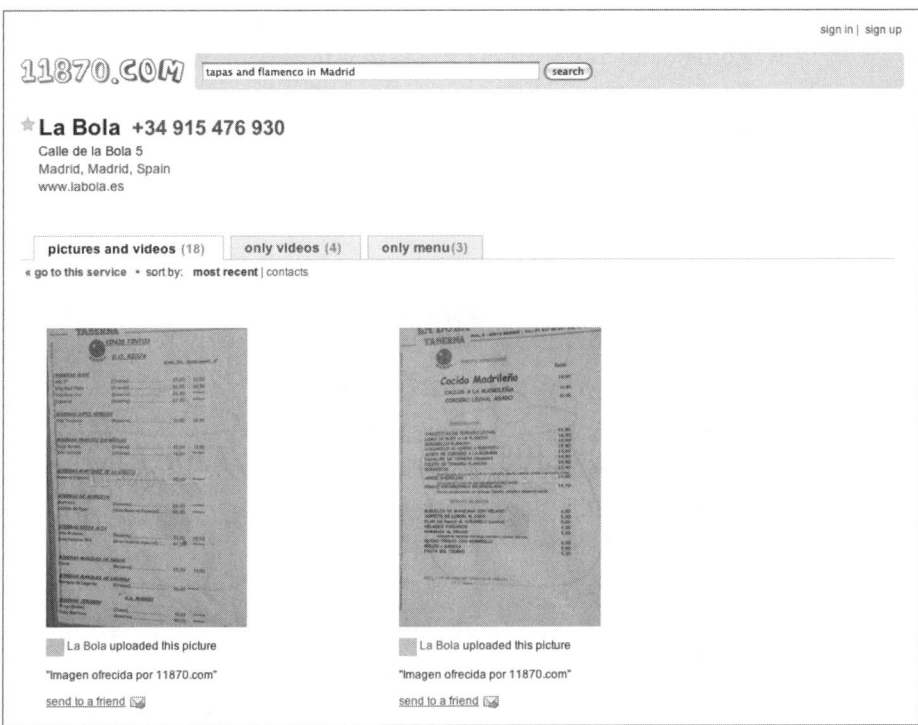

11870.com: User-generated content even shows you what's on the menu.

INTERVIEW

When did 11870.com begin?

Our company was started in 2006 as an initiative of Jesús Encinar and a group of private investors. We launched the community in 2007. During our first week, we were number one in Technorati, the website that tracks blogs. We knocked Britney Spears out of the number one position, and that was right when she had shaved her head.

How do you encourage members to join your community and participate?

The first thing that we provide is a pleasant website, with a clean interface. Our registration process is simple, and three days after registration, a community manager gets in touch with new members to welcome them. In the physical world, the community manager might offer them a coffee. In the virtual world, we welcome them and let them know that if they get lost, we're here to guide them. And we observe what the members have done. If they haven't saved any places on their profiles, we ask them if they need help.

We pay a lot of attention to the user. The center of what we do isn't technology; it's humanity.

When I registered on your website, I clicked on an activation link, and this took me straight to a page that asked me to recommend a service. This seems an effective strategy to get new users participating right away.

The first page the user sees is fundamental. We want to avoid what happens on many websites, where the user registers and then thinks, "Now what?" We want to give the user options, to avoid the blank page syndrome, so that the user never arrives at a dead end. It's a matter of usability.

Each member has a different way of participating, and we try to support the users who contribute a lot. We have a system for classifying users according to the level of contribution they make, but we don't believe that users who contribute more content are necessarily better users. Some people use the website to post content, and others only consult it, and those users might be using it more.

We've found that the users who contribute the most make up 5 to 10 percent of the population and contribute 90 percent of the content. These are our real fans. So what we do, for example, if someone adds a new place to the website, is to give this person a virtual prize, a kind of medal with the title Discoverer. Another thing we do is to run small competitions or campaigns. But we never say, "Publish X contributions and get a prize." We don't want to buy users. Instead, we recognize their contributions afterward. We might send a small gift, a real gift, but always after the fact, in a natural way. For example, one of our users was going on a trip, and we sent him a nice little book where he could take notes on the places he visited.

Also, when we add a new feature, we ask the opinions of our most active users. We organize meetings in our office, group sessions, and ask them what they want, what they like, and how we can improve.

Our offices are always open for users to visit. And it's a rare week when one or two don't stop by.

Your website addresses users in a very friendly, informal way. Why did you choose this communication style?

For us, the fundamental point is humanity. We've designed our interface to be pleasant and easy to navigate. One of our cofounders is the leading Web usability expert in Spain, and a lot of thought has gone into every feature. Usability is essential, and our communication style is part of this. Basically, it's about treating the users how we'd like to be treated. So we talk to them as humans, not as robots.

How do you make your community viral?

We offer a lot of tools for users to send a review by email, or send photos, a profile, videos. Users can also send information about a company by SMS. What's most important is not the virtual world; it's having a reference in the real world.

Users make lists of companies, and they can download their lists to a GPS. For example, if they are planning a trip to San Francisco, they save a list of interesting places there and then download it to a GPS before their trip.

How is your website set up to facilitate interaction among members?

We offer a system of internal messages, which is the current system that members use to communicate. And now we are implementing a system of recommendations that allows users to find people in different cities who have similar tastes. Members can use these recommendations to meet new people and to find new places that they might like.

What problems or challenges have you faced in your community, and how have you resolved them?

Our biggest challenge has been the reaction of business owners to negative opinions. They discover that search engines are displaying these opinions before the company's own website. Their first reaction is, "I don't want this to appear. Take it off." We have to help them see that a negative opinion can also give them credibility, and many times these opinions are a great opportunity to improve.

Your community is available in several languages. What benefits and challenges does this bring?

We offer several language options so that people will feel more comfortable. We have community managers to answer users in English and Spanish. Currently, the main website language is Spanish, since we're located in Spain. But we also offer the content in Catalan to cover Catalonia, and in English so that the community has the ability to grow outside Spain. What's great is that it's very scalable. Although we're based in Spain, the content is global, and people can recommend services all over the world.

How can companies use your platform for marketing?

Our model of business is centered on the role of intermediaries. So if someone is looking for a plumber or someone to remodel a kitchen, instead of going to a traditional directory, this person can go to 11870.com to look for professionals and request price proposals. What we do is put a huge number of clients together with companies.

We want to be a platform where companies of all sizes have a presence. The community isn't only for users—companies can also register and publish content, photos, and videos, and you see this content together with the user content. Companies can use us as a platform to get exposure and connect with clients, but it's more than this. They can also use it as a platform where their clients can comment on their experiences.

When someone is thinking of buying a product, they will often look at forums for user comments before they go to the official company website. What we offer clients is a service where they get exposure and have tools for managing client feedback. For example, recently a restaurant owner called and wanted us to delete a negative opinion that a user had published. We can't delete negative opinions. But what this restaurant really wanted was to change the user's opinion. So in the end, they invited the user to dinner to try to change his opinion, and it worked.

What advice would you offer to someone who is interested in setting up a community to support a product or brand?

My first advice would be to look at whether the brand is conducive to creating a community around it. There are brands such as Apple and Levi's that naturally create a sense of belonging in their customers. You have to ask yourself if your customers really want to identify themselves as fans.

Second, you should keep in mind that creating a community is not a project with an expiration date. It's something that requires dedication and maintenance over the long term.

Third, I'd suggest looking around at the communities that already exist because many of them provide options for marketing, and this requires much less investment and effort.

LESSONS LEARNED

The 11870.com management place a great emphasis on personal communication with users and effective website and activity design. The comfort of the user is given top priority. They pay special attention to the 5 to 10 percent of users who generate 90 percent of the content—content that adds value for all the other users.

For anyone building a community, 11870.com can serve as a positive example in many areas:

* Clean, usable Web design
* Simple registration process
* Easy-to-understand activities that engage new users right away
* Care taken to avoid "blank page syndrome"—no dead ends; users are always offered a new activity
* Written communication style that sounds "human-to-human" instead of "robot-to-human"
* Use of member feedback in website development and improvement.

TWELVE

M POWER WORLD

> "We always offer exclusive information. Our members have a highly emotional relationship to the brand."
>
> —Helmut Bruendl, community manager, M Power World

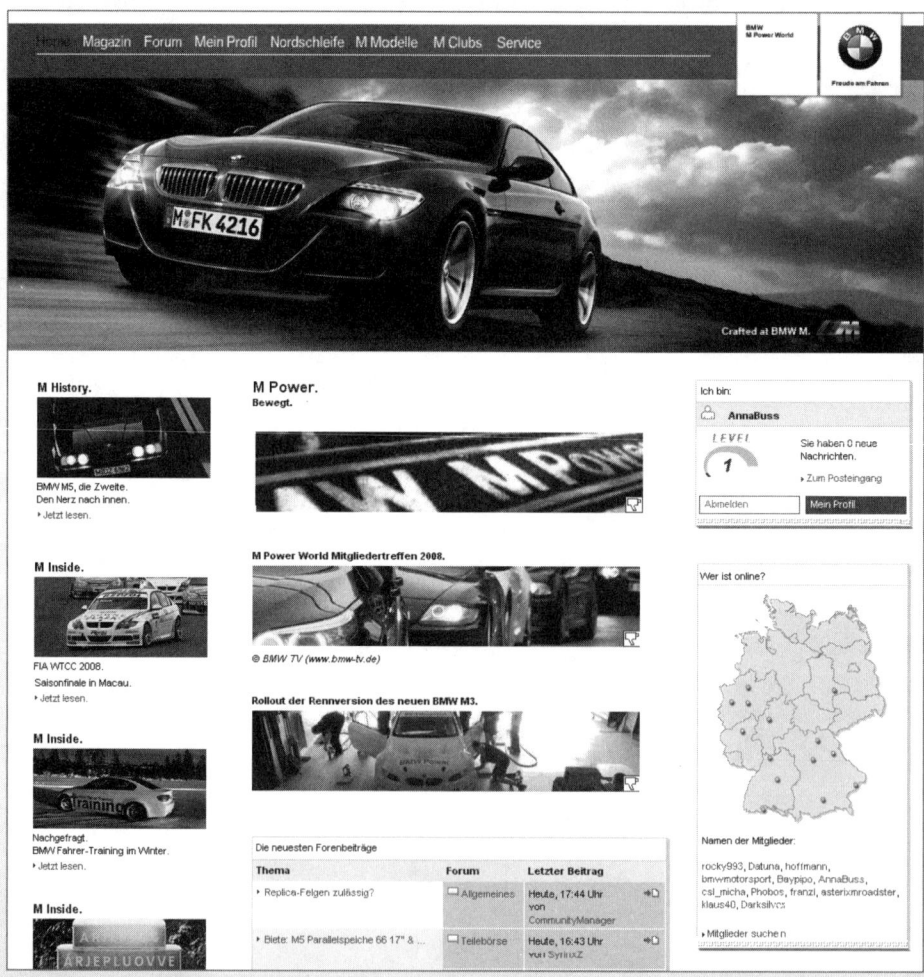

M Power World: The homepage shows a strong focus on the brand.

M Power World is an online community for people who own a BMW M model (M stands for Motorsport). The community was created by BMW M GmbH, a fully owned subsidiary of BMW AG that produces sporty modifications of BMW cars. High-end materials reduce the weight of M cars, and a new design gives them a dynamic look. These models are fairly exclusive: BMW M GmbH produces only around 20,000 units per year.

Launched in March 2007, the community is completely closed to everyone but members. Guests can only see the login page. In order to register, you need a valid chassis number of a new BMW M car. At the end of 2008, more than 25 percent of all German M model owners were members of this community. Three months after the community's launch, BMW counted some 1,000 visitors per day. The main business goal of M Power World is to strengthen brand loyalty.

Members can read magazine articles produced exclusively for the community, find user-generated content, organize events, search for other members, send private messages, have group discussions about the latest BMW innovations, or publish cool pictures of their beloved BMW Ms online. In the future, M Power World plans to offer the ability to share data about the most exciting driving routes. Members will be able to follow these via GPS and use Google Maps to find other community members who drive on the same road. It's interesting to note that M Power World supports many offline activities such as driver training.

We spoke with Helmut Bruendl, community manager at M Power World.

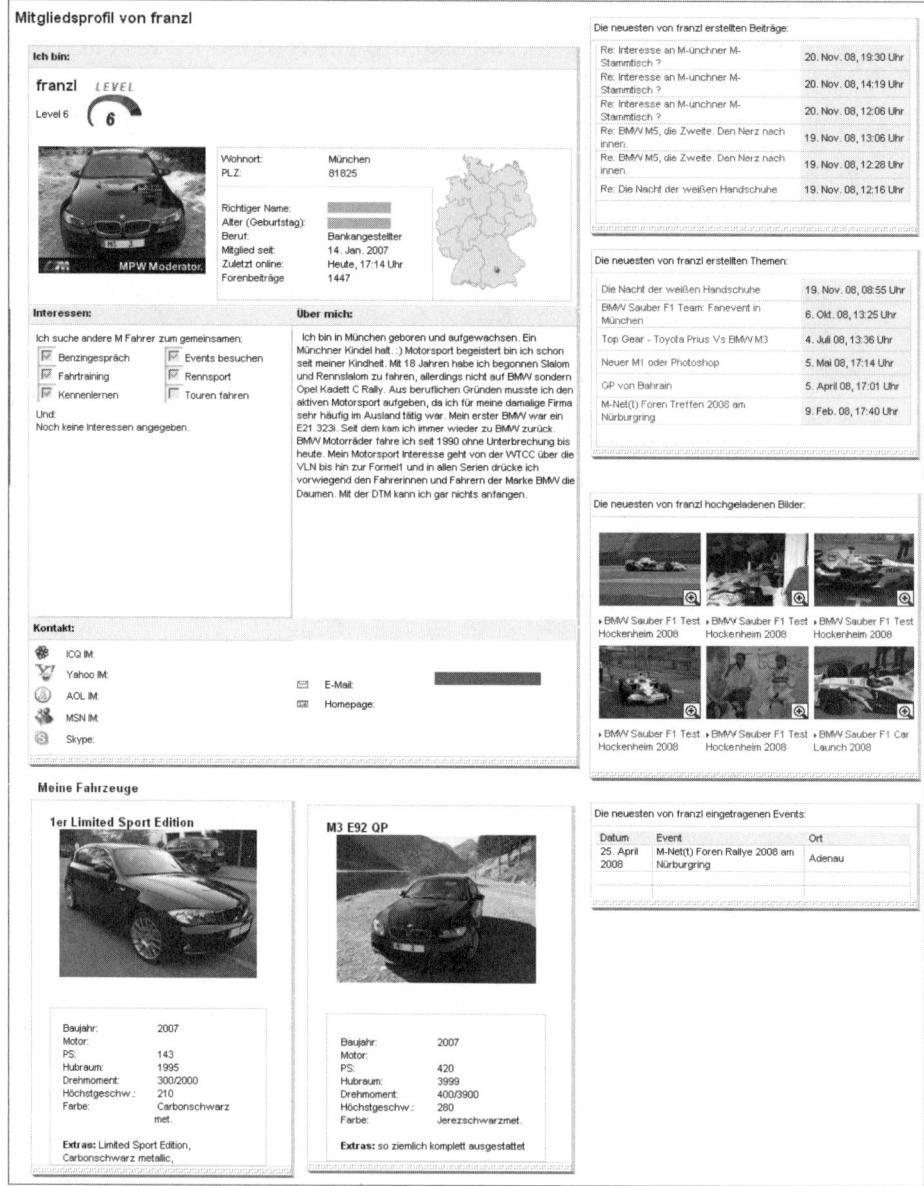

M Power World: Instead of posting pictures of themselves on their profiles, many members choose to publish photos of their beloved BMW M models.

INTERVIEW

Why does BMW offer a special community for M drivers? What makes them so special?

Owners of a BMW M car are ideal candidates for a community because they have a very strong, emotional relationship to their highly powerful cars. Their car is much more than a vehicle to drive from A to B. One of them, a user called "onkeltom," has declared that "M is a virus." Onkeltom runs his own BMW online forum with 6,000 members. Another user who calls himself "Franzl" visits the M Power World every single day, wears a little tag with the M logo on his jacket, and says: "BMW M is an attitude towards life." User "Propeller" is convinced that his BMW M3 CSL "fits me like a tailor-made business suit. As if it's built around my body. This car—it's me." If you have a look at members' profile pages, you will see that they often use a picture of an M car instead of a portrait. They have a strong empathy with the brand. But in general, a community for all BMW drivers would work, too.

How much attention do your members need?

Standard queries like "I forgot my password" go to BMW customer care. Two highly committed colleagues take care of the members: one community manager and one writer who writes magazine articles—and, of course, other departments support us. For example, if a community member has a product-related question, we try to help and look for a BMW expert who can answer that question. Direct contact with the community members is always managed by the community team.

What's the benefit of being an M Power World member?

Most of our members look for exclusive, detailed information that they cannot find elsewhere. To give an example: our community members were among the first people outside BMW who got in-depth and detailed information about the new M3. This is what members are looking for. The more product-related information the better. That's what people expect. Do not try to talk about the weather or the next holiday with them. Never publish the same texts that you can find elsewhere as press information. Press information can have a tone that does not fit your community and is widely distributed. We always offer exclusive information. Our members have a highly emotional relationship to the brand and feel that the BMW gives something back to them with this community. Some of them are looking for contact with BMW staff.

Are BMW employees community members, too?

Some of them are members. But they have a guest status and no permission to write. They can read only. Of course, there are some members who work at a BMW retailer and own an M car themselves. But we take care that no BMW employee publishes secret facts.

The launch phase is critical for every community. How did you manage this? What was your strategy to attract the first members?

Before we started, we had some workshops with BMW M customers. Some of them started the community at the beta phase. This was the "seed" for our community. We do not spend any money on advertisements, and we do not need gifts or other incentives to attract members. To make members stay and come back, we focused our attention from the very beginning on the quality of magazine content.

The profile page displays the real name of the member. This is unusual. What was the idea behind it?

During registration, it is optional to enter a real name. But lots of members register their full name. The idea behind this was to avoid pseudo-identities. We do not want users who pretend to be M drivers.

M Power World strongly supports offline activities such as regulars' tables or driver training. What's the reason?

We know that members who meet online like to see each other offline, too. The other reason is that we want to offer more than just an online platform. We want to be more useful to our members. Offline activities are the best way for community managers to stay in touch with the members. It's the perfect opportunity to talk about the M cars with drivers and to go more deeply into themes that we have found at the forums: what they love, what is missing, how often they use the car and for what purpose. Do they like the sound of the motor? Do they use child car seats? No market research method can deliver such detailed insights on customers every day.

LESSONS LEARNED

M Power World is a community with a strong product focus. This focus works well because the product in question is one that inspires intense emotions.

As a community based around a product, M Power World makes a special effort to offer members information that can't be found elsewhere on the Web. This is so important to the community's value proposition to members that their community management team includes a writer responsible for providing fresh product-related content. In addition to offering exclusive information, M Power World has chosen to limit access to the site, applying an overall strategy of exclusivity that fits the product, a car model whose appeal is partly rooted in its elite status.

Because M Power owners are so proud of their brand association, the community is strengthened by a real-world dimension. Members readily use their real names on the website and meet each other at offline events. These offline events are also an opportunity for BMW community managers to talk personally with their customers and gain valuable insights about their target market.

THIRTEEN
PRO-AGE NETZWERK

> "It's a fact that more and more users are seniors...
> Nevertheless, websites that are made for seniors are still rare."
>
> —Tanja Kindler, Senior Brand Manager, Dove

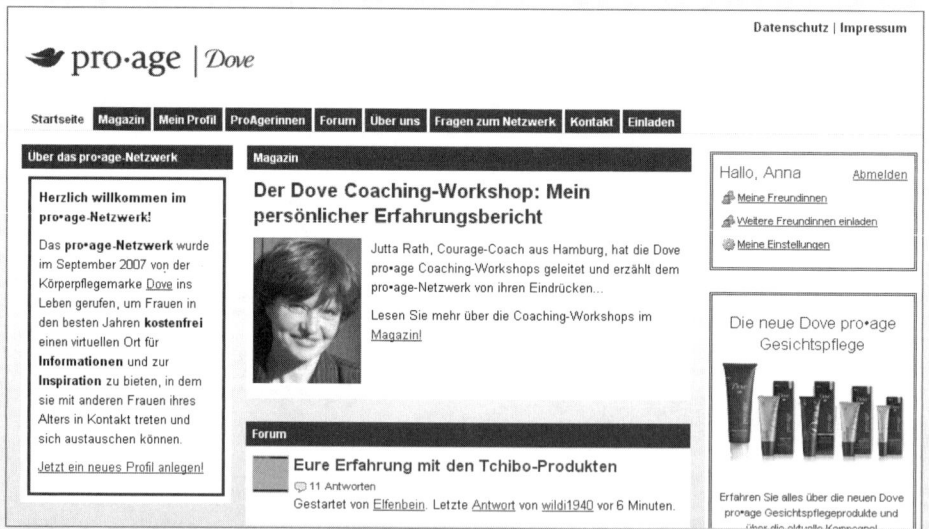

Pro-Age Netzwerk (Network): The target group is women aged 45 and over.

CHAPTER THIRTEEN PRO-AGE NETZWERK

Dove is a personal care brand of Unilever whose products include shampoos, face creams, lotions, hairspray, sunscreens, and more. In 2007, Dove caused a stir with an advertising campaign for their Pro-Age product line. These advertisements showed photos not of glamorous models, but of nude "real" women between the ages of 54 and 62. The photography was done by Annie Leibovitz.

Since 2004, Dove's communication strategy has avoided common standards of physical perfection and has emphasized the great variety of individual beauty. In fact, the brand encourages women to be more self-confident and to love every wrinkle and curve of their bodies. This unusual strategy has been used not only for advertising, but also for public relations and brand loyalty programs.

The strategy has been extremely successful for Unilever. In Germany, 90 percent of consumers are familiar with the Dove brand. On YouTube, more than 8 million visitors have now viewed Dove's "Evolution" video, which documents what makeup and computer-aided design can do with the face of a woman who doesn't look like a supermodel.

Can this communication strategy be taken further with a brand community? We spoke with Tanja Kindler, Senior Brand Manager at Dove, about the German community Pro-Age Netzwerk (Pro-Age Network).

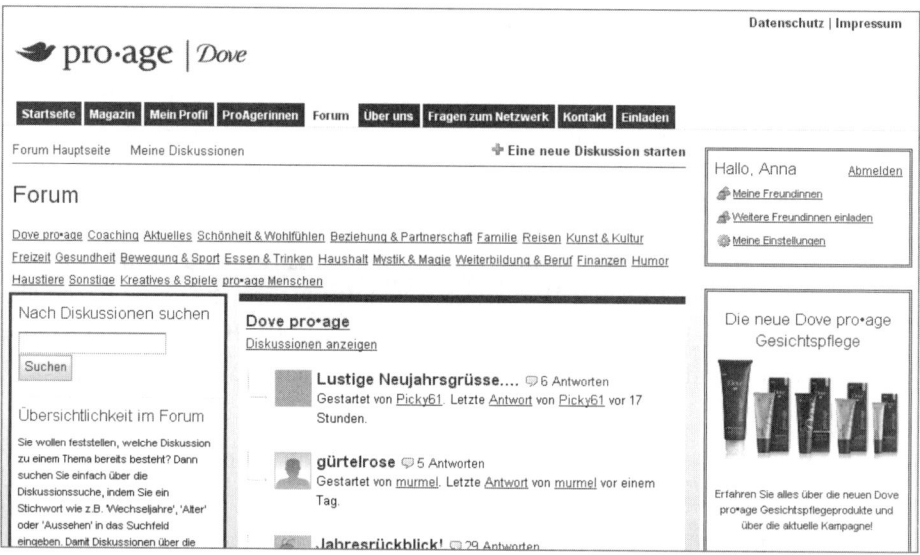

Pro-Age Netzwerk Forum: The community is focused on themes of interest to the target group. (Forum category links shown include: Dove Pro-age, Coaching, News, Health and Beauty, Relationship and Partnership, Family, Travel, Art and Culture, Leisure, Health, Exercise and Sports, Food and Drink, Home, Mysticism and Magic, Continuing Education and Work, Finance, Humor, Pets, Miscellaneous, Creative Activities and Games, Pro-age People.)

Pro-Age Netzwerk member profile page.

INTERVIEW

What was motivation behind the Pro-Age Netzwerk?

In 2007, we introduced an advertising campaign for our brand, Dove Pro-Age. The campaign's message is that getting older is something positive and beauty is not a matter of age at all. It is dated and a stereotypical point-of-view that women over age 45 are no longer attractive. We do not talk about "anti-age" but "pro-age": We want to encourage older women to be more self-confident. We know from market research studies that many women find it stressful and feel under pressure if they compare their bodies and faces with glamorous models in advertising campaigns. Pro-age shows "normal" women like you and me, not extraordinary beauties. This campaign worked successfully offline, and this was the reason for launching an online network.

What does the Pro-Age Netzwerk offer?

While there are offerings on social communities for all kind of interests, there's no community for older women. Based on the positive feedback from women all over Germany on our Pro-Age campaign we therefore decided to offer them a place to meet and discuss. The idea of the network was born and developed into a Web-based meeting place where women can read an online magazine, discuss topics in forums and—this is the most important thing for us—interact with each other. Our users talk about things that are inspiring and relevant to their everyday life. Pro-Age Network wants to inspire and inform people. We offer content in combination with a community because Web-based communication with others is important for women. The Pro-Age Network supports this need for women over 45. For example, a search function helps to find other users in your neighborhood.

Does the online magazine have a strong focus on cosmetics and beauty?

Of course, we publish themes that are interesting for every woman: social topics, love and partnership, travel reports, new books, interviews with popular community members. As beauty is a relevant topic for all women, we do also offer tips and tricks for beautiful hair and smooth skin. For example, a dermatologist gives advice to our members.

Why did you choose these topics?

This is what our target group is interested in. 66 percent like to read about cultural events, 64 percent like news, and 62 percent are interested in travel and holiday. If users are interested in a topic it is much easier to motivate them to write a comment and to start a discussion. This keeps our community lively.

Why are you focused on the target group of women aged 45 and over?

There's no community for these women; that's the original reason we made the network. It's a fact that more and more users are seniors. 40 percent of them are online regularly. 67 percent of all women who are between 45 and 59 years old are Web users. Nevertheless, websites that are made for seniors are still rare.

The launch phase is critical for every community. What did you do to attract your first members?

We supported the launch of the network through online advertising and sticky note ads in print magazines. As an incentive, we had a present for our first 500 registered members: a Dove welcome package that contained four Pro-Age products.

How successful is your community today?

I find it fascinating how many facets our members discuss online. Today we have about 7,100 registered users, and each day we recruit new members. 25 percent of all members visit the Pro-Age network daily and help to shape the platform.

LESSONS LEARNED

Pro-Age Netzwerk is a thematic community that was launched with a specific type of user in mind. The intention was to create an inspiring and useful platform for women aged 45 and older. Dove used market research to discover the real concerns of their target market and built a community to address them. This user-centered approach to designing a community is the best way to ensure its relevance to your target group.

Pro-Age Netzwerk responds to the fact that many women hate feeling pressured to look perfect. This is emotional material, and growing older is a topic that's relevant to any woman. The use of a Pro-Age product can therefore become a philosophical statement, expressing support for the messages conveyed by Dove's marketing campaign. Remember the marketing approach we discussed in Chapter Nine, Social Networks as a Platform for Your Brand: many customers aren't interested in lists of product features and rational arguments about why to buy, so engaging them emotionally is a way to distinguish your product from others. Brands that touch people's emotions have a competitive advantage—and that's what Dove does.

Another strategic point is that the brand doesn't play a major role in the community. The success of Dove's communication strategy attracts users to the community, but the brand is not intrusive once they're there.

As Tanja Kindler points out, it is very rare to find online communities specifically for older women. Traditionally, the Internet has been dominated by teenagers and young adults in their twenties. Currently, 90 to 95 percent of young people are online, meaning that there is no longer much room for Internet usage to increase among this age group; on the other hand, more and more older people are starting to use the Internet. Nielsen NetRatings found that between 2006 and 2007, four out of five newbies on the Web were aged fifty and older. In Germany, 2007 was the first year when the percentage of Internet users aged sixty and over was larger than the percentage under twenty years old. Dove saw in these developments a need and an opportunity, and the success of the Pro-Age Netzwerk is proof that the Internet can also be used for marketing to older target groups.

It is important to choose the right language to use with your target population. Few German women over 45 are familiar with English expressions that are used on community websites all over the world. Consequently, the Pro-Age Netzwerk website avoids terms such as "log out," "tag," and "thread;" such terms are replaced by German words. This makes it easier for the target group to use this community. And members can find answers to their questions in a user-friendly help section that covers many topics for community beginners.

FOURTEEN

XING

> "The members are more active, because they see that there are really active people behind the platform."
>
> —Félix López Capel, Business Development Manager, Xing Spain

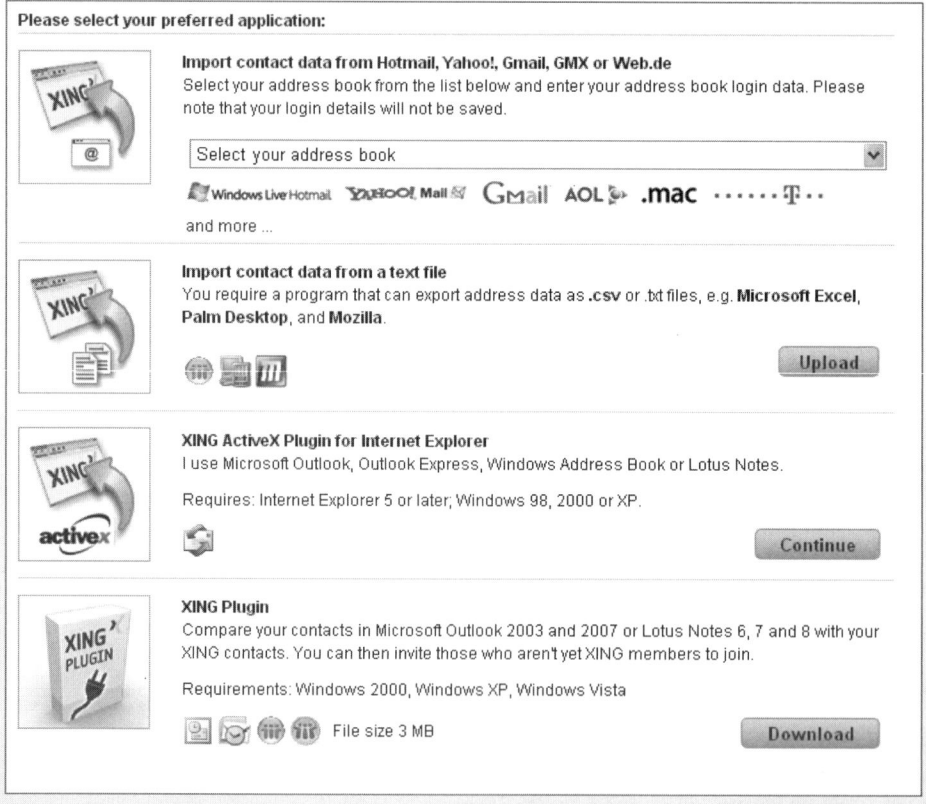

Xing: Viral tools such as the option to import contacts from other websites help this business network grow even faster. With over 6.5 million members, Xing is one of the largest online networks of any kind.

Xing is an online community focused primarily on professional networking. On Xing, members can post professional profiles, connect with other businesspeople, and manage their existing contacts, as well as organize offline events and post or search for jobs in an employment marketplace. Members can also start their own groups—or microcommunities—around any imaginable topic. Currently, Xing has over 22,000 such groups organized by members. Some companies such as IBM have taken advantage of this feature to create brand communities. Xing offers two membership levels: paying members have access to a broader range of options for contacting other professionals and are not shown advertising on the website.

With sixteen website languages and over 6.5 million members, Xing is one of the largest online networks of any kind. Of the 161 Xing employees, approximately forty are directly involved with member management activities, offering member support in eleven languages.

In addition to a successful community, Xing has a highly successful business model, with three separate income streams: advertising, e-commerce, and paid subscription. In 2007, the German-based company generated around $28 million in revenue.

We learned more about Xing from Félix López Capel, Business Development Manager for Xing Spain, and María Marín Gregorio, Manager of Corporate Communications for Xing Spain. What follows is our interview with Félix López Capel.

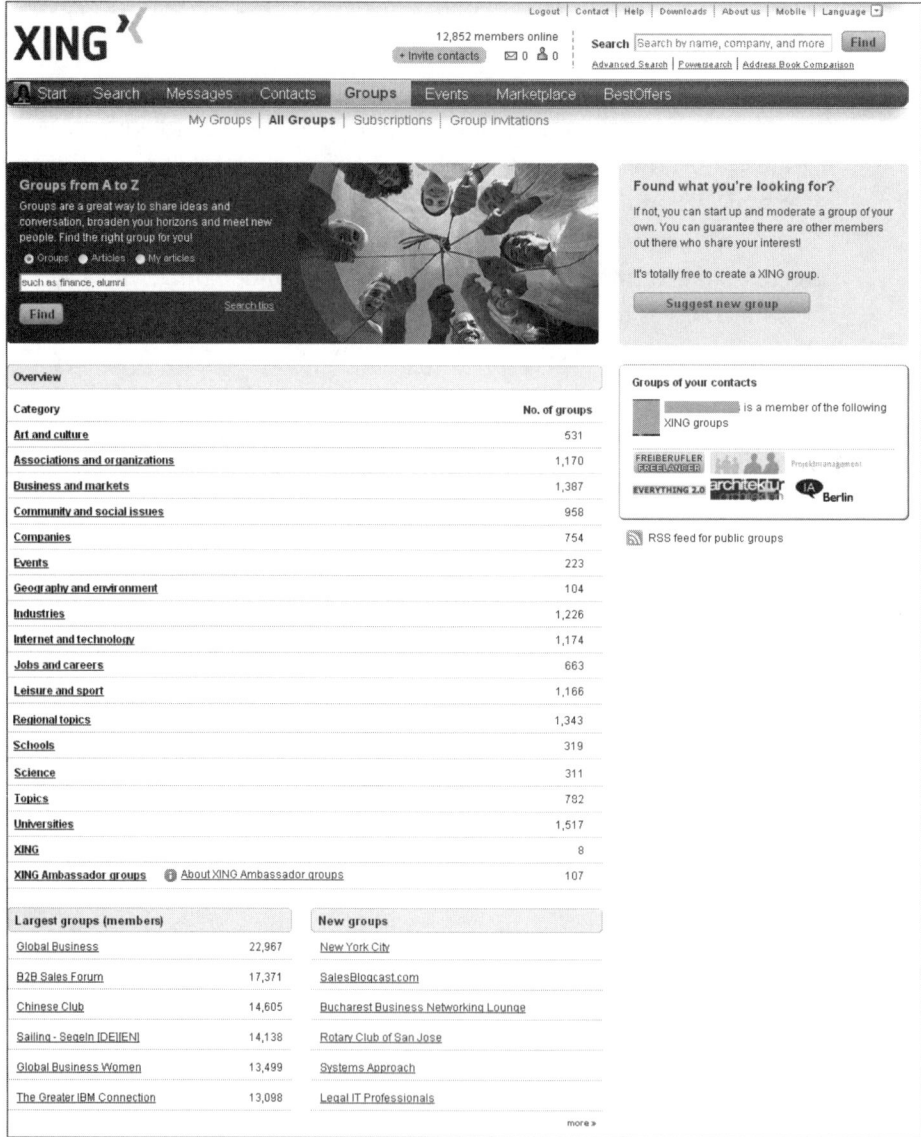

Xing groups: Most groups are formed and moderated by members. Xing offers special manuals and support for group moderators.

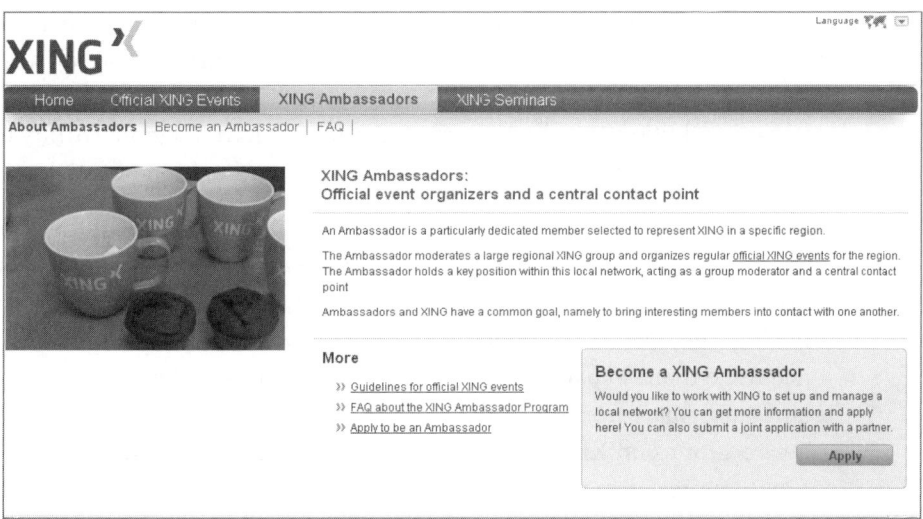

One of Xing's USPs: "Ambassadors" organize Xing events and support the business networking of other members.

INTERVIEW

Who is a typical Xing member?

The average age is between thirty and forty. More than 70 percent of members have university studies. More than 15 percent are over fifty, which indicates that Xing is easy to use for people who might be less experienced with new technology.

How is Xing different from the other online professional networks?

Basically, right now there are a lot of social networks, and very few are professional networks, maybe three or four at an international level. One of things that makes Xing different is that the members are much more active. They spend more time on the platform, they use more tools, and they're engaged in networking both online and offline. We're the only platform that has a role called the ambassador.

Ambassadors have a key role; they're natural networkers, and they organize networking events in their city. For example, there's an ambassador in Atlanta, in New York, in Los Angeles; and then on a global level, there's an ambassador in every major city—in London, in Shanghai, in Madrid, in Sidney, among others. These people are experts in managing Xing, and they organize events so that in addition to online interactions, people have the opportunity to meet offline and do business. No other platform offers this kind of activity.

As a result, the members are more active, because they see that there are really active people behind the platform, and they see that there's a real reason for participating on the platform. When members join a group or community on Xing, they see that a moderator is there to welcome them right away and encourage them to participate. And another point is that we have strict quality standards. Apart from the official groups run by Xing ambassadors, there are 22,000 groups on Xing. When we see that a group isn't active, we help them become more active and help them get people to participate. So we stand out compared to platforms that don't take care of their members in the same way.

What is the role of community managers in keeping members active?
We have various community managers. In the Xing team in Hamburg there are more than ten people who are responsible for managing the online communities. There are community managers for each region and global community managers. Above all, what we help with is getting things started—in the beginning when someone opens a new group, we give them a very complete manual to answer all of their questions, and there's also a forum called Xing Moderation for any question they might have. The other community managers will help them write a newsletter, organize an event, moderate a forum, publish news. Communities always have a lot of help and support from Xing.

How do you use the personal information that members provide in their Xing profiles?
A user's profile is completely private. We never use it to send any kind of mailing. So the news that a member receives about Xing is always through another form. If users sign up for a newsletter, which is always voluntary, the only purpose of the Xing newsletter is to help them manage their professional profiles better. So Xing's communication with our users is only to improve their online and offline networking.

Is profile information used to target the advertising that they see on the website?

Yes, a user's profile is used to recommend the best Marketplace offers, on the one hand. And basic users will see the advertising that fits their professional profile, their age, their studies, always in a noninvasive way. Companies that advertise on Xing can choose who will see it.

Why are Xing members motivated to complete their profiles?

Basically, there's a trend toward personal branding, and as a result of that, people want to be easy to reach. They want to be able to control their digital identities. Another person might talk about you on the Internet or publish information about you, but thanks to your digital identity on Xing, you manage your personal information on your personal profile. You can let people know about your experience, your interests, what you have to offer, what you're looking for, previous experience, your Web page, which groups you belong to, all of which is your personal branding. So users are looking for this, to market themselves. And when someone searches for you on Google, what's always going to appear first is your Xing profile (if you agree to this in your privacy settings). So the more complete a person's Xing profile is, the easier it is to reach the person, and to find the right information about this person.

In what ways is Xing set up to be viral?

We give basic users months of premium membership in return for referring new users. For example, for every ten people I invite to Xing, I get a month of premium membership, which allows me to know even more about what is happening in my network.

The platform started five years ago with only 500 users, and within 24 hours, there were 1,000 users thanks to viral marketing. Seeing that the tool works makes you recommend it to all of your contacts.

What are the advantages of premium membership, and why are members motivated to pay for it?

Basic membership has many advantages, and the platform was always designed to be used for free, but the premium user has additional advantages. Basic users can organize an event each month for ten people, and premium users can organize all the events they want, without limitation on the number of people. Basic users can make contacts, but are more limited in terms of communication. Premium users can send as many messages as they want to their network of contacts or to other contacts of interest in the community. Premium users can also publish employment offers in the Marketplace, while basic users can't. Premium users have access to all the benefits of the platform. And there are exclusive offers in the Best Offers section that are only available to premium users.

One factor that motivates basic users to become premium users is the ability to see who has visited their profile. If you're looking for work, you know if a headhunter or a human resources person has visited your profile, and you know who has visited your Web page, who has visited your blog, who has read a post of yours on the forum. So being a premium member allows you to have continuous and up-to-date information on what is really happening in your network.

Xing is available in a large number of languages. How do you manage a multilingual community?

Practically from the second year of Xing, it was in various languages, and we have sixteen languages now. We must be one of the few platforms in so many languages. We have a translation team, and we have community managers for every language. We have communities all over the world, but they have a centralized form, and the advantage is that if I enter the profile of users who speak a different language, I can still get quite a precise idea of their professions, the type of company where they work. Even if they don't speak the same language I do, I can get information about them. The advantage of being in so many languages is that it means more opportunities for networking and a more multicultural platform.

Your website includes a Best Offers section with promotions from partners. How have you integrated advertising on Xing?

Companies saw that we had a community of over 6 million users, and they obviously wanted to advertise on the platform. But what we didn't want was for it to turn into just another website full of banners and advertising messages. So the advertising is only for a basic member. A premium member doesn't see advertising banners.

On the other hand, there's the Best Offers section, which instead of being advertising is a place for partners. For example, some partners are Ibis and Hertz and Radisson Hotels; instead of advertising they post exclusive offers, interesting offers that offer users a chance to save money. There are also a lot of technology companies, for example Epson and HP, with exclusive offers for Xing members on their websites. So the Xing user has access to those benefits, those advantages. It's more positive than the invasive advertising we're used to seeing on television and other media. We look for partners who have offers that will be interesting to our users, from technology to hotels to travel to buying flowers. BMW has also used Best Offers.

What are some of the ways in which companies use Xing's platform to create their own brand communities?

Some years ago, some companies saw the potential of Web 2.0, which allows the users to interact freely with one another. They saw that our platform makes it possible to know not only someone's personal and professional profile, but also their interests, where they've worked and studied, and so on. And so companies started using our platform as a corporate Intranet, a meeting point for their employees, former employees, and collaborators.

The first company to ask us to create an online community was IBM. Currently there are more than 15,000 Xing users who belong to the IBM group, which is called the IBM Connection. What does this tool accomplish? Above all, what we've found is that companies are able to retain talent better through these Web 2.0 tools that permit, for example, IBM employees in Spain to connect with employees in France, England, Holland. These groups make it possible for employees to share projects and ideas, and to deliver news instantly to the whole community. A newsletter is very simple, and the IBM newsletter is even in various different languages —Spanish, French, English, German, and Portuguese, the languages in which IBM manages its employee community. Other companies like PricewaterhouseCoopers have also decided to start online communities within Xing, because it's possible instantly—in a matter of days—to have a community totally adapted not only to their organization but also to the look and feel of their website. So these companies will sometimes even have a link on their website to their Xing online community. Users going to the company website will enter the Xing community, where they will finally have the chance to interact with other members who share certain interests related to the company.

Apart from employee communities, some companies start groups with commercial aims—that's not the main reason for creating a group on Xing, which is always about networking, but some companies have a meeting point for staying in touch with a group of their clients. It's another communication channel, so for example, a hotel chain or a hotel will create a group on Xing to learn about your experience staying in their hotel, and to send you news and offers. So also on a marketing level, it's a very powerful tool. A related example is a conference company called IIR—they're a multinational operating in 100 countries, and they have also created a group on Xing to learn about the opinions of people who have attended their conferences. These communities can also be used as a tool to learn the opinions of attendees at meetings, conferences, suggestions, new ideas, and they allow you as well to meet and speak with the presenters that you've seen at a conference. So they're also a very powerful tool for managing customer service and customer satisfaction. Also, the customer is frequently the best source of inspiration for new ideas, so companies will often launch new ideas or proposals in their Xing community. They can also run exclusive offers, invite the community to events, presentations, parties, and competitions, too.

What advice would you give to a company that wants to do marketing on Xing?
That it shouldn't be completely commercial, but instead a tool for communication and for creating a positive feeling about the company. That's the main point. That the commercial aspect shouldn't be 100 percent, but maybe 50 percent, so that users will really feel comfortable. It's important to offer something really appealing for the users—interesting news, or activities they can participate in.

But above all, creating an online community takes a lot of time. It takes dedication. When users enter the community, you have to welcome them and motivate them to participate. It really takes a team in the background, not necessarily spending eight hours a day in the community, but a certain amount of time every day to manage the community, to invite new users, to answer questions about the platform. So my recommendation is the following: develop a business plan and clear motives about what you want to do with the community. Do you want it to be a meeting point, or a place to deliver news or organize events, or do you want to launch offers via this channel?

Once you've clarified your objectives, then you have to give it a look and feel that's related to the company's website to create continuity so that it becomes a discussion forum or meeting place where clients and employees of the company feel comfortable. You have to give users a reason to want to belong to that community and even to recruit new users and colleagues to join the group. Viral marketing is fundamental. If users find interesting things in the community, they're going to recommend it to their contacts. And maybe it's also fundamental that there's an offline aspect as well. There should be a newsletter at least once a month, and a physical event—if not monthly, at least once every two or three months—where users of this group can get to know each other and get to know the company, and the moderators. It's possible to do business online, but in order to trust people, you need to know them personally, so we help with this by setting up real meetings.

LESSONS LEARNED

Xing is an online community with a particularly effective business model that includes three simultaneous revenue channels: advertising, e-commerce, and paid subscription. The very concept of Xing encourages fast viral growth, since the platform becomes more useful for users the more they can increase their online networks.

Xing encourages members to create their own microcommunities. As a result, the users are constantly adding depth and activities to the Xing platform, and discussion topics are based on the users' interests rather than being imposed by the company. This raises an important point to keep in mind when designing a new community: one should take care not to overdetermine the structure of community activities. It is often better to start out with activities that are both simple and organic, and allow the users to develop the community in a natural way. Félix López Capel also emphasizes the importance of reinforcing user-generated activities by offering training, supervision, and support.

It is interesting to look at the way Xing uses offline events to add depth and relevance to its online activities. Offline networking events give real-world weight to relationships formed online, increasing Xing's usefulness as a professional tool.

For companies that want to create brand communities, Xing offers a quick and low-cost alternative to building a new platform. Using Xing's groups feature, you can create a brand community almost instantly, with very little risk or expense. These communities can be restricted to the members you wish to invite, and they can even be hidden from other Xing members.

No matter what platform you use for your community strategy, keep in mind Félix's advice for community marketers: make a business plan, focus on offering value to users instead of straight advertising, and invest the time and care needed to keep a community alive.

FIFTEEN
ECADEMY

> "Members have a feeling of being looked after, being cared for, of safety."
>
> —Penny Power, Ecademy founder and CEO

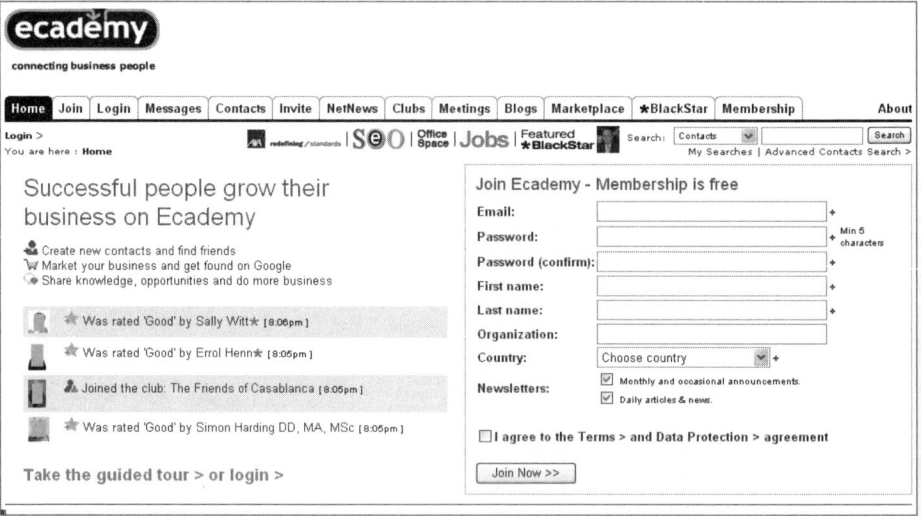

Ecademy: This professional network helps small business owners manage every aspect of their business.

Ecademy is an online networking community for businesspeople that emphasizes the development of personal as well as professional relationships among members. Ecademy members create online profiles and build networks of online contacts. They create and participate in clubs—discussion forums organized by members around specific themes; they can also create their own blogs on the Ecademy platform and comment on other members' blogs. Search-engine optimized blogs are one of the business tools that Ecademy offers, along with a jobs directory, and a marketplace section where paying members can publish offers. Members who pay a higher fee for a VIP membership are also allowed to place advertisements on the Ecademy website.

Ecademy offers three membership levels—free membership, a Power Networking membership with a monthly fee of $14.95, and a VIP Black Star membership that costs $105 per month. Although Black Star membership confers additional privileges, part of its attraction comes from the elite status associated with its higher price. BlackStar members display a special symbol next to their user names and have access to exclusive BlackStar-only clubs and meetings.

A typical Ecademy member is age 35 or older, and is self-employed or a small business owner. Over 60 percent of Ecademy members represent small and medium-sized businesses.

Founded in 1998, Ecademy was a pioneer of online networking. In November 2006, Ecademy's membership reached 100,000. Since then, the community has experienced rapid growth with over 8,000 new members joining each month.

We spoke with Ecademy founder and CEO Penny Power.

BlackStar City Leaders - BlackStar City Leaders Club

This online networking group is a business club
The discussion and promotion of commercial goods and services is encouraged

*BlackStar
City Leaders Club

 Message from Ecademy Founder, Penny Power

The most successful and forward thinking part of Ecademy is the ★BlackStar Brand. Through being a ★BlackStar, member businesses have grown and ideas have flourished.

Ecademy is traditionally an online business with clubs that as a part of their functionality also arrange offline meetings. ★BlackStar is different; it is primarily offline with the online forums and connections as an interface and support for them. The members there rely on face to face, local meetings. For this reason ★BlackStar has been most successful within London where we hold the monthly meetings and training.... (read the whole message here >>)

City Leaders Free info pack Click here

Ecademy BlackStar: The City Leaders Club is an additional service for BlackStar members.

Profile

ooooO............You touch me...You touch my world...You touch my soul...Thank you for coming here...Touch my heart now!
(......)...Ooooo
.).../......(......) You tell me, i forget. You teach me, i remember. You involve me, i learn. Benjamin Franklin.
(_ /........)..../
............(_ /

English-French-German On/Off-line Coaching. International VIPs Advisor, Wordsmith,Trainer, Lecturer, Public Speaker and Facilitator. Multinational, Multilingual, Intercultural From Casablanca. Lived in 7 countries, Visited 65 and more to come...Networks Moderator. Oximorox, Online Business and Cultural Agenda Publisher. BNI-USA - Churchill Club - Moroccan American Circle...Founder of several Companies and member of several Societies.I am a global citizen. I coach In Site...Face to face and faster via phone...skype...wherever you are...we can get together...quickly...On! And on...And on... ▆▆▆▆▆▆ Is YOUR Actual Global Coaching Hotline!

All Engines Running! Powers On! I like Fast ...Everlasting Connections...Fast Horses...Fast Boats...Fast Cars...Fast Planes...Fast Trains...And...Fast Brains! I believe that all is about speed. Speed of making mistakes and speed of fixing them! **I speak** English, Spanish, German, French, Swedish and Arabic and i would love to learn all yours one day...*Limits* of your language? Limits of your world! Ludwig Wittgenstein - Austrian-British Logician

Ecademy user profile: Profile pages include more personal information than is normally available in other business communities.

INTERVIEW

Could you talk a little bit about how your community is different from other online business networks?

The core of why Ecademy is different is related to the reasons we set it up in the first place. We set up Ecademy in 1998, after I had been home for five years with our children, and I wasn't thinking in terms of technology; I saw an issue, a problem. The core of our community is connecting people to one another, and our business model could really exist even without the Internet. It's like a modern-day version of a chamber of commerce, an answer to the question of how business people can see each other. It's very important for companies that want to start networking websites to start with this question of what problem they want to solve.

I look at the e-mails I received over the weekend, people thanking me because we have helped them, thanking us for caring. I think some of the other networking sites are in terms of their intentions. Ecademy is about making deep relationships, people who will help you, friendships. It's a real community, like a town. With LinkedIn, what you have is a tool, a directory—it's a mile wide, but an inch thick. Ecademy's about forming a smaller network, but a very deep one. You might have 4,000 contacts on LinkedIn and only 50 on Ecademy, but on Ecademy you know them well enough to help them.

Imagine a funnel. "Know me" is at the top of the funnel, "like me" is the middle, and "follow me" is the thinnest part. "Know me" is LinkedIn—it's about branding; it's about being in the right places, having links to your profile in a lot of places, using tools. "Like me" is Ecademy. It's about community, conversation, relationships. "Follow me" is when you like someone enough to follow what they are saying. That's Twitter, or becoming a reader of a blog. All three levels are linked together in a holistic view of how to help businesses. LinkedIn is like an exhibition hall, where people exchange cards. Ecademy is like a wine bar. And just like in the offline world, if you act inappropriately, people will let you know. If you go to LinkedIn and talk to people about your dogs, no one will be interested, and if you are on Ecademy and all you do is promote your business, people will see you as a spammer.

You've compared Ecademy to a wine bar, where people can build personal relationships as well as business contacts. How have you set the community up to achieve this kind of atmosphere?

Building an online community is like building a new town. You're located in Madrid—that's a town with history and an atmosphere that people know, and if someone tried to build another Madrid, it wouldn't have the same depth. We built Ecademy over eleven years, and it's really about leadership. We know our members personally; they have our phone numbers. We're like the mother and father of the community. You know the autocratic teacher at school, versus the teacher you like and don't want to disappoint. Members have a feeling of being looked after, being cared for, of safety.

A lot of people think they can start a social network and treat it as a machine. A machine is cold, but if you want to be a community, you have to care about it, you have to care about members' lives, or if one member is dying of cancer. Now, I don't have to care about all of our members individually because they all care for each other, just like in a family, where the brothers and sisters grow up and can take care of each other. This is what the world needs, people caring for each other, and community.

I recently read a book called *Hot, Flat, and Crowded*, and there was the story of a CEO whose daughter was interrupting him while he was working. So he found a photo of the world taken from space in a magazine, and he tore up the photo in little pieces and told his daughter to put it back together, thinking that this would keep her busy for a while, but to his surprise she came back to him after a few minutes and it was done. When he asked her how she had managed this so quickly, she showed him that there was a picture of people on the other side, and by putting the people back together, she put together the picture of the world. A community isn't about technology. It's about people. We think first about people and what they need, and then we create the technology to provide it to them.

So companies have to think about their intention. The community's not about *them*, it's about their customers, about what will help their customers.

Ecademy has three parts: the DNA, which is the technology; the community, which is the people; and the intention, which is what they both share.

We're the only business community that includes blogging, which is like our town square. This can be scary, and we have to be careful and spend a lot of time moderating and teaching people how to behave, that there shouldn't be arguments, swearing, or advertising in the blogs.

If Facebook is a social community and LinkedIn is a business community, we're a social business community. If you look at my blog, you'll see a video of a member's wedding that I went to recently. You don't go to Ecademy just to do business with a "me first" attitude. Just like in a wine bar, you make conversation before you hand out your business card.

In what ways does a member's Ecademy experience deepen over time as he or she participates?

Like in the offline world, it's not the same experience if you come to a community just to drive in and drive back out. On the other hand, if you move in, visit shops, spend money in the shops, go to the pubs, and become connected, then people can say, "I can recommend this plumber. I can recommend this shop." And when you're lonely, you have friends to go to. And if you lose your job, you have people to help you. A lot of people think when they lose their job that's the time to do networking; they want to take before they give, but you have to give first.

It seems that members have a lot of options to customize and shape their own Ecademy experience.

The community fits their life. Everyone uses it in different ways. Some blog every week, go to offline meetings. Everything's there when you want it. It completely mirrors the offline world.

What problems have you faced in your community, and how have you resolved them?

We have a feedback button where members can report abusive content. If someone reports you, you receive a message explaining the error that the community feel you are making, however, you do not know the identity of the complainer—they remain anonymous to ensure witch hunts do not take place. It's monitored. If someone comes on board and misuses the site, we have a conversation with that person, and see if he's willing to change. If not, we would ban him, but there have only been about twenty-five cases where that's happened in eleven years. Our community is built on mature people, and no one wants to be banned from the only wine bar in town. But all of the safeguards are in place.

Do Ecademy members feel like part of your brand?

Absolutely. They call themselves Ecademists. They have Ecademy badges and display Ecademy on their websites. It's reputation by association, and the Ecademy brand says that this is a well-connected person who belongs to a high-quality group of people.

How do you balance advertising and community on your website?

We've set it up so that paying members see fewer ads, and there are no ads in the blogs. Only 10 percent of our revenue is advertising-based; we made the decision from the beginning to use a subscription model.

What advice would you give to a company that wants to do marketing on Ecademy?

My advice would be to get involved, read the blogs, and do conversation marketing. Marketing isn't just about broadcasting your message.

Could you talk about your paid membership levels, and what motivates members to subscribe to them?

Our first level of paid membership is the Power Networker. We decided to make sure that these members paid a small amount to participate because it involves a level of commitment and results in a higher quality of membership. So these members pay a small amount and have a lot of benefits such as Google optimization for their content. The BlackStar members have a level of prestige. People said to us that they wanted to be able to collaborate at a high level with other people who were spending a lot of time on the website, and to share in-depth information about their businesses. The higher payment ensures a higher level of commitment: no one is going to pay 100 pounds a month and then abuse the community.

How have you set up your community to be viral?

Our members can write a blog and send that to anyone; they can bookmark a page for Twitter. We have a huge amount of constantly updated content, which optimizes our website for search engines. Google checks us for new content every twenty-one minutes. When someone starts a club, they can email their external network to join.

Ultimately, what we want is for our members to be able to use Ecademy to run a business. We have our Marketplace section, and members can hold meetings and charge for them, or they can start clubs and charge for membership. They can monetize their network. This all stems from our original intention, when we looked at how to make members more financially and emotionally wealthy.

If you try to be all things to all people you can't get it right, but it's very easy when you start out with the clear intention of helping business people form relationships.

How has your community evolved, and how do you envision it evolving in the future?

It's the same as what we started out to do. Our market is a business owner age 35 or over who traditionally wouldn't go online to do stuff. Now this person has more online practices, and we've experienced 142 percent growth over the last year.

People are looking to reduce travel costs, and they're finding that they can achieve a lot on Ecademy and leverage their online relationships to accomplish what might take them a week offline. So our community isn't changing, and we have no plans to change; there's just more of it now. We've always had business owners, and now a lot of unemployed people are coming to our websites to learn about working freelance.

You've compared your community to a wine bar. Yet your community offers members something that an offline wine bar doesn't, which is the opportunity to network with people across global barriers.

Yes, the Internet connects people globally. This is something we sometimes have to explain to our members. It can be interesting—the world is changing, and you have to evolve if you want to be able to feed yourself in the future.

On our website, we offer members the option of taking an IMA personality test. This is a test with profiling questions that identifies four personality types. The results are posted on members' profiles and tell you the best way to approach the person. The communication styles of Americans and Indians can be very different from those of Europeans, and the IMA is one way that we're helping people across the world communicate with each other more effectively.

For example, if you go to my profile, you see that I'm a high blue. This means that I'm people-oriented. But if you look up Glenn Watkins, you'll see he's a high red. This type of person is task-oriented. If you want to contact him and you send him an email chatting about your dog, it's likely to go right in the trash. On the other hand, if you contact me, and you write a curt email that asks, "Hi, what's your annual revenue?," that's not the best way to start a conversation. So if I get a message that seems abrupt from someone in a different country, it helps to go to that person's profile and see that this is just the way they communicate. This helps to cut down on misunderstandings.

How do you see the future of online communities?

I think they're going to be more and more people-based. If a community is built as a tool, then it's just a utility. Our members feel that they belong; they feel safe, happy, and nurtured. We ran a survey asking our members to say whether they *used* or *belonged to* the community. 70 percent of them said they belonged.

LESSONS LEARNED

Ecademy is a community that was started with a specific type of person in mind, with the intention of solving a specific problem for this person. This is an example of the user-centered approach that we recommend in this book. It is the best way to ensure the relevance of your community.

In the case of Ecademy, the problem to be solved was to help business people form relationships with other professionals, with special attention to the needs of business people working from home. Ecademy differs from other business communities in its emphasis on building deep relationships rather than growing a large network. Related to this strategy is Ecademy's use of paid membership subscriptions as a quality measure. By charging up to $105 for premium membership—an amount far higher than the membership fees charged by other professional networks—Ecademy attracts members who have made a real commitment to the community. In addition, the paid subscriptions reduce the importance of advertising revenue on the site and allow Ecademy to give advertising space to premium members.

Ecademy aims to meet the needs of its target members by mirroring the offline world as much as possible. One aspect that distinguishes Ecademy is the extent to which members can use the platform to run a business at all levels, from strategic consulting to advertising to the formation of professional relationships, and even the collection of fees for events and clubs organized through the Ecademy website.

SIXTEEN
MINUBE.COM

> "When the user who contributed the content sees that it is being shared and that it's useful to other people, the user…is motivated to contribute more."
>
> —Pedro Jareño, marketing and public relations, Minube.com

Minube: A travel community with many useful tools for trip planning. (Heading on top left means "Latest user activity." Heading over search box: "What are you looking for? A destination, a hotel…" Below the map are links to the "Most Popular Destinations.")

The Spanish website Minube.com and its French sister site MonNuage.fr offer many useful features for planning a trip, including price comparison information about plane tickets, budget hotels, and rental cars. At the heart of Minube.com is a lively community of travelers who publish travel reviews, photographs, videos, blogs, and lists of their favorite travel spots. On their personal profile pages, they can also plan and discuss their upcoming trips and get advice on them from other travelers. They can participate in discussion forums, leave messages for other members, and make lists of their favorite "globetrotters" in the community. The website is extremely rich in activities and interactive options for members. Members also are offered tools they can use on personal blogs or other websites to share information about their Minube.com activities.

Minube.com encourages member participation with virtual medals that are awarded to members who reach certain milestones. Members who list or write about fifty different travel spots earn an Explorer medal. Those who collect a certain number of medals are rewarded with a title such as Ambassador, which marks their status in the community hierarchy.

Minube.com's business model has two parts: CPA (cost per acquisition) revenue for every sale that an advertiser, such as a hotel or airline, receives via Minube.com, as well as CPC (cost per click) revenue when a user goes from Minube.com to a commercial website.

As of December 2008, Minube.com had more than 47,000 registered members.

We spoke with Pedro Jareño, who is in charge of marketing and public relations for Minube.com.

Minube.com: This detail page for a travel destination focuses on user-generated content. (Tabs at top are: "Home," "Flights," "Hotels," "Destinations," Competition," and "Forum." Tabs under the destination La Paz [Bolivia] are: "All," "What to see," "Restaurants," "Blogs," and "Flights.")

User profile previews: These two users have collected many community status symbols. The row of rectangular images to the right of the user name are virtual "medals" earned for website activity—mousing over them displays titles such as "Explorer" (*Explorador*), and "Marco Polo." The user Pedroja has also earned the title "Compulsive Traveler" (*Viajero Empedernido*), while Miskita has earned the title "Regular" (*Habitual*).

INTERVIEW

Your website has two parts: an online travel service, where users can make reservations or buy tickets, and a travel community. Could you discuss how those two parts feed each other?

The community is not only a fundamental part of our project, it's its essence. Our philosophy is very clear: Minube is a community of travelers. Starting from this base, offering users the ability to compare prices and make purchases on more than forty websites is an added service.

Our business depends completely on the community. We want our users to feel that Minube offers everything they need for their travel. If a user participates in our community, then when they think about travel, they'll automatically think of Minube instead of another travel site. The community generates loyalty. And when the user recommends a travel site to a friend, it will be Minube. And so the community gets bigger and bigger.

The users generate a lot of content about a lot of places, and all of this creates new pages that Google indexes. This brings traffic to the website. Our goal is to achieve member loyalty, so that the members will continue generating content and bringing traffic. When someone thinks of travel, we want them to think of Minube.

We have a lot of content, and we're becoming a source of travel content for other websites. Someone setting up a blog about Niagara Falls, for example, will come to Minube for photos and content about Niagara Falls. We're becoming a kind of Wikipedia about travel.

When the user who contributed the content sees that it is being shared and that it's useful to other people, the user feels valued and is motivated to contribute more.

What role does community management play in your success?

The community manager has a fundamental role in making our community grow, in recruiting new users, answering the questions of existing members, and keeping the community motivated.

The relationship with users has to be constant and very personal. It doesn't make sense to try to build a community if the organization doesn't believe in it. We are the first users of Minube, and we treat the other users as equals.

How do you motivate users to participate in the community?

When new users join the community, they get an automatic email that explains the community and how to get started. Then our management team welcomes new users personally, inviting them to be contacts, chatting with them and answering questions. There are a number of different email addresses where users can contact us, and they always receive personal answers. We try to solve their problems or send apologies if something has gone wrong. And we place a high value on user feedback. When a user makes a contribution, posting good content or publishing a lot of photos, we'll contact that user to congratulate them.

If a user becomes inactive, we'll send that user an email asking what happened, if everything's all right, and if we can help with something.

At this point, there are users who are practically part of our team. We try to make the relationship as personal as possible, and there are users who are now our friends.

You offer a system of nonmonetary rewards for participation. How does this help keep members motivated over time?

Members can earn prizes for their contributions. These are prizes without monetary value, a type of medal that appears on the website. For example, if you post fifty travel spots, you earn the title Explorer. If you publish over a hundred photos, you are a Photographer. There are various statuses on the website, for Recent Arrivals and for members at all stages of participation. The more you participate, the more status you have in the community.

The idea is exactly like a video game where you earn points, which bring you to different phases. Visitors to the site see that a member has earned prizes and trust that person's content more. And the members who earn the prizes get visibility, recognition. They know that they're becoming popular in the community. So this is a benefit for them.

How are you using Facebook to attract new users to Minube?

We've developed a Facebook application called Tus Rincones Favoritos (Your Favorite Spots). This has two benefits for us. First, it brings new users to the community. Second, when you create an application with good content on Facebook, it adds value for users and strengthens your brand.

Facebook is an important platform, and they have an enormous network of content, but they don't have content specific to travel. So we think that users can proudly share their "Favorite Spots" on Facebook. On the one hand, it's an opportunity for them to share. On the other hand, it's an opportunity for other users to discover this content.

Facebook Connect makes it possible to synchronize accounts on Facebook and Minube. If I add a Favorite Spot on Minube, I can click a "Share on Facebook" button, and a line will appear on Facebook, "Pedro just shared etc." and users there will see that I'm active on Minube. It's a way to share content and generate interest.

What other strategies do you use to make Minube viral?

Our website has been designed to be useful. The viral content has been generated in parallel to let people know about our project. It's about using social tools to offer something interesting to users, something that they'll naturally want to share with their friends.

Our greatest viral success has been "Around the World 2.0." We thought, if we're travelers, why not show it? So we traveled around the world, visiting bloggers and Spanish-speaking entrepreneurs, going to major tourist sites and sharing them on Minube in real time and, at the same time, doing interviews and publishing them on the blog that was set up for this.

This generated a lot of interest in blogs and in the media. We were featured for a week on a Spanish television program, and it helped us get into places that would otherwise be hard to access and to meet people that would otherwise be difficult to meet. It was one of the most successful marketing ideas of the year in Spain.

As a company using social media, it's important to have marketing that's not intrusive and that shows the human factor. We're a business, behind it there are people, and when the users see who we are, that we're people like them, it gives us credibility.

Do Minube members feel that they are part of your brand?

As we mentioned earlier, this is one of our objectives. But at the same time, this is something that the users have to decide for themselves. We're in the middle of a revolution that has changed the way brands reach users. Nowadays, it isn't the brand that generates its image but the users who shape it to their tastes. Minube will end up turning into what the users want it to be.

In the past, brands dictated their opinions to users, but if a brand tries to do that now, it doesn't work. You have to give a voice to the users. This is our philosophy. It's about humanization. Users see us as a different kind of company, a company that shares ideas with them. Companies that don't do this are condemned to lose.

LESSONS LEARNED

Minube.com know that by making their website useful, they increase the likelihood that members will share it. They aim to offer everything a traveler needs to plan a trip, from user-generated reviews to price comparison and online reservations, and a viral effect emerges naturally from the valuable content.

They have used several viral marketing strategies that can work for other communities. Some of these involve the social network Facebook. Minube has incorporated Facebook Connect, a Facebook application that allows users to share information between their account on Minube.com and their Facebook account. In addition, they have developed a travel tool for Facebook users.

Another successful viral effort was the campaign "Around the World 2.0," in which Minube.com management traveled around the world. Since Minube.com is a community of travelers, the management chose to center this campaign around travel. However, a similar strategy could be used for other types of communities: *participate in offline activities related to your community's theme, and discuss them on your site.* In addition to generating media attention, this type of campaign gives your company a human face. Users follow the experiences of specific staff members and get to know the people behind the company. And this creates trust in your brand.

SEVENTEEN
TOPRURAL.COM

> "A user who searches on Toprural.com sees both the positive and negative experiences of other travelers, and this creates trust."
>
> —François Derbaix, Toprural.com founder and CEO

Toprural.com: This community has focused on a single vertical market—rural tourism in Southern Europe—and has come to dominate that niche.

Toprural.com is an online directory of rural vacation homes and rural tourism in Southern Europe. In Spain, where the company is based, they dominate the rural tourism market. Owners of rural vacation homes in seven countries pay for listings on Toprural.com, and community members post reviews of their accommodations. Traveler reviews of rural accommodations are the focus of Toprural.com's community, which also includes discussion forums.

Founded in 2000, by 2008 Toprural.com included 77,125 traveler reviews and over 75,000 registered members, supported by two community managers, and was averaging around 1.5 million visits a month. Their website is available in eight languages, including an English-language version at en.toprural.com.

We talked with Toprural.com's founder and CEO François Derbaix.

Toprural.com photo pages: User feedback indicated that photographs were important for trip planning and merited extra space on the website.

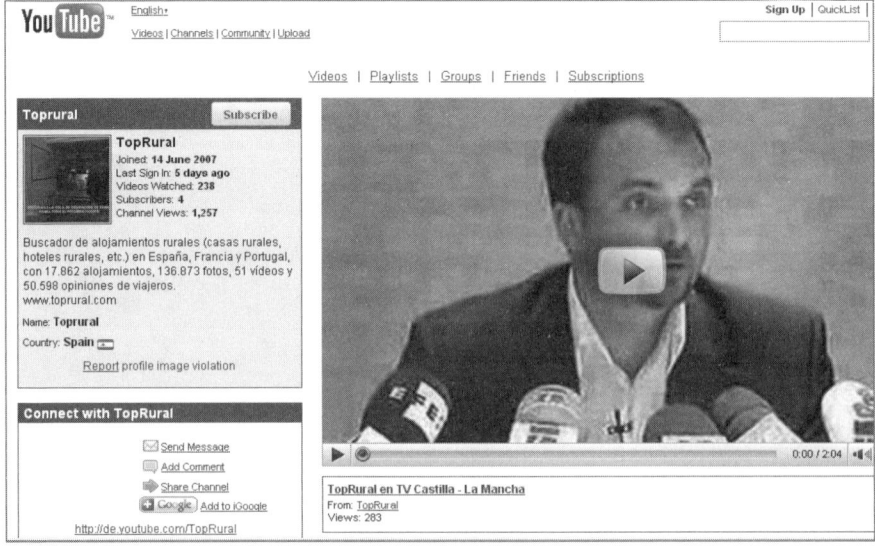

Toprural.com on YouTube: Toprural.com posts on social networks including YouTube, Facebook, LinkedIn, and Twitter.

INTERVIEW

Could you talk about why you decided to include the community element in your website? How does that add to your service?

Our website was launched in July 2000, and by September it already included traveler opinions. Our community has three parts—the opinions, a discussion forum, and a blog—but the opinions are the most strategic part for us. Without traveler opinions, the only information would be promotional material from the accommodation owner.

A user who searches on Toprural.com sees both the positive and negative experiences of other travelers, and this creates trust. In the rural tourism market, there's a very broad range of services: the accommodations are very different from each other and it's important to have user opinions to help distinguish among the offerings. There are also details that you don't find out from the owners but that might be important if you're planning a trip, and the users talk about them. For example, if a house has activities for children, some people will like this, while others won't like it because they might be looking for a romantic weekend away.

We ran a survey where we discovered that users trust the opinions of other users more than the recommendations of friends and family members. The user-generated content makes our website more useful. Users therefore recommend us to others, and this brings more visits, which means more reservations, which means more revenue for our advertisers, and thus more revenue for Toprural.com.

Our clients are the house owners, but in our case, the client isn't king. Our long-term success depends on the users, not on the advertisers. We publish traveler opinions on the accommodation pages, and we do not censor the opinions no matter how much the advertiser is paying us. Just as with television, the main point is to have the audience, and the satisfaction of the owner-advertisers ultimately depends as well on the satisfaction of our traveler-users.

How do you encourage users to participate and post opinions?

The main motivation for publishing opinions is to thank a good service provider or punish a bad one.

We do invite users to publish opinions if they've contacted the accommodation through our site. If they've reserved a house on November 10, we'll send them an email on November 11. But that's about the only action we take to motivate the users. We don't run competitions or anything along those lines.

What is the role of community management in your success?

We have a team of two people in contact with the users full-time. They're constantly receiving suggestions and passing information on to us. In the end, if you're not in contact with the users, there's no way to improve your service.

Could you give some examples of useful feedback that you've gotten from your users?

Practically everything we do is based on user feedback. During the last two years, we've run a survey on a panel of our users, and this has helped us to improve. For example, in July 2008 we started including photographs in user opinions, because we saw that this was very important to users who are making travel plans. The next step will be to include videos in opinions as well.

What problems or challenges have you faced in your community? How have you overcome them?

The main challenge is to prevent fake reviews, for example from friends of the owners, or people who want to discredit them. We don't check the content published by users; we allow free expression, except in the case of insults. Instead, we focus on identifying the users. When they create a new account, we send them an email confirmation, and we require them to provide personal details—not in order to publish this information, which is for internal use only, but to establish their identity and create a sense of responsibility for the content they publish.

What are the advantages and challenges of managing a community in multiple languages?

When Internet users look for information, they look for it in their own language. Therefore, if we want them to use our website, we have to give it to them in their own language. Toprural.com was launched in multiple languages from the beginning. Originally, it was in four languages, and now we're up to eight. There's a snowball effect, where the languages with the most users are the ones that attract the most new traffic. Our strongest language is Spanish. Of every two people who search for a rural house in Spain, one of them does it through Toprural.com.

In other languages where we have fewer users, we can't rely as much on this snowball effect, and we have to invest more in growth.

Could you talk more about this snowball effect?

In the offline world, everyone's concerned with economies of scale. But on the Internet, it's not the volume of production that matters, it's the volume of users. So there's a network effect. The more users you have, the better the service you can provide, and the stronger your position in the market.

What advice would you offer to someone who is launching a community to support his or her brand?

I would suggest setting up a blog instead. A blog can work for any company. And it's very easy for the users to respond by leaving comments. It's very important not to censor user comments. The point of the blog is to project an image of transparency and participation, and if the company censors comments, the effect will be exactly the opposite. Users will always post criticism, but that gives the company credibility. And you will have to respond to the criticism in very specific terms. This is hard, but it's the way of the future, and companies that don't do it are going to be left behind.

I'd recommend setting up a blog and participating in existing communities such as Facebook, Twitter, LinkedIn, and Flickr. I'd do this instead of creating a new community, because it's difficult to make that successful. For example, (the Spanish phone company) Telefónica recently created an online community, and I don't think it's going to work. I just don't think that young people will want to belong to a Telefónica community. They'd rather be on Facebook, which is closer to them, instead of a community that belongs to a big company.

At Toprural.com, we have pages on Facebook and LinkedIn. We post photos on Flickr and videos on YouTube. We use Twitter. And we have blogs in multiple languages—Spanish, French, Portuguese, Catalan, Italian (not in English yet).

Another recommendation: use standard tools like a Wordpress blog instead of hiring a programmer to develop new ones. If you want to build a community, there are standard tools for that such as Ning or Drupal for instance. These tools allow you to customize, and they allow you to grow. You don't need your programmers to update the platform because these tools are constantly evolving. The main point isn't technical development—it's getting users who will participate.

Also, it's important to think first of just one feature and generate a level of activity there before you start to expand. Toprural.com began with only opinions, and everything else came afterward. Don't start with everything all at once. The same with languages—start with just one, and start strong. If you start with too many things at once, then the activity will get dispersed.

LESSONS LEARNED

Toprural.com is an online community that has chosen a single vertical market—rural travelers in Southern Europe—and has come to dominate that niche. François Derbaix talks about the "network effect," whereby market strength on the Internet is directly related to user volume. Toprural.com therefore prioritizes the satisfaction of their users even before that of their paying customers and advertisers, and allows negative reviews about the advertised accommodations to be published.

This "network effect" is also why François recommends focusing a new community on just one feature and language before launching others. By narrowing the community's scope, you can generate more volume in a particular area than if the content and activity were more dispersed. These strategies have been most effective for Toprural.com. By choosing depth over breadth and focusing content on traveler reviews of rural accommodations, Toprural.com has succeeded in building a very rich directory that would be extremely difficult for any competitor to match.

François also recommends focusing on content over technological development when creating your own online community strategy. This could mean using existing tools rather than investing in custom technology, or it could mean marketing through blogs and social networking sites rather than investing money and time to start a dedicated brand community.

EIGHTEEN
INTERVIEW WITH LEESA BARNES

> "A key is insuring that you use the right viral campaign for your target market."
>
> —Leesa Barnes, author, *Podcasting for Profit*

Leesa Barnes is an influential social media marketing expert and author of the book *Podcasting for Profit*. You can learn more about social media strategies on her website www.marketingfit.com. She spoke to us about marketing with social media.

INTERVIEW

Could you name some online communities that marketing professionals need to know about?

Absolutely. Some of the best places to start are social networking websites such as LinkedIn and Facebook. I know that many marketing professionals will hear that and think: wait a minute, they are sharing recipes and the fact that they broke up with their boyfriend on Facebook. So definitely start with LinkedIn, a network geared toward business professionals. And then Facebook will give you a more social aspect, but will connect you with people who are in your target market.

What should marketing professionals know about the best way to approach people in online communities?

If a marketing professional wants to be taken seriously and not looked upon as someone who is peddling their wares all the time, they should make sure that they have a completed profile on the site. Complete your profile as much as possible—include your URL because that helps to make you look transparent, and if you are the CMO or the VP of Marketing or Marketing Director with a big name brand company, make sure you identify that in your profile. It is all about transparency and that is what people are looking for.

Then it is time to reach out. Don't start off with your coupons or the fifty percent off sale or the fact that you are liquidating all your resources. Instead, start off with something where you are asking for help. A good way to do that is to start off with a survey—perhaps you are looking for feedback on a Christmas campaign you have coming up. That is so key because there is an example of a company that did it so wrong and got publicity for all the wrong reasons; I have to mention it because this is a great example of what *not* to do and demonstrates how asking your target markets for help is the least expensive thing you can do online.

There was a campaign that was launched on a Friday (every marketing person knows that you never launch on a Friday!) in late 2008 by McNeil Consumer Healthcare—the makers of the painkiller Motrin. They launched this viral video that was obviously targeted to moms because it said that moms go through a lot of pain wearing those baby slings, and they tried to make it humorous by saying it may be trendy to carry your child in a sling across your chest, but it causes back pain, and so on. It was meant to be tongue-in-cheek, but it was obviously written by someone who is not funny because none of the moms saw the humor in it—they took huge offense. Moms had all day Friday, all day Saturday, all day Sunday to commiserate with each other about how awful the video was and it was not until Monday, or late Sunday, that the VP of Communications issued an apology. But then there was a second mistake: instead of taking the opportunity to connect personally with all of these moms by sending a personalized message, it was a canned "We apologize for the inconvenience" response, so they missed the market again.

The video has since been pulled from the Motrin website, but I mention it because Motrin got publicity but for all the wrong reasons. All the company had to do was ask—send out the video, find out where moms are hanging out online, which is very easy, and say, "We are thinking about launching this as a viral campaign; give us your feedback." You don't have to pay them the fifty thousand dollars for a focus group; you don't have to pay them anything—just give them a chance to offer you feedback. They would have avoided such pain and heartache had they just asked. That is the very first thing marketers can do in these online communities, social communities in particular: just ask. And by doing so you are engaging people with your brand.

Besides doing your market research first, what do you think are the keys to a successful viral campaign?

A key is insuring that you use the right viral campaign for your target market. There's a great tool that Forrester put together called social technographics; it's an online survey that anyone can use to determine how their target market uses social media. You can find the survey at www.forrester.com/Groundswell/profile_tool.html. That will give you insight into how people are using social media. Some people lurk, some people in your target market are only going to lurk; they will watch what you are putting together and then they will go away. If your target market does that, a viral campaign is not going to work because they are not going to share it, they are not going to comment, all they are going to do is peep and run away.

Now, moms in particular love to share, they love to comment, and so a viral campaign for them, done the right way, is going to be key. If they see a video they like—done the right way—they are going to share it, comment on it. And then there is a certain element of your target market—they love to create. If you are launching a viral marketing campaign for say, young males, then you need to ensure that there is an element where they can create as well. An example of that might be doing something on Facebook: perhaps you have a video that you are sharing, and then you invite your target market—young men—to contribute a video response. In that case, they are creating on top of your viral campaign, whereas moms will not create but they will provide feedback and share your video. It all depends on your target market—how do they engage with social media? If they are creators, then you need to incorporate an element of creation: here is a viral video, but here is a chance for you to create and contribute and so forth. That is what is going to be so important for marketing professionals: to understand the mindset of their target market when developing their viral campaign.

Besides viral marketing, how are companies using online communities to promote their brands?

There are a number of companies using what is called a fan page on Facebook, and that allows you to add thousands of people as followers on your fan page. Really, it is developing a page around your brand, or maybe someone who represents your brand, and getting people to comment on photos. Some celebrities have fan pages, but companies can use this as well to post information about their brand or product. Podcasting is another great area that companies are using to build communities and so they will publish an audio or video podcast and invite their communities to call in with ideas or comment on a discussion board. Coming at this well is Butterball Turkey—around Christmas time or Thanksgiving, they have a series of audio podcasts that teach people how to prepare their turkey for the holiday season. I think that's so clever. They do not publish any episodes at any point of the year except right before Thanksgiving and into the Christmas season. It is brilliant! You don't have to do a ten-thousand week serial—you can do it for a very specific event. And then you can invite them to call your 1-800 line for more tips or if they have more questions, or if they have feedback. Here's a company that merges both new media and old media in order to create a community around their brand. It's very clever.

Twitter member page: This is the profile page of Peachpit Press, publisher of this book.

Another good one is Twitter, which is being used by companies as a customer service tool. Companies such as Verizon and AT&T have some of their executives on Twitter, so that as soon as someone says something or complains about their brand, that person calls the person directly to help them solve that issue. You have companies like AT&T and Verizon having ten thousand followers who are all customers of theirs. Verizon and AT&T are using Twitter to monitor feedback—who is tweeting about it, who is using Twitter, and what are they saying? If it's something negative, they get their customer service right on them. Call that person and solve their problem.

These are just some awesome ways that companies and businesses are using social media to build a community. What's key here is that these companies are not driving people to their complicated Web pages to click, click, click until they get to the help desk or until they get to that phone number. Instead, they are being proactive by contacting that customer directly or giving them just one place to go to follow up with them. In the case of Butterball, it is that 1-800 number. That is going to be key, because if you lead people back to your complicated website where it takes ten thousand clicks to get where they really want to go, then you are not meeting your community and instead you are creating more barriers.

Can you think of more examples of companies that are successfully using social media for marketing?

I can mention another disaster, which is equally important. Starbucks Coffee launched an audio podcast about three years ago, in 2006. They published about three episodes and that was it. I don't think they are still online, but listening to them they sound beautiful, they are perfect, the audio quality is amazing, and you can tell that a lot of thought went into them. But, the reason it got such bad publicity is because they did one thing wrong: they focused their audio podcast on the coffee bean, the cultivation, so they actually went to someplace in Kenya and interviewed one of the coffee farmers, or coffee cultivators, and they have a coffee sommelier who swishes coffee as if swishing wine. The reason why so many people hated the podcast is because it focused on the coffee bean instead of focusing on the customer experience. So here is an opportunity to focus on interviewing customers—going through the stores, asking them how they choose coffee, what mood they're in when they buy a particular brand of coffee, why they go for tall versus grande. Or they could have interviewed some of the people serving coffee and asked them about some of the weirdest coffee combinations they've ever heard ordered.

Instead of focusing on the coffee bean, Starbucks should have focused on the customer experience. People don't care how the coffee gets into their cup; they want to hear the experience stories that are told around that coffee—the customer experience is what would have saved Starbucks. At the end of the day, your customer wants to hear drama, they want to hear a story being told, and if you can't tell a story through your brand—if you can't create drama through your brand—then don't use social media. As I said earlier, it's not about pushing your product or talking about that sale, although that will come. First you need to tell a story; your brand needs to be a story. Who is the CEO—what is he about? Why is he where he is? Is he a family man? Does he love to golf? What about your VP of Marketing who's putting all of this stuff together? What's her story? What is she about? Put a face to your brand, and if it is not a face then use the faces of your target market to create that story for your brand.

That's what will make many brand managers, many marketing professionals successful at social media. Once you tell a story, people start to identify with that story, and that's when you start to build a community.

You have talked about some of the things that can go seriously awry when companies try to use social media. Do you see any risk for companies in not developing a social media strategy?

Oh, yes. The risk is that either your competitor is going to do it and take all of your customers with them, or a customer is going to launch things on your behalf and may not do it according to your key points or your key message—or worse yet, they could be an unhappy customer who starts a movement on Facebook against your company, how your company sucks. And that's the biggest danger that many companies risk by not taking advantage of social media—they risk their competitors being there, showing that they care and stealing all their customers, or that a customer—particularly a disgruntled one—will look to social media and launch something. The most famous case was that of Dell computers. This happened about three or four years ago. For the longest time, if you did a Google search for "Dell computers," the number one result was a negative blog about Dell. So, here is an unhappy customer who is using a blog to complain about the company, and the blog was number one on Google.

That's the risk. But I often hear people say, "Well, we should not get involved in social media because there is no ROI," and that usually comes from a place where people are looking for the ad revenue—they are looking for the hard number. Unfortunately with social media you can have ten thousand followers on Twitter, you can have five thousand friends on Facebook, you can have 2.9 million connections on LinkedIn through six degrees of separation, but oftentimes that doesn't translate into cold, hard cash. That's what many marketing professionals have to realize and build a case around—social media is going help you do that one-to-one communication, often one-to-many, and it is going to help you connect with your customers in a way that other media channels cannot. It's more of a long-term approach, rather than something that is going to be quick.

You mention connecting to customers in a way that you can't through other media channels. Could you talk a bit more about that and the kind of relationships brands can build with their customers through social media?

Sure. In my book, I mention that advertising is a multibillion-dollar industry; I'm sure you can find those stats online. One of the things that I often point out is that when an ad is run on television—it's a thirty-second ad, and let's just say it's for a car company—that dealership has no idea if the reason why I walked into the dealership is because I saw an ad on television two nights ago: no idea, none. So, this mass approach to getting the eyeballs and getting the interest in products and services costs a lot of money—a thirty-second spot during the Super Bowl costs millions and millions of dollars, and those companies have no clue whether that person went to their website as a result of seeing the ad. But with social media because you have more of a one-to-one interaction, you can get that feedback right away. You can set up different tools online to track how people are going from one place to another. Let's just say in Facebook you post a link on a fan page. If you are a smart marketing professional, you'll create that link so it goes to a separate page from your website so you can track those clicks and see how many of those clicks transition to downloading your white paper or registering for a lunchtime Webinar that you are having. That's where I say that traditional media channels don't work. It's not that they don't work, but you don't have the ability to track what's happening once that person has viewed your ad, whereas online—especially by using social media—you can set up a way for people to be able to click on things, and you can track where they are clicking and where they are headed. There are many tools online that can help you do that.

What are some common misconceptions about marketing through social media?

I remember working with one client who launched an audio podcast; she did three episodes and was angry with me that there was nobody coming from her audio podcast to buy her product, but yet when she did radio interviews, she got a thousand sales after she did the interviews, a thousand sales of her product. Another client didn't quite grasp that when we launched her video series online, it was a serial so that one episode would come out a week, just like a television show. She thought they would all come out at the same time. Other clients misunderstand that a blog is something you can update on the fly when you want, and it is not supposed to be a static Web page that you forget.

There are tons of misconceptions, but the most common I hear is that social media is just for teenagers. In fact if you go to Facebook they have a page that shows that the fastest growing age group on their website is people between the ages of twenty-five and fifty. Every stat I have been able to pull up about blogging, about podcasting, about Facebook, about Twitter, about online usage, shows that the heaviest users tend to be between twenty-five and fifty years old. The massive growing group is the baby boomers. That is a huge misconception that we still have to fight. Too often I hear that we can't use social media because it's too young, when in fact the opposite is true.

Another misconception is that many people believe they won't have the time to do this. Granted, yes, social media is going to be something to add to your marketing plate and it is going to require time—it's not like a television ad where it runs, you forget it, and then if feedback comes in it is okay. Social media is going to take some of your time. But, there are so many tools online that you can use to automate social media. For example, if you are on Twitter, you can use a tool that will automate your updates. Once a week I sit down and schedule different posts to go out live on a future date, so I am not using all these tools every day, although it looks like I am. There are automatic tools out there that you can use, and you spend one, maybe two or three hours a week and you automate everything, and it goes live, and that way it's not consuming your time.

Another misconception is that it is expensive or that the learning curve is huge. In fact, most of the tools are free and it's not expensive. As far as the learning curve, I usually tell people if you know how to send an email, you can update a blog. If you know how to click with your mouse, you can create a Twitter account or a Facebook account. From there what people get confused about is creating a profile and connecting with people. But to get started, it's easy.

Another one I hear is about privacy and security. I often hear this from bigger companies who are afraid someone is going to release a virus through Facebook and it is going to damage their system. That objection is not rooted in fact, but in fear. The other one is that we're going to have our private information out there. But what I hear most from marketing managers is that they are going to lose their ability to control their key messages or their key points. To that I usually say, you have to either adjust it or, better yet, you can create guidelines. If employees are using social media, they know what the guidelines are. IBM put together a list of blogging and podcasting guidelines for its employees, so that they are very aware of what can and cannot be disclosed as an employee of IBM. I've heard dozens of different objections but I have an answer for all of them because I keep hearing them all the time.

What would be your main advice to a company that was planning to start an online community for their own brand?

When you are starting an online community, remember that the tools are just tools. They enable you to do something. If you just think of the tools as tools, you will understand that there's a bigger perspective that you need to take into account. Marketing's your chance to promote your message, and in order to promote your message you use various tools. Social media is one of the tools in your toolkit. But, if you take a look at what you're doing as sharing information, as helping your target market do something better, and solving a key problem for your target market—if you look at your role as helping, giving, and sharing, then you're going to be very successful at building an online community around your brand. That's it – that's your role. Go on social media, help your target market solve a pressing problem, give information, share your expertise and suddenly you become a company that cares—a brand that cares. Then, when they're ready to buy, the first brand they are going to think about is yours because you help, you share.

How do you see the future of online communities?

They're going to continue to evolve. I think that mobile technology is going to be huge, and if marketers think that social media online is scary—wait until social media tools become accessible on a mobile device. I just got my iPod Touch and I'm accessing Facebook, Twitter, my blog, all these tools. The first thing I do now is go to a website or a blog, and make sure I can actually see it on my mobile device. So get ready, because online communities are going well beyond the desktop, and now people are going to be able to access your brand from their hip, from their mobile device. It's time that marketers also consider that as another tool in the marketing tool kit.

Any final thoughts?

I just want to mention that your customer no longer needs your permission to talk about your brand. They are now in a position where they have the power—stats that I keep seeing show that television viewership is declining, radio listenership is declining; people are engaging with your brand on their time.

Consumers know they have that power, so remember that they don't need your permission to talk about your brand. The key points, key messages that many marketing professionals hold onto need to be adjusted, they need to be updated. Remember that you are on your consumer's time. You are now entering their universe, their neighborhood, and you need to be very aware of what their role is and how you can interact with that.

LESSONS LEARNED

In our interview, Leesa Barnes offers many important tips on effective marketing through social media. Her advice is relevant for any online community marketing strategy, whether you are marketing on social networks or building a dedicated community for your brand:

* Don't start out by pushing your products or promotions
* Create a user profile
* Be transparent
* Ask for feedback from users before launching a campaign
* Respond to feedback in a personal way, not with canned messages
* Make sure viral campaigns fit your target market
* Be proactive about contacting your customers, or give them a clear communication channel such as a 1-800 number rather than forcing them to navigate through a website
* If you tell a story around your brand, focus this on customer experience
* Remember that social media is just one tool in your marketing toolbox
* Use social media to help your target market, and you will be seen as a company that cares

* Leesa also offers useful responses to common misconceptions about social media:

    1. Misconception: sales should immediately increase after a social media campaign (Results come over time).

    2. Misconception: you can create a blog and forget it (Blogs need to be updated regularly).

    3. Misconception: social media is just for teenagers (Baby boomers are an increasing presence on social networks).

    4. Misconception: social media is too time-consuming (There are tools to automate updates).

    5. Misconception: social media is expensive (Most of the tools are free).

    6. Misconception: the learning curve is huge (If you can send an e-mail, you can update a blog).

    7. Misconception: a virus will be released into your system (This is not a realistic concern).

    8. Misconception: you'll lose control of your message (You can set communication guidelines for your organization).

WEB 2.0 GLOSSARY

ACTIVE RECRUITMENT: The process of actively pursuing new website members through advertising banners, email campaigns, or other means (versus *passive recruitment,* where members find the website on their own).

ADMIN PANEL: Software that allows staff to access and manage website member accounts and content.

AVATAR: An image or figure that represents a specific website member and becomes his or her online identity in a specific community. The avatar often appears next to content published by the member with whom it's associated. In communities that allow live chat, members can often make their avatars move on the screen like characters in a video game.

BANNER BLINDNESS: The habit that experienced Internet users develop of ignoring or overlooking anything that looks like an advertising banner.

BETA: The test mode of a website or software. New websites are often launched with the word "beta" near their logo to let users know that bugs and problems are still being worked out.

BLOG: Short for weblog. A website where the author publishes content in a journal or diary format; every time the author publishes a new entry, it appears with a date and time stamp on top of the previous entry, in a vertical column. Blog entries are normally quite short and conversational in style. A blog is normally written by a single author, or a small group of authors, although readers are often able to publish comments on the entries.

BLOGOSPHERE: The interrelationship of blogs. Blogs often link to and refer to other blogs, creating the effect of a global conversation.

BOOKMARKS: See *Social bookmarking.*

CAPTCHA: An image of letters or numbers that an Internet user must type into a box to prove that he or she is a person and not a computer program. CAPTCHA images are commonly used on website registration forms to prevent computer-generated registrations. (CAPTCHA is a trademark owned by Carnegie Mellon and stands for Completely Automated Public Turing test to tell Computers and Humans Apart.)

CHAT: A written conversation that takes place online in real time; one person types a sentence, which appears instantly on the second person's computer screen, and the second person responds.

CLICK PATH: The sequence of links that a user follows when navigating a website.

CLOSED COMMUNITY: An online community whose membership is limited. Closed communities might accept new members on an invitation-only basis and/or have a maximum number of members allowed to join.

CLOSED USER GROUP: A limited group of users who have access to an area of a website requiring login. Closed user groups are not necessarily online communities. In some cases, the closed areas of websites are used for community features; in other cases they are used for purposes unrelated to the interrelationship of users, such as online shopping, managing account details, or customer support.

COMMUNITY MANAGEMENT: See *Community manager*.

COMMUNITY MANAGER: The person tasked with managing an online community. This person's responsibilities typically include some or all of the following: answering member questions, resolving member disputes, moderating discussions, removing inappropriate content, and policing and energizing the community.

CONTENT NAVIGATION: A way of organizing a website in which one content piece or activity leads organically to another (versus *structural navigation* which uses a menu of links or a navigation bar).

CONTENT TAGS: Key words that are used to label website content pieces to help users find them in online searches. For example, an article about mystery novels might be tagged with the key words "mysteries," "detectives," "novels," and "books." When a user searches on the website with one of those words, the article will come up. Many websites also display the most popularly used tags in the form of a menu of these key words; when users click on a tag, they are shown all content that has been labeled with that word.

CONTEXT-SENSITIVE ADVERTISING: An advertising method that uses technology to match advertising content with the content on a Web page. For example, if a website member publishes an article about Spain, ads for Spanish wines and Spanish travel packages might automatically appear on that page.

COOKIE: A temporary Internet file that is stored on a website user's computer. For example, if you click an option on a website to view the page in Spanish, a cookie might be used to remember this preference, so that, in the future, the same website will always be displayed in Spanish on that particular computer.

COREGISTRATION: An advertising partnership arrangement between websites in which users registering on one site are offered the opportunity to register for the other site at the same time.

CPA: Cost Per Acquisition—an advertising arrangement in which the advertiser pays according to how many ad viewers perform a specific action, such as registering for a website.

CPM: Cost per thousand impressions—an advertising arrangement where the advertiser pays according to how many times the page is displayed (M here is the Roman numeral for 1,000).

DOMAIN NAME: The name that identifies a website's address.

EMOTICON: An image used in online conversations to express the speaker's emotions. Basic emoticons are smiley faces and frowning faces. Since people conversing online normally can't see each other's actual facial expressions, emoticons are used as a stand-in to make the conversation feel more personal.

FAQ: Frequently Asked Questions. A help page that displays answers to common user questions.

FOLD LINE: An imaginary line in an email dividing the content that is immediately visible in the recipient's email viewer from the content that cannot be seen without scrolling down. Since marketing email recipients do not always bother to scroll, it is important to keep key content above the fold line.

FRIEND LIST: A feature that allows online community members to display a list of their friends or contacts in the community.

GENERATION Y: Refers to people born between 1977 and 1995. The young people in this group have radically different media consumption habits than the generations before them.

IGNORE BUTTON: A community website feature that offers a user the option not to see content from another specific user. This is helpful to prevent community conflicts from escalating and to alert community managers to potential problems.

IM: Instant Messenger—a tool for online chats.

LOGIN NAME: See *User name*.

LOL: Laugh Out Loud—used in online chat and conversation when someone wants to say that he or she is amused.

MESSAGE BOARD: An interactive technology that allows members of a website or the general public to publish their comments on specific topics or questions. As is the case on blogs, the comments are normally displayed in reverse chronological order, in a vertical string with timestamps showing when each one was posted.

MICRO-BLOGGING: Publishing very short blog-type posts—the term normally refers to posting on the social network Twitter, where users are allowed a maximum of 140 characters per post.

NAVIGATION BAR: A menu of links on a website, often arranged in a vertical or horizontal strip.

NETIQUETTE: The etiquette norms of the Internet.

NEWBIE: A recent member of an online community, a novice.

NICK: See *User name*.

ONLINE COMMUNITY: A website where users form online relationships with each other.

PAGE IMPRESSIONS: The number of times that a particular Web page has been viewed. Online advertising is often paid for according to the number of page impressions.

PAGE REAL ESTATE: The distribution of space on a Web page.

PASSIVE RECRUITMENT: See *Active recruitment*.

PPA: Pay Per Action (or PPL—Pay Per Lead)—an advertising arrangement where the advertiser pays according to the number of ad viewers who perform a specific action, such as registering for a website.

PPC: Pay Per Click—an advertising arrangement where the advertiser pays according to the number of clicks on the ad banner or link.

PPI: Pay Per Impression—an advertising arrangement where the advertiser pays according to the number of times an ad is displayed.

PPL: Pay Per Lead. See *PPA*.

PUBLISHER: In the context of Internet marketing, a website that displays third-party advertising.

ROFL: Roll on the Floor Laughing—used in online chat and conversation when someone wants to say that he or she finds something hilarious.

RSS: Really Simple Syndication—code that allows a user to subscribe to content from a website. This content is then received and updated automatically.

SEARCH ENGINE MARKETING: See *SEM*.

SEARCH ENGINE OPTIMIZATION: See *SEO*.

SEARCH ENGINE RANKING: The position in which a Web page appears on the results lists of search engines such as Google when someone searches for words related to the website content. The higher a Web page appears on the list, the more visible it is to search engine users.

SEM: Search Engine Marketing—marketing through sponsored links on search engines such as Google. Google AdWords is a well-known SEM program.

SEO: Search Engine Optimization—the science or art of improving a website's search engine ranking by making it appear higher on the results lists of search engines such as Google.

SERVER: See *Web server*.

SOCIAL BOOKMARKING: The public display and sharing of website bookmarks, or saved web links. Social bookmarking tools are offered by websites such as Digg and Del.icio.us.

SOCIAL NETWORK: An online community where user relationships are the main focus and activity.

SOCIAL SHOPPING: Describes online communities where shopping is the focus of social activities. Typical social shopping activities include sharing shopping wish lists and shopping advice, and discussion of items purchased.

SOFT LAUNCH: The gradual release of a product or website, e.g., to test it on a small population before it is publicized more widely.

SPAM: (Noun) Unsolicited junk email. (Verb) To send unsolicited bulk emails.

START PAGE: An introductory website page that often allows the visitor to choose among different versions of the website (for example, versions in different languages, for different geographic locations, or for different sub-brands).

STICKY: The quality of a website that "hooks" visitors into spending a lot of time there during a visit. Some techniques for creating stickiness include setting up website activities to lead naturally from one to another so that there is no natural stopping point. In general, stickiness is highly desirable for community websites.

STRUCTURAL NAVIGATION: See *Content navigation*.

SYNDICATION: See *RSS*.

TAGS: See *Content tags*.

THREAD: On an online message board, a particular topic with its associated string of comments.

TROLL: A person who joins online communities in order to create conflict and disruption.

TWEET: (Noun) A post on the social network Twitter. (Verb) To post on Twitter.

USER NAME: Also *Login name* or *Nick*. A nickname that becomes a website user's public online identity. The user name is often used for logging onto a website, and, on community websites, is generally displayed next to content published by the associated member and on the member's profile page. A user name allows an online community member to become known to other members while keeping his or her offline identity private.

WEB 1.0: See *Web 2.0*.

WEB 2.0: A term coined by media consultant Tim O'Reilly to describe trends in the Internet which began after the dot-com bubble burst in 2001. An important aspect of Web 2.0 is interactivity; in other words, technology which allows website visitors to modify the content of the websites by posting messages and articles, publishing photos, and so on. Before Web 2.0 there was Web 1.0, where website visitors could only read content published by the authors. Web 1.0 was a monologue; Web 2.0 permits a dialogue.

WEBCAM: A camera that displays video on the Internet.

WEBINAR: An online seminar.

WEBLOG: See *Blog*.

WEB SERVER: The computer that hosts a website.

WIKI: A website that allows visitors to publish and edit the website's content. The term wiki is generally applied to websites where the focus is on the content, rather than on the authors.

INDEX

11870.com, 169–177
    internationalization, 135–136
    overview, 171–173
    rewarding members, 89
    virtual prizes, 95

A

About Us page, 54
abusive content, 33, 104–105, 213
activation links, 80, 174
active members, 95–97
active recruitment, 62, 251
activities
    design principles, 44
    examples of, 43
    facilitating, 102–103
    participation in, 9
    popular, 43
    shared, 5, 9
Adidas Streetball Challenge, 151
admin panel, 57, 107–108, 251
AdSense, 125
advertising. *See also* banners; marketing
    considerations, 118–119
    context-sensitive, 125, 253
    display, 124–125
    earning money via, 123–127
    Ecademy.com, 214
    feedback on, 120
    games and, 118–119
    Generation Y and, 146–147
    Google AdSense, 125
    Google AdWords, 67
    incentivized, 123–124
    injecting into discussions, 103
    membership levels and, 202–203
    negative reactions to, 119, 125
    page impressions, 41, 66, 253, 254
    PPA (pay-per-action), 123, 255
    PPC (pay-per-click), 66, 123, 255
    PPI (pay-per-impression), 66, 123, 255
    PPL (pay-per-lead), 66, 255
    PPS (pay-per-sale), 123
    recruiting from, 66
    selling, 124–125
    on social networks, 145–148
    Super Bowl commercials, 245
    targeted, 148
    via email, 126–127
AdWords, 67
agreements
    coregistration, 66, 126, 253
    Terms of Use, 33–34, 53–54, 75
alerts, email, 96, 97, 126
alert services, 96, 126
aliases, 10
announcement email, 96
anonymity, 10
antisocial behavior, 105
aSmallWorld, 72, 73
AT&T, 242
audio podcasts, 241, 243
avatars, 10–11, 85, 251
Axiom, 64

B

B2B (business to business) pages, 40
B2B products, 153
B2C (business to consumer) pages, 40
baby boomers, 153, 246

backups, 108
banner blindness, 119, 145–146, 251
banners
    advertisements, 202–203
    recruiting from, 66
Barbiegirls.com, 15
Barnes, Leesa, 71, 149, 237–249
beta mode, 251
beta testing, 76, 251
Bfriends, 62
blogosphere, 8, 251
blogs. *See also* message boards; online communities
    described, 7–8, 251
    examples of, 8
    intention of, 8
    micro-blogging, 254
    search-engine optimized, 209
    vs. online communities, 7–8, 235
BMW.de website, 65
BMW M Power World, 179–185
    exclusive content in, 47, 183–184
    launch of, 76
    overview, 181–182
    profile pages, 182–183, 184, 190
    promoting community, 65
    restrictions on joining, 12
bookmarking, social, 256
bookmarks, 69
brand awareness
    Barnes on, 241, 245, 247
    creating loyalty, 20–21
    social networks and, 149–155
brand communication, 111
brand communities. *See* online communities
branded gifts, 88
brand loyalty, 20–21
brand-related content, 46–47
brands. *See also* products
    control of, 20–21
    criticism of, 21–22, 32, 36, 150, 175
    defining role of, 44–47
    emotional engagement and, 151–152
    examples of, 45–46, 47
    friend lists and, 149, 151, 155
    integrating with communities, 46–47, 149–150, 176
    Jareño on, 226
    key messages about, 21–22
    media exposure for, 29
    personal branding, 201
    profile pages for. *See* profile pages
    on social networks, 147–155
    testimonials, 22, 123, 152
brand-to-customer communication, 147
Brigitte.de, 62, 64, 82
Bruendl, Helmut, 47, 111, 180, 181–185
budget control, 89, 127
bulletin boards. *See* message boards
businesses. *See* companies
business networks
    Ecademy.com, 21, 25, 33, 207–217
    LinkedIn, 91, 144, 211, 239
    Xing. *See* Xing
business to business (B2B) pages, 40
business to consumer (B2C) pages, 40
Butterball Turkey audio podcasts, 241–242
buzzmachine.com, 22
buzz marketing, 68–71

C

campaignforrealbeauty.com, 15
Campina, 28
Capel, Félix López, 23, 196, 197, 199–206
Capessa.com, 13
CAPTCHA (Completely Automated Public Turing Test to tell Computers and Humans Apart), 75, 252
CAPTCHA images, 75, 252
cash rewards/gifts, 88–91
censoring content, 104–105, 114
censorship, 33, 35, 36, 57
chat, live, 108, 252, 254
Chefkoch.de, 103
ChocolateandZucchini.com, 8
Ciao.com, 159–167
    converting visitors to members, 66
    internationalization, 136–137
    language support, 165
    overview, 161–162
    rewards, 86, 87, 89
    status/social hierarchy, 86, 87
click paths, 46, 252

closed communities, 12–14, 62, 252
closed user groups, 14, 252
clubs, 16
comments. *See also* feedback
    feedback on, 164
    negative, 21–22, 32, 36, 150, 175
    threads, 256
communications policies, 36
Communispace, 14, 27, 28, 120
community content, 46–47
"Community Effects 2008" study, 118
community management, 100–115.
    See also community managers
    admin panel, 57, 107–108, 251
    importance of, 114
    increasing efficiency of, 111–113
    infrastructure, 56–57
    keeping up-to-date, 132
    long-term, 132
    overview, 100
    peer management, 113–114
    role of members, 113–114
community managers
    admin panel, 57, 107–108, 251
    authority needed, 57, 107
    censoring content, 104–105
    duties of, 56, 57, 100, 101–105
    email to/from, 94, 102–103, 108, 109
    facilitating activity, 102–103
    "functionary" mindset, 132
    liaising between members/company, 103
    member support, 101–102
    Minube.com, 224
    need for additional, 133
    objectives, 105–106
    overidentification with members, 132
    overview, 100, 252
    planning for, 56–57
    qualifications for, 100–101
    requirements for, 105–111
    support from company experts, 109–111
    tools needed, 107–109
    Toprural.com, 234
    training of, 106
    website policing, 105
    website updates, 131
    Xing, 200

community members. *See* members
community points, 164
community representatives, 114
community websites. *See also* online
    communities; websites
    About Us page, 54
    adding languages, 135–138
    adding new features, 96
    advantages of, 9–12
    analyzing traffic/activity, 130
    "bad word filters," 112
    blogs on. *See* blogs
    bookmarks, 69
    challenge examples, 95
    checklist for, 48
    company information, 54
    components of, 81–83
    considerations, 56
    development costs, 31
    domain names, 57–58
    features of, 55
    help page, 54
    homepages. *See* homepages
    increasing traffic to, 24, 41
    keeping up-to-date, 131–132
    languages, 56, 165
    launch strategy, 75–77, 184, 192
    login links, 51
    measuring success of, 130
    member profile pages, 11, 52–53
    mission statements, 49
    partner sites, 66, 126
    planning, 40, 48–56
    policing, 105
    press exposure, 41
    profiting from. *See* revenues
    public criticism and, 32–33
    registration page, 50–51, 73–75
    "stickiness" of, 81–83, 256
    undesirable content, 32–33
companies
    benefits of online communities, 20–30
    brands. *See* brands
    contact information, 54
    creating loyalty, 20
    increasing website traffic, 24, 41
    information leaks, 34–35

companies (*continued*)
    making money, 29–30
    perception of, 130
    public awareness, 130
    rumors about, 36
    saving money, 29
company newsletters, 63
competition, 44, 244
conduct, standards of, 33–34
confidentiality statement, 34
content
    abusive, 33, 104–105, 213
    censoring, 33, 35, 36, 57, 104–105
    controversial, 70
    created by specific members, 55
    dynamic, 25
    exclusive, 47, 183–184
    "fold line," 63, 253
    forwarding, 69
    generating, 24–25
    ignoring, 146
    links to, 69
    location on page, 50
    managing, 56–57, 112
    mixing brand/community content, 46–47
    off-topic, 104
    optimizing for search engines, 25, 67–68, 255
    republishable, 69
    "stickiness" in, 81–83, 256
    undesirable, 32–33
content navigation, 48, 252
content tags, 252–253. *See also* keywords
context-sensitive advertising, 125, 253
contracts, Terms of Use, 33–34, 53–54, 75
contribution. *See* participation
controversy, 70
cookies, 253
copyright protection, 33–34
copyright violations, 104
coregistration agreements, 66, 126, 253
corporate websites
    recruiting from, 64–66
    traffic to, 130
cost per acquisition (CPA), 66, 253
cost per thousand impressions (CPM), 253
costs, 31, 66, 253

country domains, 58
Cox, Ana Marie, 8
CPA (cost per acquisition), 66, 253
CPM (cost per thousand impressions), 253
CRM (customer relationship management) program, 40–41, 108–109
customer feedback, 130. *See also* feedback
customer help desk, 23
customer mailing lists, 40, 63
customer relationship management (CRM) program, 40–41, 108–109
customers
    brand communication, 147
    long-term relationships, 148
    sense of entitlement, 35–36
    testimonials, 22, 123, 152
customer service, 34, 35, 242

D

data mining, 28
defamation, 104
Del.icio.us, 256
Dell Computer, 22, 244
demographics, 85
Derbaix, François, 26, 31, 77, 231–236
developers, 56
development costs, 31
Digg, 69, 256
direct email campaigns, 63
direct mail marketing, 75
discounts, 88
discussion moderators, 114
display advertising, 124–125
domain names, 57–58, 253
domain registration, 57–58
domains, country, 58
double-byte alphabets, 56
Dove brand, 15, 70, 188, 189–193
Drupal, 236
Dusoulier, Clotilde, 8
dynamic content, 25

E

eBay, 5
Ecademy.com, 21, 25, 33, 207–217

E-circle, 64
e-commerce websites
    adding community elements to, 163
    earning money via, 122–123
    shorter sale cycle and, 148
    traffic to, 130
email
    advertising via, 126–127
    alert options, 96, 97, 126
    announcements, 96
    "fold line," 63, 253
    forwarding content, 68, 69
    to inactive members, 97
    inviting/referring friends, 68, 69, 75
    jokes/humor, 70
    marketing, 75
    mass, 127
    registration process, 75, 80
    reports, 108
    sharing, 70
    sorting, 113
    spam, 63, 104, 108, 127, 256
    templates, 113
    to/from community managers, 94, 102–103, 108, 109
email addresses, 12, 54
email campaigns, 63, 130
email lists, 63–64
email newsletters, 94
emoticons, 253
emotional brand experiences, 151–152
employees, as community members, 47, 184
Encinar, Jesús, 173
entitlement, sense of, 35–36
etiquette, Internet, 254
events, 151–152

F

Facebook
    Barnes on, 239
    fan pages, 241, 245
    growth rate of, 144
    Minube.com, 225
    revenues from, 118
Facebook Connect, 225
fan pages, 241, 245

FAQs (Frequently Asked Questions), 31, 54, 112, 113, 253
feedback. *See also* comments
    advantages of, 120
    on advertising, 120
    analyzing, 130
    Ciao.com, 164
    negative, 21–22, 32, 36, 150, 175
    product testing, 26
    success metrics, 130
    Toprural.com, 26, 132
    user, 234
FIFA World Cup, 151
FIM (Fox Interactive Media), 118
Flickr photo sharing site, 121
fold line, 63, 253
foreign languages. *See* languages
Fox Interactive Media (FIM), 118
fraud, 90
Frequently Asked Questions (FAQs), 31, 54, 112, 113, 253
friend lists, 53, 149, 151, 155, 254

G

games, advertising and, 118–119
Generation Y, 146–147, 254
German Tour 1993, 151
gifts, 85, 87–89, 92, 151. *See also* rewards
globalization, 134–139, 165
Google AdSense, 125
Google AdWords, 67
Google Answers, 91
Google keyword analysis, 41
GPS devices, 171, 175, 181
Gregorio, María Marín, 197, 199–206
groups, 16
Gruner & Jahr, 29, 30
guest status, 72, 80–81

H

Habbo.com, 10
Hamsterster.com, 14
help desk, 23
help page, 54
hierarchies, 86–88

hierarchy, social, 86–88
homepages. *See also* community websites; websites
    featuring members on, 50
    importance of, 49
    links on, 50
    member, 11
    mission statement, 49
    navigation, 50
    planning, 48–50
    recent contributions, 49
humor, 70

I

IAB (Interactive Advertising Bureau), 146
IBM, 246–247
IBM Connection, 203
identities, online, 10
ignore button, 112, 254
IM (Instant Messenger), 254
images
    avatars, 10–11, 85, 251
    CAPTCHA, 75, 252
incentive programs, 123–124. *See also* rewards
incentivized advertising, 123–124
information leaks, 34–35
instant messaging, 252, 254
Instant Messenger (IM), 254
Interactive Advertising Bureau (IAB), 146
interactivity, 119, 257
international communities, 134–139, 165
internationalization, 134–139
interviews
    Barnes, Leesa, 237–249
    Bruendl, Helmut, 180, 181–185
    Capel, Félix López, 196, 197, 199–206
    Derbaix, François, 231–236
    Jareño, Pedro, 220, 221–227
    Kindler, Tanja, 188, 189–193
    Musikant, Stephan, 160, 161, 163–167
    Power, Penny, 208, 209–217
    Puell, Nacho, 171, 173–177

J

Jareño, Pedro, 221–227
jokes, 70
junk email, 63, 256

K

keywords
    analyzing, 41
    described, 252–253
    Search Engine Optimization and, 67–68
    tips for, 67
Kindler, Tanja, 188, 189–193
Kleiman, Debi, 14, 28, 100, 101, 120
Kraft.de, 64

L

languages
    11870.com, 176
    adding to communities, 135–138
    Ciao.com, 165
    double-byte alphabets, 56
    foreign-language support, 138
    newsletters, 203
    Toprural.com, 234–235
    translation, 126, 137, 138, 139
    Xing, 202
Laugh Out Loud (LOL), 254
launch strategies, 75–77, 184, 192
lawsuits, 104
learning curve, 246
legal exposure, 33–34
legal issues, 74, 104
Lego.com, 15, 71, 74
Leibovitz, Annie, 189
libel, 104
Linden dollars, 85
LinkedIn, 91, 144, 211, 239
links
    activation, 80, 174
    to community, 23
    to content, 69
    on homepage, 50
    login, 51
    for product purchase, 122

registration, 51
RSS, 69
on search engines, 67
sharing, 68
sponsored, 67
live chat, 108, 252, 254
Livingathome.de, 29, 30
login links, 51
login names, 10, 256. *See also* user names
login problems, 112
LOL (Laugh Out Loud), 254
long-term customer relationships, 148
Lostzombies.com, 14
"lovemarks," 153
loyalty programs, 84–85

M

mailing lists, 40, 63
marketing. *See also* advertising
    Barnes on, 245–247, 248
    buzz, 68–71
    considerations, 204–205
    Ecademy.com, 214
    to Generation Y, 146–147
    misconceptions, 245–247
    on social networks, 145–148
    viral, 23, 68–71
marketing email, 75
marketingfit.com, 239
market research department, 110
McDonald's, 22, 152
McNeil Consumer Healthcare, 240
mega events, 151–152
member profile pages, 11, 52–53
members. *See also* membership; users
    abusive, 33, 104–105, 213
    active, 95–97
    activities. *See* activities
    advice from, 23
    anonymity of, 10
    autonomous participation, 55
    avatars, 10–11, 85, 251
    banning, 213–214
    communications between, 12
    converting guests to, 80–81
    demographics, 85
    employees as, 47, 184
    fading, 97
    false, 103
    featuring on homepages, 50
    fraud and, 90
    friend lists, 53, 149, 151, 155, 254
    guest status, 72, 80–81
    home pages, 11
    ignoring, 112, 254
    inactive, 97, 225
    integrating, 92–93
    interactions between, 175
    inviting/referring friends, 68–69, 75, 164
    level of experience, 11
    login problems, 112
    loyalty programs, 84–85
    multiple accounts, 90
    names. *See* nicknames; user names
    new, 80–81, 92–93, 254
    number of, 62
    online identities, 10
    participation. *See* participation
    passive, 93–95
    passwords, 75, 112
    popularity, 85–87
    premium. *See* premium membership
    privileges, 84–85
    profiles. *See* profile pages
    public display of information, 52
    rankings, 84–85
    reactivating, 97
    recruiting. *See* recruitment
    registering. *See* registration
    relationships between, 53, 58
    rewarding. *See* rewards
    role in community management, 113–114
    scores, 84–85
    seniority, 86–87
    shared activities, 5, 9
    social hierarchy, 86–88
    support of, 101–102
    Terms of Use agreements, 33–34, 53–54, 75
    trolls/trolling, 105, 256
    viewing content created by, 55

membership. *See also* members
    benefits of, 72, 73
    lifecycle of, 92–97, 102
    paid subscriptions, 120–122
    premium. *See* premium membership
    types of, 201–202
message, brand, 20–21
message boards. *See also* blogs; online communities
    described, 254
    threads, 9, 256
    trolls/trolling, 105, 256
    vs. online communities, 9
micro-blogging, 254
micro-communities, 16, 144
Mini Space, 46
Minube.com, 70, 85, 219–227
mission statements, 49
moderators, 9, 114
Modo community, 27
monetary rewards/gifts, 88–91
MonNuage.fr, 221
Motrin website, 240
M Power World. *See* BMW M Power World
Müller, Frank, 28
Musikant, Stephan, 66, 160–167
MySpace
    display advertising, 125
    McDonald's customer testimonials on, 22, 152
    Puma v1.08 Speed Boot, 154–155
    targeted advertising, 148

N

navigation
    content, 48, 252
    homepages. *See* homepages
    importance of, 48, 50
    structural, 252
navigation bar, 48, 254
negative opinions/comments, 21–22, 32, 36, 150, 175
netiquette, 254
"network effect," 236

networks
    business. *See* business networks
    recruitment and, 148
    social. *See* social networks
newbies, 92–93, 254
newsletters
    direct mail opt-in, 75
    editorial services, 126
    engaging members with, 94
    promoting communities on, 63
    translation, 126
nicknames, 10, 53, 75, 256. *See also* user names
Nielsen, Jakob, 119
Nielsen Company, 144
Nielsen Norman Group, 146
Ning.com, 16, 236

O

offline events, 151–152
Olympic Games, 151
online communities. *See also* community websites; message boards
    activities. *See* activities
    adding languages, 135–138
    adding new features, 96
    authenticity, 165
    business benefits of, 20–30
    charging members, 91, 120–122
    closed, 62, 252
    common activities, 9
    competition, 44, 244
    defined, 254
    disadvantages of, 31–36
    features of, 9–12
    future of, 216, 247
    getting started, 42–44
    goals for, 41–42
    identities, 10–11
    increasing Web traffic to, 24
    infrastructure, 56–58
    integrating brands with, 46–47, 149–150, 176
    international, 134–139, 165
    inviting/referring friends, 68–69, 75, 164
    learning curve, 246

links to, 23
management of, 56–57
measuring success of, 130
members of. *See* members; membership
member thoughts on, 6
micro-communities, 144
moderation of, 56–57
open vs. closed, 12–14
optimizing efficiency of, 133
overview, 4–6
planning for, 40–47, 56–58
power of, 17
preparing for success, 37
product testing/feedback, 26
profiting from. *See* revenues
revenue generated by, 29
saving money via, 119–120
shared communications, 12
social hierarchy, 86–88
social networks. *See* social networks
social shopping, 15, 256
strategies for, 40–42
themes, 14–15, 42–43
trolls/trolling, 105, 256
types of, 12–16
vs. blogs, 7–8, 235
vs. message boards, 9
vs. wikis, 7
well-managed, 114
online events, 151–152
online identities, 10–11
online seminars (Webinars), 41, 257
open communities, 12–14
Optiwell, 28
O'Reilly, Tim, 6, 257
ourbania network, 4

P

page impressions, 41, 66, 253, 254
page real estate, 50, 255
pages. *See* Web pages
Parship site, 122
participation
  analyzing, 130
  encouraging, 173–174, 224, 233–234
engaging passive members, 93–95
maintaining active members, 95–97
motivating new members, 80–81
reactivating fading members, 97
rewarding. *See* rewards
website "stickiness" and, 81–83, 256
partner websites, 66, 126
passive members, 93–95
passive recruitment, 62, 251
passwords, 75, 112
pay-per-action (PPA), 123, 255
pay-per-click (PPC), 66, 123, 255
pay-per-impression (PPI), 66, 123, 255
pay-per-lead (PPL), 66, 255
pay-per-sale (PPS), 123
peer management, 113–114
peer-to-peer communication, 147
personal branding, 201
personality tests, 216
Philips, 110
phone numbers, 54
podcasting, 241, 243
Power, Penny, 21, 25, 33, 208, 209–217
PPA (pay-per-action), 123, 255
PPC (pay-per-click), 66, 123, 255
PPI (pay-per-impression), 66, 123, 255
PPL (pay-per-lead), 66, 255
PPS (pay-per-sale), 123
premium membership
  ad-free benefit of, 125
  Flickr, 121
  Parship, 122
  tips for, 80, 120–122
  Xing, 121, 202–203
press attention, 130
press opportunities, 29
press releases, 29, 41
PricewaterhouseCoopers online
  community, 203
print advertising, 66
privacy issues, 246–247
privileges, 84–85
Pro-Age Netzwerk, 45, 187–193
product development, 26
product-related discussions, 150
product-related rewards, 88

products. *See also* brands
    B2B, 153
    criticism of, 21–22, 32, 36, 150, 175
    links to purchase pages, 122
    "lovemark" status, 153
    reviews, 123
    sales cycle, 148
    soft launches, 256
    testimonials, 22, 123, 152
    testing, 26–27, 42
professional networks
    Ecademy.com, 21, 25, 33, 207–217
    LinkedIn, 16, 91, 144, 211, 239
    Xing. *See* Xing
profile pages
    BMW M Power World, 182–183, 184, 190
    for brands, 149
    Ciao, 161
    completion of, 239
    Ecademy, 210, 216
    Minube.com, 223
    Pro-Age Netzwerk, 190
    Puma v1.08 Speed Boot, 154–155
    Wrigley's Airwaves chewing gum, 153
    Xing, 52, 200–201
profile pages, member, 11, 52–53
promotions, 124
proteacher.net, 14
publicity, 240
publishers, 123, 255
Puell, Nacho, 171, 173–177
Puma v1.08 Speed Boot, 154–155

R

raffles, 89
rankings, member, 84–85
Really Simple Syndication. *See* RSS
recruitment, 62–71. *See also* registration
    active, 62, 251
    adapting strategies for, 134
    from advertising, 66
    avoiding "spam" appearance, 63
    community, 148
    from corporate websites, 64–66
    in-house, 164
    large-scale, 76–77
    from mailing lists, 63
    Musikant on, 164
    passive, 62, 251
    referral programs, 69
    from rented email lists, 64
    social networks and, 148
    strategies for, 62–71
    via search engines, 67–68
    viral/buzz marketing, 68–71
referral programs, 69
registration, 71–77. *See also* recruitment
    activation links, 80, 174
    charging members for, 91, 120–122
    converting guests to premium members, 80–81
    coregistration agreements, 66, 126, 253
    email confirmation, 80
    false, 90
    guest status, 72, 80–81
    Terms of Use agreements, 33–34, 53–54, 75
registration forms, 73–75
registration links, 51
registration pages, 50–51, 73–75
registration process, 50, 71–73
relationships, 40–41, 53, 58, 148
return on investment (ROI), 127
revenues, 118–128
    from advertising, 123–127
    considerations, 118–119
    e-commerce websites, 122–123
    paid subscriptions, 120–122
    saving money, 119–120
reviews, product, 123
rewards, 83–91
    abusers of, 90
    advantages of, 83
    Ciao.com, 164
    discounts, 88, 151
    gifts, 85, 87–89, 92, 151
    ideas for, 87–88
    loyalty programs, 84–85
    Minube.com, 225
    monetary, 88–91
    privileges, 84–85
    product-related, 88

samples, 151
social hierarchy, 86–88
virtual, 83–88
Roberts, Kevin, 153
ROI (return on investment), 127
ROFL (Roll on the Floor Laughing), 255
Roll on the Floor Laughing (ROFL), 255
RSS (Really Simple Syndication), 69, 255
RSS feeds, 96
RSS links, 69
rumors, 36

S

Saatchi & Saatchi, 153
sale cycle, 148
sales leads, 130
Schwab, Charles, 27
scores, member, 84–85
scrapbookeronline.com, 14
search engine marketing (SEM), 67, 255
Search Engine Optimization (SEO), 25, 67–68, 255
search engine ranking, 25, 130, 255
search engines
    drawing visitors from, 41
    keywords. *See* keywords
    optimizing content for, 25, 67–68, 255
    performance, 25
    recruiting via, 67–68
    sponsored links on, 67
search functionality, 108
Second Life, 11, 85, 166
security issues, 246–247
SEM (search engine marketing), 67, 255
seniority, 86–87
Senseo forum, 110
SEO (Search Engine Optimization), 25, 67–68, 255
servers, Web, 58, 257
shared items
    activities, 5, 9
    email, 70
    links, 68
    photos, 121
shopping points, 124

shopping websites, 15
"Shop" tab, 122
social bookmarking, 256
social hierarchy, 86–88
social media, 245–247
social networks, 143–156
    advantages of, 147–148
    brand promotion on, 147–155
    described, 256
    growth rate of, 144–145
    marketing on, 145–148
    overview, 16, 144–145
    recruitment and, 148
    target groups and, 153
social shopping, 15, 256
social shopping websites, 15
social technographics survey, 240–241
soft launch, 256
spam, 63, 104, 108, 127, 256
special offers, 124
Spiegel.de, 33
Spiegel Online, 24
spokespeople, 114
staffing costs, 31
Starbucks, 243
Stardoll community, 91
start page, 135, 256
statistics, 113
status symbols, 86–88
"stickiness," in websites, 81–83, 256
structural navigation, 252. *See also* content navigation
studiVZ, 24
StumbleUpon, 69
subscriptions, paid, 120–122
Super Bowl advertising, 245
sweepstakes, 89
syndication. *See* RSS

T

tags, 252–253. *See also* keywords
target demographics, 85
targeted advertising, 148
target users, 58
Telefónica community, 235

telephone numbers, 54
templates, 113
Terms of Use agreements, 33–34, 53–54, 75
testimonials, 22, 123
themed communities, 14–15
themes, 42–43, 46
Threadless.com, 15
threads, 9, 256
Timberlake, Justin, 155
Toprural.com, 229–236
    handling of abusive content, 105
    internationalization, 135
    overview, 231–232
    user feedback, 26, 132
    Web 2.0 tools, 31
translation, 126, 137, 138
Tremor, 45
trolls/trolling, 105, 256
"trustmarks," 153
Tus Rincones Favoritos, 225
TV advertising, 66
TV channels, 36
tweet, 256
Twitter, 145, 211, 242, 254, 256

U

Unilever, 28, 189
user groups, 14, 252
user names, 10, 256–257. *See also* login names; nicknames
user profiles. *See* profile pages
users. *See also* members
    activities. *See* activities
    banning, 213–214
    guest status, 72, 80–81
    ignoring, 254
    inactive, 225
    participation. *See* participation
    passwords, 75, 112
    relationships between, 53, 58
    rewarding. *See* rewards
    target, 58
    Terms of Use agreements, 33–34, 53–54, 75

V

Verizon, 242
video podcasts, 241
viral marketing
    11870.com, 175
    Barnes on, 238, 240–241
    Ecademy, 215
    examples of, 23
    McNeil Consumer Healthcare, 240
    Minube.com, 226, 227
    recruitment, 68–71
    social technographics survey, 240–241
    Xing, 201, 204–205
viral recommendations, 147
virtual rewards, 83–88
virtual worlds, 11, 85, 166
viruses, 246

W

Web 1.0, 6, 257
Web 2.0, 6, 203, 257
webcam, 257
Webinars (online seminars), 41, 257
weblogs. *See* blogs
Web pages
    content location on, 50
    FAQ, 31, 54, 112, 113, 253
    page impressions, 41, 66, 253, 254
    page real estate, 50, 255
    profiles. *See* profile pages
    start page, 135, 256
    typical components of, 81–83
Web servers, 58, 257
website analytics, 130
website developers, 56
website domains, 57–58
website policing, 105
websites. *See also* community websites
    "bad word filters," 112
    banners. *See* banners
    beta testing, 76, 251
    bookmarks, 69
    closed areas of, 14, 252
    content. *See* content
    cookies, 253
    e-commerce. *See* e-commerce websites

homepages. *See* homepages
increasing traffic to, 24, 41
optimizing for search engines, 25, 67–68, 255
partners, 66, 126
publishers, 123, 255
sense of entitlement and, 35–36
start page, 135, 256
"stickiness" in, 81–83, 256
Web tracking statistics, 41
Web traffic, 24, 41, 130
Wikipedia, 7
wikis, 7, 257
William Victor company, 126, 139
Wonkette.com, 8
Wordpress blog, 236
Wrigley's Airwaves chewing gum, 153

X

Xing, 195–206
    ambassadors, 199–200
    community managers, 200
incentivized advertising, 124
internationalization, 135, 136
inviting friends example, 68
marketing on, 204–205
micro-communities, 144
overview, 197–199
product discussions on, 150
registration page example, 51, 73
reporting spam/abuse, 104
revenues from, 118
types of memberships, 121, 201–203
user profiles, 52, 200–201
viral marketing, 23

Y

Yahoo Answers, 84, 91, 93, 96
YouTube, 232

Z

ziitrend.com, 15

Get free online access to this book!

And sign up for a free trial to Safari Books Online to get access to thousands more!

With the purchase of this book you have instant online, searchable access to it on Safari Books Online (for a limited time). And while you're there, be sure to check out the Safari on-demand digital library and its Free Trial Offer (a separate sign-up process)—where you can access thousands of technical and inspirational books, instructional videos, and articles from the world's leading creative professionals with a Safari Books Online subscription.

Simply visit www.peachpit.com/safarienabled and enter code XROZYBI to try it today.